Native Vote

American Indians, the Voting Rights Act, and the Right to Vote

The right to vote is the foundation of democratic government; all other policies are derived from it. The history of voting rights in America has been characterized by a gradual expansion of the franchise. American Indians are an important part of that story, but they have faced a prolonged battle to gain the franchise. One of the most important tools wielded by advocates of minority voting rights has been the Voting Rights Act. This book explains the history and expansion of Indian voting rights, with an emphasis on more than seventy cases based on the Voting Rights Act and/or the Equal Protection Clause. The authors describe the struggle to obtain Indian citizenship and the basic right to vote and then analyze the cases brought under the Voting Rights Act, including three case studies. The final two chapters assess the political impact of these cases and the role of American Indians in contemporary politics.

Daniel McCool is a professor of Political Science at the University of Utah and the director of the American West Center and the Environmental Studies program at the University of Utah. He is the author, co-author, or editor of six other books, including: *Native Waters: Contemporary Indian Water Settlements and the Second Treaty Era* (2002); *Staking Out the Terrain: Power and Performance Among Natural Resource Agencies* (1996, second ed., with Jeanne Clarke); and *Contested Landscape: The Politics of Wilderness in Utah and the West* (1999). He has appeared as an expert witness in Indian voting rights cases and has served as a consultant for the National Oceanic and Atmospheric Administration, the U.S. Justice Department, and the Southwest Center for Environmental Research and Policy.

Susan M. Olson is a professor of Political Science at the University of Utah, where she has been teaching since 1986. Since 2000 she has also been Associate Vice President for Faculty at the University of Utah. She has been an active member of the American Political Science Association and the Law & Society Association since 1978, serving on the Board of Trustees of the latter. She is the author of *Clients and Lawyers: Securing the Rights of Disabled Persons* (1984). She has published numerous articles in the *Law and Society Review, Polity, Journal of Politics*, and *Law and Policy*, among other journals.

Jennifer L. Robinson currently works for the Center for Public Policy and Administration at the University of Utah as a research associate. She is completing her Ph.D. in Political Science, focusing on American Government and Public Administration, at the University of Utah. In 2003, she was awarded the Scott M. Matheson Fellowship in Political Science at the University of Utah.

Native Vote

American Indians, the Voting Rights Act, and the Right to Vote

DANIEL McCOOL,
SUSAN M. OLSON, and
JENNIFER L. ROBINSON
University of Utah

CAMBRIDGE UNIVERSITY PRESS
Cambridge, New York, Melbourne, Madrid, Cape Town, Singapore, São Paulo

Cambridge University Press
32 Avenue of the Americas, New York, NY 10013-2473, USA

www.cambridge.org
Information on this title: www.cambridge.org/9780521839839

First published 2007

Printed in the United States of America

A catalog record for this publication is available from the British Library.

Library of Congress Cataloging in Publication Data

McCool, Daniel, 1950–
Native vote : American Indians, the Voting Rights Act, and the right to vote / Daniel McCool, Susan M. Olson, Jennifer L. Robinson.
p. cm.
Includes bibliographical references and index.
ISBN 0-521-83983-1 (hardback) – ISBN 0-521-54871-3 (pbk.)
1. Indians of North America – Suffrage. 2. Indians of North America – Legal status, laws, etc. 3. Indians of North America – Civil rights. 4. Voting rights – United States – History. 5. United States – Race relations. 6. United States – Politics and government. I. Olson, Susan M. II. Robinson, Jennifer L. (Jennifer Lynn), 1967– III. Title.
E91.M25 2007
324.6′208997073–dc22 2006013649

ISBN 978-0-521-83983-9 hardback
ISBN 978-0-521-54871-7 paperback

Miguel Trujillo, Isleta Pueblo
Frank Harrison, Mohave Tribe
– DCM

Paul and Olivia
– SMO

My parents, Scott and Valerie
– JLR

Contents

Preface

When the Founding Fathers designed our government at the Constitutional Convention, their concept of "democracy" was quite different from what that term means to most people today. They held the view that the "consent of the governed" came from only a small fraction of the populace – propertied white males. Article I, Section 4, of the U.S. Constitution gave states the power to prescribe rules for the "times, places, and manner of holding elections," but it also gave Congress the right to "make or alter such regulations." This split control over election laws led to dramatic conflicts between the states and the federal government regarding who is entitled to vote. Eventually this conflict led to the Fifteenth Amendment to the Constitution and ultimately to the Voting Rights Act of 1965 (VRA) and its amendments. This book examines the impact that landmark legislation has had on the voting rights of American Indians.

The right to vote is the foundation of democratic government; all other policies are derived from it. Yet there is an "astounding lack of research" on Indian politics, especially Indian voting (Wilkins 2002, 188). Many textbooks on Indian law and Indian policy hardly mention it, and when Indian voting is discussed, the focus is almost always on tribal elections. There is virtually no coverage of the role of Indian voting in federal, state, and local elections. Voting studies usually ignore Indians, and national data sets often lump Indians into an "other" category. As a result, there has been very little systematic study of Indian voting, and there is a "dangerous paucity of data and analysis of actual participation" (Lehman and Macy 2004). Jacqueline Johnson, executive director of the National Congress of American Indians, recently referred to this problem: "Indian people have never been a regularly documented population in voter demographics, exit polls or in the mind of the American public as a population that can help determine election results. There has never been a nation-wide study of Native American voters..." (Johnson 2004a).

Due to this lack of attention in the literature, one might get the impression that, after Indians gained citizenship in 1924, their voting rights suddenly equaled those of non-Indians. But the truth is far less ideal; Indians have faced a prolonged battle to gain the franchise on a footing equal to that of whites. Much like the struggle for black voting rights in the South, this conflict has been long, arduous, and often bitter. There are many facets to the conflict, but without doubt one of the most important tools wielded by advocates of minority voting rights has been the VRA. It has literally changed the face of America's electorate and eventually brought to office a much more diverse set of people – a process that continues today.

In Indian Country there have been at least seventy-four voting rights cases based on the VRA and/or the Equal Protection Clause since the law was passed. Most of these cases have been fairly recent, and thus the impact of this act is still evolving. But in just a few short years, it has enabled a significant number of Indian people, and candidates of their choice, to get elected to federal, state, and local governments. The history of voting rights in America has been characterized by a gradual but persistent expansion of the franchise; American Indians are an important part of that story.

Chapter 1 of this book describes how Indians achieved citizenship and the right to vote. It traces the long history of Indian–white relations from the earliest attempts to define the political relationship between tribes and the new American nation to the granting of the right to vote to Indians through a series of court cases and statutes. The VRA refers to attempts to deny or abridge the right to vote. Chapter 1 deals with the former; the remainder of the book is primarily about the latter, although even recently there have been efforts to deny Indians the right to vote.

Chapter 2 explains the evolution of the VRA and its amendments. The VRA has been amended several times to expand its coverage and effectiveness. After the passage of the original act in 1965, some political jurisdictions found ways to limit or abrogate the impact of minority voters; the U.S. Congress responded by closing loopholes, extending and strengthening certain aspects of the act, and expanding its provisions into new areas. Chapter 2 explains how these successive amendments have changed the nature of VRA cases, especially as they apply to American

Indians. The chapter also introduces the organizations principally responsible for bringing the lawsuits under the act.

Chapter 3 presents a broad summary of the seventy-four cases in Indian Country and explains how they fit together as a body of law. Given the volume and complexity of the litigation, this chapter presents only an overview of the case law and points out important trends and developing legal constructs.

The book then turns to three case studies illustrating how VRA cases are litigated or settled. The first case study, in Chapter 4, focuses on two of the earliest VRA cases in Indian Country, both brought by the U.S. Justice Department against San Juan County, Utah. One of those cases, a challenge to at-large elections for county commission, was settled and resulted in the election of a Navajo to the commission. The other case, dealing with information and assistance for Navajo-speaking voters, was also settled and resulted in changes to election procedures.

Chapter 5 tells the story of a VRA case in Montana that pitted Indians on the Fort Belknap Reservation against Blaine County. *United States v. Blaine County* concerned an at-large election system in which all three county commissioners were elected by the entire county – a county that included a substantial Indian minority that had never elected one of its members to the commission. This case went to trial in the U.S. district court and was appealed to the Ninth Circuit Court of Appeals, with the county losing at both levels. The county appealed to the U.S. Supreme Court but was denied certiorari in 2005.

Chapter 6 describes the litigation in *Bone Shirt v. Hazeltine*, which involved Lakota Sioux voters in two legislative districts in South Dakota. The principal issue concerned how the relative number of Indian voters in these adjoining districts affected the ability of Indians to elect a candidate of their choice. The Indian plaintiffs won this case, and the state of South Dakota appealed. In August 2006, the Eighth Circuit ruled in favor of the Indian plaintiffs.

Each of these case studies reveals a different facet of VRA litigation, and each clearly illustrates the complexity and difficulty of winning such a claim. The various sections of the act produce different sets of cases; the facts of the cases vary across tribes, states, and jurisdictions. In addition, the issues change with the development of new case law. We chose our three case studies to illustrate this diversity in legal issues, levels of government, and means of resolution.

The final two chapters focus on results. Chapter 7 examines the impact of VRA cases after the judges have issued their decisions, when the voters and candidates begin their odyssey through the election process. Chapter 8 looks at Indian political participation on a national scale, with an emphasis on the 2004 elections. In that election, an unprecedented effort was made to get Indians to the polls. A nationwide campaign by the National Congress of American Indians produced thousands of bumper stickers and lapel pins proudly announcing "I'm Indian and I Vote" and "Native Vote." The latter slogan provided the title for this book.

When we began our research for this book, we knew there had been quite a few VRA cases in Indian Country, but as we delved more deeply into the issue, we were surprised that the total number eventually climbed to seventy-four. With so many cases, it is clear that the time has come to analyze them and assess their impact. Indeed, there is so much material on these cases that we experienced considerable difficulty controlling the length of this book; VRA cases are so complex that an entire book could be written on most of them. Thus, this book is an overview of what has grown into a voluminous body of case law and election policy. A significant number of these cases involve the sections of the Voting Rights Act that were reauthorized in 2006, just months before this book went to press (see McDonald 2004; Hasen 2005; National Commission on the Voting Rights Act 2005).

In surveying the literature on VRA cases in Indian Country, we found that no one had assembled all of these cases into a single accessible file. We consulted many sources just to put together the case list. Such an effort, of course, requires assistance from a diverse group of attorneys, scholars, and colleagues. We must begin our expression of appreciation by thanking two groups of individuals who went far beyond the call of duty in assisting us. The staff of the Voting Section of the U.S. Department of Justice, particularly Peyton McCrary, Christopher Coates, and Gaye Tenoso, provided incalculable assistance. The same can be said of Laughlin McDonald and Bryan Sells of the American Civil Liberties Union's Voting Rights Project. Together, these two organizations brought most of the cases examined in this book. We could not have completed it without their assistance, cooperation, and generosity.

Our colleague, Professor Pei-te Lien, provided useful and insightful comments on an early draft of the manuscript. Another colleague, Professor Matthew Burbank, also gave us invaluable advice and insights. Jason Hardy, of the American West Center at the University of Utah, assisted us greatly in our research for Chapter 7. The American West Center provided release time for both Jason and Jennifer Robinson to work on the book. We also owe our appreciation to John Bevan and Lee Warthen, librarians at the S. J. Quinney Law Library, and Peter Kraus, librarian at the J. Willard Marriott Library, for their assistance with research. Donald Burge, reference librarian at the Center for Southwest Research, University of New Mexico, provided invaluable assistance with the archives of the National Indian Youth Council. Sheila Olson-Cator assisted with the list of sources cited. We also want to thank Dean Steven Ott of the College of Social and Behavioral Science for his encouragement and support, as well as Ron Hrebenar, chairman of the Political Science Department. In addition, we extend our thanks to the numerous elected officials who graciously agreed to telephone interviews for our analysis in Chapter 7. On a larger scale, we would be remiss if we did not mention the inspiration we received from Vine Deloria, Jr. And finally, we would like to thank our families for tolerating our absences while we worked on this book.

1

From Vanishing American to Voter

The Enfranchisement of American Indians

The struggle for Indian suffrage has been a long one; it took nearly 200 years of effort to award U.S. citizenship to Indians and make them eligible to vote in national, state, and local elections. Thus the focus in this chapter is on overcoming the *denial* of Indian suffrage; most of the remainder of the book is about the *abridgment* of the Indian vote. The first section of this chapter describes the incremental bestowal of citizenship on American Indians. The second section focuses on state election laws and how they prohibited or impeded the Indian franchise. The conclusion interprets these developments in light of the passage of the Voting Rights Act (VRA).

Subjects Become Citizens

The authors of the Constitution did not envision Indian people as a part of the electorate. Congressional districts were apportioned among the states based on population, but "Indians not taxed" were excluded from the enumeration (Art. I. Sec. 2). This was in apparent recognition that most Indians were not under the jurisdiction of the fledgling U.S. government, and therefore taxes could not be levied against them. Indians are mentioned again in Article I, Section 8, where Congress is given the power to "regulate commerce with foreign nations, and among the several states, and with the Indian tribes." The phrase clearly indicates that the Constitution's authors considered Indian tribes to be extrajurisdictional, lying somewhere between foreign nations and American citizens. For the next 200 years, the nation would struggle to define exactly where tribes fit in along that continuum.

The first major effort to define legally the relationship between Indian tribes and the United States was a set of three Supreme Court cases known as the "Marshall trilogy" (see Wilkins and Lomawaima 2001, 52–63).[1] Chief Justice John Marshall admitted that the Cherokee tribe was a "distinct political society," but due to its association with the federal government he characterized it as a "domestic dependent nation" and stated that the tribe's relationship to the federal government "resembles that of a ward to a guardian" (*Cherokee Nation v. Georgia* 1831). The contradictions in these phrases are readily apparent; they combine the notion of dependency with that of nationhood. To make matters even more confusing, the opinions written by other justices ranged from a position that Indians had no sovereignty to one that Indians had complete sovereignty (Deloria and Lytle 1983, 30–1). The other two cases further confused the issue (Wilkins 1997).

The ambiguities of the Constitution and the contradictions within the Marshall trilogy of cases virtually guaranteed that the legal status of Indians, especially in regard to citizenship and the right to vote, would remain shrouded in confusion and conflict for many years. In an attempt to clarify the status of Indians, the U.S. attorney general, Caleb Cushing, issued an opinion in 1856, concluding:

> The simple truth is plain that the Indians are the subjects of the United States, and therefore are not, in mere right of home-birth, citizens of the United States. . . . This distinction between citizens proper, that is, the constituent members of the political sovereignty, and subjects of that sovereignty, who are not therefore citizens, is recognized in the best authorities of public law. (Official Opinions of the Attorneys General 1856, 749–50)

Thus, the Indians' relationship to the U.S. government was similar to that of people in an occupied land under the control of a foreign power – a strange relationship indeed for a country that purported to be a democracy.

The place of the Indian in the body politic again became a major issue when Congress began formulating the Fourteenth Amendment in 1866. The nation had just emerged from a brutal four-year civil war, and Congress was intent on freeing southern slaves and making them part of the political fabric of the nation. The three amendments ratified after the

[1] The three cases of the Marshall trilogy are *Johnson v. McIntosh* (1832), *Cherokee Nation v. Georgia* (1831), and *Worcester v. Georgia* (1832).

Civil War were the first that were not written by the Founding Fathers.[2] Because of the North's victory in the war and the absence of southern members of Congress, the government was finally free to act decisively against slavery. The Thirteenth Amendment abolished slavery in 1865, just seven months after the conclusion of hostilities. But the Republicans who dominated Congress felt that more had to be done to protect the freed slaves and ensure them all the rights and privileges of citizenship. In 1866 Congress passed the first civil rights act, which declared: "That all persons born in the United States, and not subject to any foreign power, excluding Indians not taxed, are hereby declared to be citizens of the United States" (Civil Rights Act of 1866). However, there was concern that this law was unenforceable in the southern states unless it was made part of the Constitution. So, a constitutional amendment was introduced in Congress, but the phrase "Indians not taxed" was omitted from the first section of the proposed amendment. Thus, the first section of the amendment was exactly like the 1866 Civil Rights Act, but without the exemption for Indians not taxed.[3] During the Senate floor debate, Senator James Doolittle of Wisconsin proposed to add "Indians not taxed" to the first section of the amendment, arguing that

> there is a large mass of the Indian population who are clearly subject to the jurisdiction of the United States who ought not to be included as citizens of the United States.... The word "citizen," if applied to them, would bring in all the Digger Indians of California. Perhaps they have mostly disappeared; the people of California, perhaps, have put them out of the way; but there are the Indians of Oregon and the Indians of the Territories. Take Colorado; there are more Indian citizens of Colorado than there are white citizens this moment if you admit it as a State. And yet by a constitutional amendment you propose to declare the Utes, the Tabhuaches, and all those wild Indians to be citizens of the United States, the Great Republic of the world, whose citizenship should be a title as proud as that of king, and whose danger is that you may degrade that citizenship. (*Congressional Globe* 1866, 2892)

Senator Doolittle was making two arguments against Indian suffrage – arguments that would be heard time and again throughout the years. His first point was that Indians were an inferior race and therefore were simply not good enough to hold the title of citizen. His second point was that, if granted citizenship, and implicitly the right to vote, they could vote in

[2] The Twelfth Amendment was ratified in 1804 under the guidance of President Thomas Jefferson.

[3] The phrase does appear in the second section of the amendment, which deals with the apportionment of House seats; that section simply repeats the language from Art. I, Sec. 2.

sufficient numbers to change the power structure and overwhelm their white neighbors.

Other senators responded to these arguments by making two points. First, they argued that Indians were not under the jurisdiction of the United States, and therefore were excluded from the provisions of the proposed amendment even without the phrase "Indians not taxed." Senator Lyman Trumbull of Illinois, the chairman of the Committee on the Judiciary, argued this point:

> What do we mean by "subject to the jurisdiction of the United States?" Not owing allegiance to anyone else. That is what it means. Can you sue a Navajoe [sic] Indian in court? Are they in any sense subject to the complete jurisdiction of the United States? By no means. We make treaties with them, and therefore they are not subject to our jurisdiction. If they were we would not make treaties with them. [This proposed amendment] by no means embraces, or by a fair construction – by any construction, I may say – could embrace the wild Indians of the Plains or any with whom we have treaty relations. (*Congressional Globe* 1866, 2893)

In other words, although Indians were "subjects" of the United States, they were not "subject" to its jurisdiction. This implies that tribes were still considered extrajurisdictional entities.

Senator Trumbull offered a second reason why the phrase "Indians not taxed" should not be added to the proposed amendment; it would, he argued, be completely contrary to the progressive notion that the franchise is not limited to those who are well moneyed:

> I am not willing to make citizenship in this country depend on taxation. I am not willing... that the rich Indian residing in the State of New York shall be a citizen and the poor Indian residing in the State of New York shall not be a citizen. If you put in those words in regard to citizenship, what do you do? You make a distinction in that respect, if you put it on the ground of taxation. (*Congressional Globe* 1866, 2894)

The argument over the connection between Indians voting and Indians paying taxes continues to this day.

Ultimately the Senate approved the first section of the proposed amendment without the phrase "Indians not taxed," but not before receiving assurances from the amendment's sponsors that it would not apply to Indians. Senator Jacob Howard of Michigan undoubtedly expressed the common will of the Senate when he averred: "I am not yet prepared to pass a sweeping act of naturalization by which all the Indian savages, wild or tame, belonging to a tribal relation, are to become my fellow-citizens and go to the polls and vote with me..." (*Congressional Globe* 1866,

2895). This viewpoint – that the amendment did not affect the status of Indians – was reiterated two years later in a report by the Senate Judiciary Committee (see Deloria and Wilkins 1999, 142–4).

The debate over the Fourteenth Amendment took place within a larger debate regarding the long-term objectives of the nation's Indian policy. This context included passage of the Fifteenth Amendment, which was a profound development but at the time had little relevance to Indians because of their citizenship status. Thus, it had virtually no impact on the right of Indians to vote.

In the nineteenth century, the larger policy context veered between two visions of the Indian's future. One approach was basically genocide, replete with statements that all Indians should be exterminated forthwith, or, in Senator Doolittle's quaint phrase quoted earlier, "put... out of the way." Colonel George Armstrong Custer clearly demonstrated this objective when he slaughtered a Cheyenne village on the Washita River in 1868 – the year the Fourteenth Amendment was ratified. A Nebraska newspaper at that time editorialized: "Exterminate the whole fraternity of redskins" (Connell 1985, 127).

Other events in 1868 reflected a second approach to Indian policy, which was to create a system of reservations set aside for Indians until they could become "civilized" and amalgamated into the great mass of white people. Treaties with the Navajos, and the Lakota Sioux and Arapahoe, both in 1868, created extensive reservations; the latter treaty also contained a provision whereby the Indians could gain citizenship by "receiving a patent for land under the foregoing provisions... and be entitled to all the privileges and immunities of such citizens, and shall, at the same time retain all [their] rights to benefits accruing to Indians under this treaty" (Treaty of Fort Laramie 1868, Article 6).

The citizenship clause in the Fort Laramie treaty was just one of several laws and treaties that permitted select Indians to become citizens under certain conditions. The significant point regarding the Sioux treaty was that it allowed Indians to become citizens and still maintain their status and rights as Indians. Many policymakers at that time felt that Indian citizenship should be granted only if individual Indians gave up their tribal affiliation and culture and adopted the "habits of civilization." In other words, citizenship, and the right to vote, would be contingent upon abandoning one culture and adopting another. However, this was not yet official policy. The law was not at all clear as to whether an individual Indian could leave his reservation, adopt the habits of the white race, pay taxes, and thus earn the right to vote. In 1884 the Supreme Court provided an answer. John Elk, an Indian who lived in Omaha, Nebraska, attempted to register to vote in local elections. He was refused a ballot, even though he had severed his tribal relations and was living among white people. In *Elk v. Wilkins*, the Supreme Court ruled against Mr. Elk, reasoning that the Fourteenth Amendment did not apply to Indians and that they were "no more 'born in the United States and subject to the jurisdiction thereof' . . . than the children . . . born within the United States, of ambassadors or other public ministers of foreign nations" (*Elk v. Wilkins* 1894, 102). Thus, it was clear that, to obtain citizenship, Indian people would need a statute or other official action to bestow that status upon them.

That statute was passed in 1887 after a long debate about how to break up the reservations and convert Indians into the Jeffersonian image of the yeoman farmer. The Dawes Act, or General Allotment Act, divided up reservation lands into individual landholdings for tribal members and then sold off the remainder to white settlers. The act provided an avenue to citizenship, but only for those Indians who availed themselves of the act's provisions and accepted allotments or completely abandoned their tribe and adopted Anglo culture:

> And every Indian born within the territorial limits of the United States to whom allotments shall have been made under the provisions of this act, or under any law or treaty, and every Indian born within the territorial limits of the United States who has voluntarily taken up, within said limits, his residence separate and apart from any tribe of Indians therein, and has adopted the habits of civilized life, is hereby declared to be a citizen of the United States. . . . (Dawes Act 1887, 390)

In 1901 President Theodore Roosevelt called the allotment policy a "mighty pulverizing engine to break up the tribal mass. . . . Under its provisions, some sixty thousand Indians have already become citizens of the United States" (Roosevelt 1901, 6672). Allotment cost Indians dearly, reducing their landholdings by more than half in less than a decade. But it did provide a conditional avenue to citizenship. As Prucha described the process, it "was not a matter of legal citizenship but of cultural amalgamation of the Indian into the mass of white citizens, a much more comprehensive matter" (1984, 686).

By the dawn of the twentieth century, after a "century of confusion" (O'Brien 1989, 71), the 250,000 American Indians who had survived the onslaught of European settlement were still in a legal state that has been described as a "legal vacuum" (Wolfley 1991, 175), a "kind of legal limbo" (Phelps 1991, 65), an "anomalous legal status" (Prucha 1984, 682), and a "large no-mans' land" (Cohen 1942, 122). Perhaps the bluntest assessment was offered by Joseph Muskrat: "The major consequence of the wars between the Indians and the Whites was that the Indians became a politically castrated and administered people" (1973, 46–7).

Indians continued to be added to the citizenship rolls on a piecemeal basis. In 1907, as part of the abolishment of the Indian Territory (what is today the state of Oklahoma), Indians living in that territory were made citizens (Oklahoma Enabling Act 1906, 267–8). Another major citizenship grant occurred in 1919 when Congress offered citizenship to every Indian who had served in the military during the First World War and received an honorable discharge (Act of November 6, 1919). Two years later, Congress granted citizenship to every member of the Osage tribe (Act of March 3, 1921). The underlying assumption of each of these acts was that these particular Indians had demonstrated that they had become part of the larger Anglo culture and were no longer wholly Indian. By the early 1920s, about two-thirds of the Indian people in the United States had been granted citizenship, and Congress began considering a bill to make citizens of the remainder (Tyler 1973, 110). The principal question was whether such an offer of citizenship would require that individuals relinquish their tribal membership and reservation and adopt Anglo culture, as in the Dawes Act. In 1922 the Office of Indian Affairs submitted a report to Congress regarding Indian citizenship. It identified eight different legal procedures or sets of conditions that had enabled select Indians to become citizens. This document reflected not only the racism of the time, but also the sexism. It stated that "legitimate children born of an Indian woman and a white citizen father are born to citizenship" (Office of Indian Affairs 1922).

When a bill to grant universal Indian citizenship was introduced in Congress, Secretary of the Interior Hubert Work wrote to the chairman of the House Committee on Indian Affairs, endorsing the bill and noting that it "will bridge the present gap and provide a means whereby an Indian may be given United States Citizenship without reference to the question of land tenure or the place of his residence" (U.S. House of Representatives, Report No. 222, 1924). In other words, Indians would not have to give up being Indian in exchange for citizenship; an Indian could be an enrolled member of a tribe, live on a federally recognized reservation, practice his or her own culture, and still be a U.S. citizen. Not every Indian welcomed the unilateral extension of citizenship, but at least they were not required to abandon their culture and homeland. The Indian Citizenship Act became law on June 24, 1924.

Citizenship for all Indian people did not automatically create the right to vote for Indians. In the congressional debate over the bill, the following exchange took place on the floor of the House of Representatives:

> Mr. Garrett of Tennessee: I would like very much to have the gentleman's construction of the meaning of this matter as applied to State laws that will be affected by this act; that is, the question of suffrage.
>
> Mr. Snyder: I would be glad to tell the gentleman that, in the investigation of this matter, that question was thoroughly looked into and the laws were examined, and it is not the intention of this law to have any effect upon the suffrage qualifications in any State. In other words, in the State of New Mexico, my understanding is that in order to vote a person must be a taxpayer, and it is in no way intended to affect any Indian in the country who would be unable to vote unless qualified under the State suffrage act. That is my understanding....
>
> Mr. Garrett: ... the principal thing I wanted to ask about was with regard to suffrage rights. It is the construction, then, of the chairman of the committee, and speaking for the committee, that this in no way affects the suffrage rights under State laws.
>
> Mr. Snyder: That is the understanding of the chairman of the committee, and he is carrying to the House that understanding, after careful consideration on that particular question, by a unanimous vote of the committee. (*Congressional Record* 1924, 9303–4)

Not everyone interpreted the Indian Citizenship Act in that manner. The Indian Bureau made the assumption that citizenship equaled enfranchisement. In 1928, the U.S. Department of the Interior issued an optimistic statement regarding Indian voting:

> Two-thirds of the Indians of the United States had acquired citizenship in one way or another prior to 1924. That year Congress passed a law which gave citizenship to all native-born Indians. The franchise was so newly granted that no great use was made of it in the election of 1924. The election of this year is the first general election at which American Indians will have a fair chance to exercise the franchise.

The Department of the Interior clearly did not anticipate the opposition to Indian voting that would be expressed in a number of western states.

The confusion and conflict concerning Indian policy at that time were due in large part to the fact that the nation had not yet decided to allow Indians to remain a separate and politically distinct part of the populace. To many people, Indians were the "vanishing Americans" who would soon be engulfed by the dominant culture. The "Indian problem," as it was termed, was simply a matter of deciding on the most effective means of ridding the nation of the remnants of these formerly independent societies. But at the same time, an alternative view was gaining ground; according to that approach, Indians were here to stay, and the best way to accommodate that reality was to recognize tribal governments, honor treaty rights, and give Indians access to the political process so that they could protect those rights. Rather than vanishing, the Indians would become voters. The 1934 Indian Reorganization Act was the pivot on which Indian policy changed from the first perspective to the second.

The passage of the Indian Citizenship Act marked the end of an era characterized by efforts to gradually obtain citizenship for American Indians. It did not, however, automatically bestow the franchise on Indians. To achieve that, Indians would have to overcome a panoply of state laws, constitutional clauses, and court decisions that blocked the way to Indian suffrage.

From Citizenship to Suffrage

The 1924 Indian Citizenship Act granted citizenship to Indians at the federal level, with the implication that they would also be considered citizens at the state and local levels. The 1934 Indian Reorganization Act recognized the legitimacy of tribal governments and permitted limited self-rule on reservations. Thus, Indians held a unique status of citizenship at four levels of government.

Some states, however, were not willing to accept Indians as equals, especially when it came to political rights. This was evidenced by numerous constitutional provisions, state laws, and court cases. In 1936 the attorney general of Colorado opined that Indians had no right to vote because they were not citizens of the state (Cohen 1942, 158). According to Peterson, as late as 1938, seven states "still refused to let Indians go to the polls" (Peterson 1957, 121). This situation finally began to change, along with many other dramatic social changes, because of World War II.

When the draft was instituted at the beginning of World War II, a Choctaw chief wrote to President Franklin Roosevelt: "[our] white friend[s] here say we are not allowed to vote.... If we are not citizens, will it be right for Choctaws to go to war"? (quoted in Bernstein 1991, 24). The answer turned out to be yes; Indians who were denied the right to vote were nevertheless expected to fight for their country. The 1947 report of the President's Committee on Civil Rights noted that "In past years, American Indians have also been denied the right to vote and other political rights in a number of states.... Protests against these legal bans on Indian suffrage in the Southwest have gained force with the return of Indian veterans to those states" (40). Indian veterans, returning home after service in World War II, played a pivotal role in fighting for the right to vote. By the end of the war, over 25,000 Indians were in military uniform – a larger proportion than that of any other ethnic group in the nation (Holm 1985, 153). Their attitude was summed up by a Navajo veteran: "We went to Hell and back for what? For the people back home in America to tell us we can't vote?" (Rawls 1996, 19). Clearly, the struggle for Indian suffrage would require more than a federal declaration of citizenship; it would require a concerted effort at all levels of government. The resistance to Indian voting ran deep and had a long history.

Limitations on Indian Voting

Official opposition to Indian voting goes back to the formative era of the nation and continues throughout its history. Several different strategies were used by states to prevent or limit Indian voting.

State Constitutions

Limitations on Indian voting were written into a number of state constitutions. In California, the writers of the state constitution in 1850 faced a special challenge

> ... while California was not opposed to admitting true Mexicans to the suffrage, there was great opposition to giving the Indians any chance to vote.... The convention passed the burden on to the legislature. All white male citizens were to vote, including Mexicans ... and the legislature was given the duty of excluding Indians in appropriate terms. (Porter 1918, 127)

The California legislature took the hint and limited the voting right to white citizens (Cohen 1942, 157). Other state constitutions withheld the right to vote from Indians not taxed. The constitutions of Idaho, New Mexico, and Washington contained such language (Cohen 1942, 158). The North Dakota Constitution restricted voting to "civilized persons of Indian descent who shall have severed their tribal relations" (Art. 2, Sec. 121). The South Dakota Constitution limited suffrage to citizens of the United States, which effectively excluded most Indians at that time (1889). Minnesota took a slightly different tack, granting the right to vote only to those Indians who had "adopted the language, customs, and habits of civilization" (Art. 7, Sec. 1).

The passage of the Fifteenth Amendment in 1870 barred states from limiting voting on account of race, so states had to find other ways to limit Indian voting. The following section examines six rationales used by states to prevent Indians from voting.

Residency

Despite the passage of the Indian Citizenship Act (1924), some states still argued that Indians were not residents (i.e., citizens) of the state in which they resided. The state of New Mexico so argued in 1948 (*Trujillo v. Garley*, 1948*, Defendant's Objections to Conclusions of Law 1). Perhaps the best-known residency case was brought in Utah, *Allen v. Merrell*, in 1956. That case is discussed extensively in Chapter 4.

Residency again became an issue in New Mexico in *Montoya v. Bolack* (1962). That case was brought by a non-Indian who had lost a close election because many Navajos voted for his opponent. The losing candidate sued, arguing that the Indian voters were not residents of the state and therefore were ineligible to cast ballots. The New Mexico Supreme Court ruled otherwise and let the election outcome stand. Residency was also one of the issues in *Shirley v. Superior Court* (1973). The Arizona Supreme Court ruled that Mr. Shirley's residence on the Navajo Indian Reservation had no effect on his eligibility to hold county office.

Self-Termination

Much of the debate concerning Indian residency was caught up in the controversy over termination – the legal process whereby Indian tribes lost their federal trust status. Some states attempted to tie Indian voting rights to a process that could be described as "self-termination" – the act of abandoning tribal ties in order to vote. In the *Allen* case, the Utah Supreme Court opined that Indians could gain the right to vote by essentially self-terminating: "All he has to do is to establish a residence in a part of the county where his living is not both supervised and subsidized by the Federal government; where he foregoes the paternalistic favors there conferred, and where he assumes his responsibilities as a citizen" (1956, 495). Once again, Indians were being given the choice between being Indian and being allowed to vote. This choice is reflected in a second method of preventing Indians from voting; some states required Indians to give up their cultural identity and tribal affiliation in order to qualify to vote. The North Dakota constitutional provision cited earlier is an example. In 1903 South Dakota passed a law stipulating that Indians "cannot vote or hold office" while "maintaining tribal relations" (South Dakota Revised Civil Code, Chapter 26).

* Unpublished cases are cited with year of filing, not court opinion, and appear throughout with an asterisk after the date. See the explanatory note with the reference list of Cases for further informations.

In the 1917 case of *Opsahl v. Johnson*, the Supreme Court of Minnesota established a cultural test for voting based on the language in the Minnesota constitution quoted previously:

> It also appears that these Indians have adopted the habits and customs of civilization to quite an extent, in that they live in separate dwellings, constructed and furnished after the manner of the surrounding white settlers. Most of them can understand and speak English, and even write their names, are members of Christian churches, and make a living much the same way as people in the vicinity of the reservation. (988)

The North Dakota Supreme Court established a similar test of cultural purity:

> ...these Indians live the same as white people; they are law-abiding; do not live in tribes under chiefs; that they marry under the civil laws of the state the same as whites, and that they are Christians; that they have severed their tribal relations and adopted civilized life for a period dating back at least 20 years. (*Swift v. Leach* 1920, 439)

These quotes indicate some of the perceived differences between Indians and whites that had to be erased before the former were given the same voting rights as the latter. Another difference between Indians and whites concerned taxes.

Taxation

Numerous states, mimicking the language in the U.S. Constitution, withheld the franchise from "Indians not taxed." A compendium of state voting laws compiled in 1940 by the Council of State Governments found that five states (Idaho, Maine, Mississippi, New Mexico, and Washington) excluded "Indians not taxed" from the voting booth (Council of State Governments 1940, 3). In 1938 the solicitor of the Interior Department issued an opinion regarding these laws: "The laws of Idaho, New Mexico, and Washington which would exclude Indians not taxed from voting in effect exclude citizens of one race from voting on grounds which are not applied to citizens of other races" (quoted in Cohen 1942, 158). The President's Committee on Civil Rights (1947) also made note of these laws: "The constitutionality of these laws is presently being tested. It has been pointed out that the concept of 'Indians not taxed' is no longer meaningful; it is a vestige of the days when most Indians were not citizens and had not become part of the community of people of the United States" (40). This did not, however, prevent states from using such laws to prevent Indians from voting.

The issue of Indians not directly paying local taxes and property taxes while living on a federally recognized Indian reservation is a recurrent theme in the voting literature. In addition to the constitutional provisions cited earlier, numerous state laws and state court decisions have focused on this issue. In *Opsahl v. Johnson* (1917), the fact that the Indians were not subject to taxation helped convince the justices to vote against allowing the Indian plaintiffs to vote (989, 990).

New Mexico's constitutional provision regarding Indians not taxed was litigated in the case of *Trujillo v. Garley* (1948*). Miguel Trujillo was from Isleta Pueblo. He volunteered for the Marines in 1942 and served until the end of the war. He then became a teacher at the Laguna Pueblo day school. When he attempted to register to vote in 1948, the county clerk refused because he was an "Indian not taxed." Mr. Trujillo pointed out that although he did not pay property taxes, he did pay federal income tax, gasoline taxes, and sales taxes, as well as paying for a state motor vehicle license. Still, he was denied the right to vote. Thus, to the state of New Mexico, the relevant phrase was construed to apply to Indians who did not pay certain taxes, even though they might pay other taxes. Both sides in the case agreed that "there are great numbers of Indians situated within the State of New Mexico who have been denied the right to vote for the same reason that the above-named plaintiff was denied the right to vote" (*Trujillo v. Garley*, 1948*, Stipulation of Fact, 2).

Judge Orie Phillips spoke for a three-judge panel:

> . . . it is immaterial whether or not from a constitutional standpoint "Indians not taxed" means Indians who do not pay an ad valorem tax or means Indians who do not pay state taxes of any character. . . . [The constitution of New Mexico] says that "Indians not taxed" may not vote, although they possess every other qualification. We are unable to escape the conclusion that, under the Fourteenth and Fifteenth Amendments, that constitutes a discrimination on the ground of race. Any other citizen, regardless of race, in the State of New Mexico who has not paid one cent of tax of any kind or character, if he possesses the other qualification, may vote. (*Trujillo v. Garley* 1948*, Conclusions of Law, 6–7)

The defendant's attorney objected to the court's decision and argued that the constitutional phrase in question referred to a "special class of persons and not to a race as such" (*Trujillo v. Garley*, Defendant's Objections to Conclusions of Law 1948, 1). The court ignored that argument and ordered a permanent injunction against enforcing the Indians-not-taxed provision of the state constitution. For the first time in history, Indians in New Mexico were free to vote.

This did not prevent the issue from returning to the New Mexico Supreme Court. In 1975 a group of white citizens asked the court to throw out the results of a school district bond election because Navajos had participated in the election. Navajo children made up two-thirds of the pupils in the district, but the non-Indians argued that Indians should not be allowed to vote in a bond election because they did not pay property taxes – the source of revenue used to repay the bonds. In *Prince v. Board of Education* (1975), the court ruled against the Anglo plaintiffs and pointed out that much of the revenue in the school district arose from the reservation, either in the form of federal subsidies and services, payments in lieu of taxes, or taxes paid by non-Indian corporations that did business on the reservation.

At about the same time, another case arose in Arizona that involved the issue of Indians and property taxes. Tom Shirley, a Navajo, had won a seat on the Apache County Board of Supervisors, but the Anglo members of the board refused to certify his election, arguing that, among other things, Shirley did not own any property that was subject to taxation by the state of Arizona. The court ruled in Mr. Shirley's favor, noting that the fact that he was "not a taxpayer [had] been declared no obstacle to voting or holding office" (*Shirley v. Superior Court* 1973, 945).

Most of these tax cases involved what the court in *Prince* referred to as the "representation without taxation" issue (*Prince v. Board of Education* 1975, 1178). In other words, Indians should not be allowed to vote on issues regarding taxes because they did not directly pay those taxes (see Phelps 1985). The defendant's brief in the landmark case of *Harrison v. Laveen* (described in detail later), put it succinctly: "If a man is not subject to taxation, he should not impose taxes on others" (*Harrison v. Laveen*, Appellee's Reply 1948, 48). Even though Indians do pay taxes, directly and indirectly, this issue remains contentious and has played a role in many Indian voting cases litigated under the VRA. There is still considerable resistance among non-Indians to Indians voting in state and local elections because of the tax issue.

Guardianship

Nearly every state in the Union limits voting to sane, competent individuals. In most cases the relevant statutes refer to the "insane," or "idiots" and "incompetents," or use the Latin equivalent, "*non compos mentis*." Fourteen states withhold voting privileges from persons "under guardianship," a phrase that "applies to people who are legally under the supervision and control of a person or agency designated by the Court" (Smith 1960, 23).

The applicability of the guardianship clause in the North Dakota constitution was litigated in 1920 in *Swift v. Leach*. Sioux Indians from the Standing Rock Indian Reservation had voted in a referendum to relocate the county seat. All of the Indians who voted in the election were trust-patent Indians, meaning that they had followed the procedures established in the Dawes and Burke Acts to settle on allotted lands. But non-Indians on the county board sued to prevent the Indian votes from being counted on the basis of two arguments. The first one, that the Indians had not given up tribal relations, has already been discussed. The second argument was that the Indians were under federal guardianship and therefore did not qualify as electors, and that this guardianship "negatives the right to recognize such Indians as civilized persons" (*Swift v. Leach* 1920, 441). The court held in favor of the Indians, noting that their abandonment of Indian ways was indicative of their competence to vote and that their participation in state elections "discloses no interference with this federal policy of wardship" (443).

The outcome was quite different when a similar case arose in Arizona. A guardianship clause became a rationale for Arizona to deny Indians the right to vote in the case of *Porter v. Hall* (1928). The Arizona Constitution provides that "No person under guardianship, non compos mentis or insane, shall be qualified to vote at any election..." (Art. 7, Sec. 2). This clearly refers to the mental condition of an individual, but when two Pima Indian men from the Gila River Reservation tried to register to vote in Pinal County, they were refused on the grounds that they were persons under guardianship and thus ineligible.

This case was important because it occurred during the first full presidential election campaign after the passage of the Indian Citizenship Act, and thus served as a test case to probe the link between citizenship and suffrage. Both sides in the *Porter* case stipulated that "there are many other Indians besides plaintiffs whose right to vote at the coming general election will be determined by this case" (*Porter v. Hall* 1928, 413). The state of Arizona made two arguments against the plaintiffs: that Indian reservations in Arizona were not within the political and governmental boundaries of the state and that the guardianship clause prevented Indians from voting. For the latter, they cited Chief Justice John Marshall's language in *Cherokee Nation v. Georgia*: "Their relation to the United States resembles that of a ward to his guardian" (1831, 17).

The Arizona Supreme Court quickly dispensed with the first argument but completely accepted the second one. They held that an Indian living on a reservation, unlike "a normal person" or an "ordinary citizen," is a person under guardianship within the meaning of the Arizona Constitution (*Porter v. Hall* 1928, 416–17). The court took pains to specifically disagree with the holding in *Swift v. Leach* (1920, 418–19). After rendering this verdict, the court engaged in an extensive digression into policy prescription and offered its support for a concept that became known thirty years later as "termination":

> We heartily approve the present announced policy of the federal government that, as soon as its Indian wards are fitted therefore, they should be released from their guardianship and placed in the ranks of citizens of the United States and of the state of their residence. (419)

Apparently the court did not notice that Indians had been awarded citizenship four years earlier. In a dissent, Chief Justice C. J. Ross pointed out that the guardianship phrase was repeated in the state's election laws, but with the addition of "idiots" and "insane persons," and thus obviously referred to the capacity of an individual who has been legally declared incompetent. He also noted that Justice Marshall used the phrase metaphorically; the relationship "resembles" a guardianship (419).

The opinion in *Porter v. Hall* stood for twenty years. In 1944 the attorney general of Arizona opined that the Porter ruling also applied to any Indian who had moved off the reservation and "goes on his own" (quoted in Houghton 1945, 19). This meant that every Indian living in Arizona, even if he or she lived far from a reservation, was still ineligible to vote. This was galling to the Indian veterans of World War II who returned home to Arizona only to find that they could not vote.

One of those veterans, Frank Harrison, decided to do something about it. He and his friend Harry Austin, both Mohave Indians from the Fort McDowell Indian Reservation, attempted to register in Maricopa County. The county auditor, Roger Laveen, rejected their registration, citing *Porter*. Harrison and Austin sued in Maricopa County Superior Court, lost, and appealed to the Arizona Supreme Court. Their case generated national attention. An amicus brief was filed on behalf of the Indians by the National Congress of American Indians (NCAI) – a pan-Indian organization formed in 1944 – and the American Civil Liberties Union (ACLU). This marked the first time that the ACLU became involved in an Indian voting rights case. The U.S. assistant attorney general also filed an amicus brief on behalf of the Indians.

The extensive briefs filed by both sides in the *Harrison v. Laveen* case provide a clear picture of how the issue of Indian voting was perceived in the late 1940s. The brief filed by the attorneys for Harrison and Austin argued that the situation had changed since the *Porter* case because Congress had passed the Nationality Act and the Selective Service Act, which "emancipated the Indians from this guardianship" (Opening Brief of Appellants, 11). They asked dryly that if Harrison was incompetent, then how could he bring suit before a state court? (12). Their brief then made a pointed comparison:

> The Arizona Constitution does not use the words "resembling a guardianship," but the words "under guardianship." The relationship of a domineering wife to a meek husband often "resembles guardianship" but the meek husband is not thereby disfranchised. One may "resemble" his brother, but he is not the brother. (Opening Brief of Appellants, 19)

The fifty-five-page amicus brief filed by the NCAI and ACLU made many of the same points as the appellant's brief, but also noted that the Indian Reorganization Act of 1934 had substantially altered the wardship relationship between Indian tribes and the federal government, and thus *Porter v. Hall* was no longer applicable (26–7). Their brief also approached the guardianship issue as a question of racism:

> The denial of the franchise to Indians as "persons under guardianship" is in fact a racial discrimination as shown by the fact that other classes of citizens who are "under guardianship" only in the same extended or metaphorical sense in which Indians are "under guardianship" are not denied the right to vote. (44)

The brief filed by the U.S. attorneys took a somewhat different tack. In effect, they argued that full political rights were part of the process of termination: "The government's policy aims at the full integration of Indians into the political, social, and economic culture of the Nation" (Brief, *Amicus Curiae*, of the United States of America, 2). The U.S. attorneys also made an issue of the hypocrisy of sending Indians to fight wars in the name of democracy and then denying them that same right at home:

> During the last war, when large numbers of Indians left the reservations for service in the armed forces and industrial jobs, they were made intensely aware of the discriminations which are enforced against Indians, and they rightly resented a situation where they are allowed to participate in upholding democratic principles as soldiers, but are considered unprepared to share in protecting those principles in peace time. (7)

The appellee's brief filed by Maricopa County attorneys offered the opposing rationale. They argued that race was not an issue: "The Indian problem is unique and must be looked upon as such and not as a problem of a class, nationality or race of people" (Appellee's Reply, 12). Instead, Indians "are a special class of people" who do not have to pay property taxes and are not subject to state law, and therefore "did not assume the burdens of citizenship" (27). Rather, "Congress still holds a tight rein on the reservation Indian" (43), and thus, "we have a class of people not considered to be capable of handling their own affairs.... Certainly while this condition exists, the Indians affected, even though citizens, should not be permitted to vote" (46–7). The appellee's brief then launched into an argument for termination, and argued that voting rights should not be extended until the "wardship" is terminated (49–50).

Justice J. J. Udall wrote the opinion of the court. He began with an allusion to Shakespeare: "The right of American Indians to vote in Arizona elections for state and federal officers has after two decades again arisen, like Banquo's ghost, to challenge us" (*Harrison v. Laveen* 1948, 457). He then noted that the payment of taxes or service in the military was not the issue. Rather, it was whether the guardianship provision of the Arizona Constitution, as interpreted in *Porter*, violated the Fourteenth and Fifteenth Amendments (458). The court also noted that, in *Porter*, the court engaged in policymaking when it presented an argument for termination and that policymaking is best left to the legislative branch of government (460). Justice Udall then took direct aim at the *Porter* decision: "it is a tortious construction by the judicial branch of the simple phrase, 'under guardianship,' accomplishing a purpose that was never designed by its framers" (461). He then noted that many states had a similar constitutional clause regarding guardianship, but only Arizona had used it to deny Indians the right to vote (461). The court then expressly overruled *Porter*. For the first time in history, Indians in Arizona had the right to vote – *if* they could pass Arizona's literacy test (which was not addressed in the *Harrison* case).

Literacy

According to the Council of State Governments' 1940 survey of election laws, eighteen states prohibited illiterates from voting; among those were six western states with substantial Indian populations. Arizona had a statutory requirement that only those who could read the U.S. Constitution in English could vote (Phelps 1985, 136).

In the mid-twentieth century, there were still thousands of Indians who spoke only their native tongue. And due to the inadequacies of reservation schools, many Indians were still illiterate. Thus, literacy tests dramatically reduced the number of Indians eligible to vote. This problem was especially severe on the Navajo Reservation, where traditional language and culture remained strong. In the early 1960s, the chairman of the Navajo Nation estimated that half of the voting-age population on the reservation could not vote because of the literacy test (Steiner 1968, 238).

Of course, the negative impact of literacy tests on voting was not limited to Indians in western states; such tests were used in the South and other regions to prevent blacks and Hispanics from voting. This problem was not remedied until passage of the Voting Rights Act.

Protecting the Status Quo

The rationales just outlined – residency, self-termination, taxation, guardianship, and literacy – have all been used to prevent Indians from voting. In many cases, these strategies are part of a larger effort by those in power who prefer not to relinquish dominance. It is human nature to try to maintain one's power; it is also human nature to contest the status quo when one is excluded from it. Throughout the literature, case law, and media coverage of the Indian voting issue, there are references to this power struggle, often with racist overtones. For example, the Utah Supreme Court, in the 1956 case of *Allen v. Merrell*, addressed this issue, making reference to a fear that Indians would have too much power if they voted (see Chapter 4).

Opposition to Indian voting began to increase in some areas as Indians experienced success in electing their own candidates. After two Navajos were elected to the New Mexico state legislature in 1964, a local non-Indian leader reacted with fear: "If this keeps up the Indians will take over" (Steiner 1968, 232). According to Glenn Phelps, areas where Indians were particularly effective in electing their own candidates became an inducement for non-Indians to contrive "much more constitutionally sophisticated objections to Indian suffrage" (Phelps 1991, 70). These efforts became the focus of the VRA.

Conclusion

As Indians gradually gained the right to vote, controversies over voting gradually shifted to the abridgment of voting rights. Despite these barriers, Indians experienced some electoral success, especially in areas where they were numerous and concentrated. Peterson lists a number of elections in the 1950s, all in western states, where the Indian vote was a "decisive factor" (Peterson 1957, 124). Jack Holmes relates how tribal leaders from all over New Mexico were invited to appear with President Lyndon B. Johnson during the 1964 presidential campaign, noting that such appearances had been symbolic in the past but were now policy related (Holmes 1967, 100). That same year, two Navajos were elected to the New Mexico state house. Two years later, a Navajo became the first Indian to serve in the New Mexico senate. That same year saw the first Indian serving in the Arizona state legislature (Steiner 1968, 233).

In the 1970s and 1980s, Indian voters had even more impact. In the 1976 elections, Navajos voted in large numbers: "A record turnout among Navajo voters Tuesday helped elect a new democratic senator and one new democratic congressman in Arizona" (Bosser 1976, 1). Not only were Indians voting in larger numbers, they were engaging in some sophisticated ticket splitting that made it clear that they knew which politicians held a pro-Indian point of view (McCool 1985, 123–4). Politicians were quick to realize that the Indian vote could make the difference between victory and defeat. In a speech before the Arizona Indian Town Hall in 1975, State Attorney General Bruce Babbitt acknowledged his debt to Indians:

> The reason why I am here is because you have developed a level of participation in state politics and it shows in the results at the polls. The governor of this State and I are particularly aware of that. At the last election, if you look at the returns from the Indian tribes around the State, you don't have to be very good at arithmetic to know that we owe you a great deal. (Babbitt 1975)

But the goal of Indian suffrage, on a par with that of their fellow citizens off the reservation, was only partially achieved. State and local officials soon learned that the impact of Indian voting could be reduced or neutralized by employing a host of election rules that made it difficult, if not impossible, for Indians to vote and elect their candidates of choice. These devices had been used to great effect in the South to prevent blacks from winning elections; some political jurisdictions realized that they could also be used against Indians. Language barriers also presented problems for American Indians, many of whom spoke primarily their native tongue. We now turn to the effort to overcome these problems, first through the passage and expansion of the VRA and second through its application in Indian Country.

2

On Account of Race or Color

The Development of the Voting Rights Act

The U.S. Congress passed the Voting Rights Act (VRA) of 1965 to complete the work started by the Fifteenth Amendment to the Constitution, ratified in 1870. The act has been amended and extended several times because of continuing discrimination against African Americans and other minorities. It is enforced through administrative action and the combined efforts of governmental and private litigation. This chapter reviews the evolution of the act and the various organizations that enforce it.

The Legislative and Judicial Evolution of the Voting Rights Act of 1965

With the end of Reconstruction in the South in 1877, formal and informal efforts to keep African Americans from voting quickly neutralized the political gains they had made. Poll taxes, literacy tests, all-white primary elections, and sheer intimidation were just a few of the many devices that kept African Americans from exercising their right to vote (Zelden 2002, 70–84; Valelly 2004). Even where they could vote, southern states reduced the votes' impact by turning elective offices into appointive ones, annexing new areas to bring in more white voters, moving to at-large elections where whites in the larger area outnumbered blacks, and making other changes. After twenty-five years and several lawsuits, the National Association for the Advancement of Colored People (NAACP) eventually succeeded in getting courts to eliminate the all-white primary, but facially race-neutral deterrents continued to permit discriminatory application. Even by 1964, average black voter registration in Alabama, Georgia, Louisiana, Mississippi, and South Carolina was only 22.5 percent of those eligible, and in Mississippi it was only 6.7 percent (Davidson 1992, 13).

The civil rights movement that emerged in the mid-1950s generated political pressure for greater federal protection of voting rights. The first twentieth-century civil rights legislation, the Civil Rights Act of 1957, created the U.S. Commission on Civil Rights and authorized it to investigate allegations of deprivation of the right to vote on account of color, race, religion, or national origin (§101 and §104). Section 131 of that statute outlawed interference with the right to vote in federal elections and empowered the U.S. attorney general to bring civil actions to prevent such interference. This provision was strengthened modestly in the Civil Rights Acts of 1960 and 1964 but without great effect, since challenges to discriminatory voting practices required case-by-case litigation (Laney 2003, 8). Jurisdictions determined to resist could do so for a long time. For example, only 2.2 percent of eligible blacks had registered to vote in Selma, Alabama, after four years of litigation challenging discriminatory practices (Hancock and Tredway 1985, 385).

This intransigence led President Johnson to call for the "goddamnedest toughest" voting rights law possible (Davidson 1992, 17, quoting Raines 1977, 377). What emerged was the VRA of 1965. Codified as 42 U.S.C. §1973, this law imposed tough new standards on all districts meeting certain objective criteria and shifted the burden to them to prove that they had not discriminated in the application of their voting laws. The law is complex, so it is worthwhile to describe its various sections in some detail. We initially describe the law as it passed in 1965; later amendments will be discussed chronologically.

The Original Statute

After Section 1 announced the law's title, Section 2 essentially restated the Fifteenth Amendment, declaring, "No voting qualification or prerequisite to voting, or standard, practice, or procedure, shall be imposed or applied by any State or political subdivision to deny or abridge the right of any citizen of the United States to vote on account of race or color." Unlike some later sections, Section 2 was permanent and applied nationwide to voting practices regardless of when they were initially passed.

Section 3 detailed the remedies courts could impose when they found a jurisdiction in violation of Section 2. These included suspending the discriminatory test or device, appointing federal election examiners, and maintaining jurisdiction to ensure that new discriminatory practices were not instituted.

These two sections still required case-by-case litigation, in contrast to the most innovative parts of the law, the "special provisions" in Sections 4 through 9. These were temporary and not nationally applicable, applying only to jurisdictions defined by a formula articulated in Section 4b. The formula targeted all states and political subdivisions that used a literacy test or any sort of "test or device" as a condition for voter registration on November 1, 1964, and in which less than 50 percent of voting-age persons were registered to vote or had voted in the presidential election of 1964. Under what is known as the "bailout" provision, Section 4a permitted jurisdictions to be removed from coverage by proving to a three-judge federal district court of the District of Columbia that they had not used such tests in a discriminatory manner in the preceding five years.

The most intrusive section of the statute was Section 5, which essentially froze all voting laws in the jurisdictions covered under Section 4. These jurisdictions had to seek "preclearance" from either the attorney general or the U.S. District Court for the District of Columbia (in an action for declaratory judgment) and establish that the proposed change in "voting qualification or prerequisite to voting, or standard, practice, or procedure with respect to voting" had no racially discriminatory purpose or effect. This section was intended to prohibit districts from allowing minority voters to register and vote but then manipulating other aspects of the electoral system to abridge the impact of their votes.

Sections 6, 7, and 8 authorized the attorney general to appoint federal examiners to register voters in covered jurisdictions and to appoint election observers where examiners were serving. Section 9 provided a mechanism for resolving challenges to voters who registered through this process.

Section 10 authorized the attorney general to bring litigation challenging poll taxes in state or local elections. The Twenty-Fourth Amendment, ratified in 1964, had outlawed poll taxes in federal elections.

Section 11 established criminal penalties for anyone "acting under color of law" or otherwise from intimidating people from voting or impeding vote counting in federal elections. It also set penalties for committing fraud in such elections. Section 12 authorized the attorney general to bring civil actions to protect the election process and provided penalties to protect ballots and voting records for a year after elections.

Finally, Section 13 provided conditions for terminating federal oversight of the voter registration process, and Section 14 stated a broad definition of "vote" and "voting" that made coverage of the law quite expansive.[1]

The jurisdictions covered by the trigger formula in Section 4 were the states of Alabama, Georgia, Louisiana, Mississippi, South Carolina, Virginia, Alaska, numerous counties in North Carolina, and a few counties in Arizona, Hawaii, and Idaho (Davidson 1992, 18). The attorney general consented to bailout suits initiated on behalf of Alaska and counties in Arizona, Idaho, and North Carolina, as he was required to if "he [had] no reason to believe" that voting tests or devices had been used to discriminate in the preceding five years (Hancock and Tredway 1985, 390, 392). Thus, the common public perception that the 1965 VRA concerned only the South, rather than other parts of the country as well, is not accurate, but clearly the emphasis was on southern states.

The constitutionality of the VRA was promptly challenged and upheld. The U.S. Supreme Court in *South Carolina v. Katzenbach* (1966) ruled emphatically that the act was a proper use of congressional power to enforce the Fifteenth Amendment. One justice, Hugo Black, dissented with respect to Section 5's preclearance requirements, which he viewed as subjecting the southern states to a violation of federalism "reminiscent of old Reconstruction days" (358).

During the first five years after the law went into effect, African American voter registration in the South increased rapidly. The discriminatorily applied tests that had been the major vehicle for deterring such registration disappeared, sometimes under the supervision of federal examiners. Registration in Mississippi grew from 6.7 percent before the act to 59.8 percent in 1967; the gap between black and white registration rates in the seven southern states principally affected decreased from 44 percent in 1965 to 11 percent in 1971–2 (Davidson 1992, 21; see also McDonald 2003a, 129).

In the face of these gains, whites who were determined to maintain their traditional hold on political power turned to other means of reducing blacks' electoral influence (Derfner 1973). These included practices that continued to make registration difficult, such as reducing hours or locations for registering, declining to provide assistance, requiring multiple

1 "The terms 'vote' or 'voting' shall include all action necessary to make a vote effective in any primary, special, or general election, including, but not limited to, registration, listing [of eligible voters] pursuant to this Act, or other action required by law prerequisite to voting, casting a ballot, and having such ballot counted properly and included in the appropriate totals of votes cast with respect to candidates for public or party office and propositions for which votes are received in an election."

registration for different elections, or purging rolls and requiring reregistration. Other policies reduced opportunities to vote by changing electoral offices to appointive ones or making running for office more difficult through filing fees and petitions. Finally, some jurisdictions made electoral changes that potentially reduced the effect of votes once cast, such as annexations, majority runoff requirements, at-large districts, and gerrymandered district boundaries. Such electoral practices have come to be known as "vote dilution": "Ethnic or racial minority vote dilution may be defined as a process whereby election laws or practices either singly or in concert, combine with systematic bloc voting among an identifiable majority group to diminish or cancel the voting strength of at least one minority group" (Davidson 1992, 24).

In 1969, in *Allen v. State Board of Elections,* the U.S. Supreme Court broadly defined the Section 5 preclearance requirement to include election law changes with the potential to dilute minority votes. Section 5 had not been used much until that time (Ball, Krane, and Lauth 1982). The number of Department of Justice objections to proposed changes grew from 6 in the three and one-half years before the *Allen* decision to 118 in the same length of time after it; 88 of the latter involved vote-diluting changes (Davidson 1992, 28). *Allen* also held that private litigants have standing to sue if jurisdictions fail to follow the preclearance requirements of Section 5, opening up Section 5 enforcement to the private civil rights bar (1969, 556–7).

The Amendments of 1970 and 1975

Continuing efforts to restrict voting rights led to the VRA Amendments of 1970. The bailout provisions of the 1965 act required only that jurisdictions had not used "tests or devices" to discriminate in the past five years. Thus, jurisdictions with a long history of discrimination that had eliminated such tests as required by the law in 1965 could bail out of preclearance requirements and the other "special provisions" even if other vote-deterring or diluting tactics were in use.

The 1970 amendments made the ban on literacy tests and other devices nationwide, updated the formula determining the jurisdictions under the special provisions by using participation in the 1968 presidential election as the benchmark, and extended for five more years the period in which such jurisdictions would have to prove that they had not used discriminatory tests or devices. The new formula brought no new states under the special provisions, but did bring in numerous political subdivisions including towns and counties in New York State and New England (Hancock and Tredway 1985, 396). Some Alaska and Arizona political subdivisions that had bailed out after their 1965 coverage were covered again.

In 1975 the U.S. Commission on Civil Rights issued a major report, the *Voting Rights Act: Ten Years After*, which characterized the period since the passage of the VRA as "years of catching up, a process well under way but far from complete" (U.S. Commission on Civil Rights 1975, 329). "[T]here is still hostility and resistance to the free and effective political participation" of America's minorities (330). Noting that the 1970 coverage formula picked up jurisdictions in "every corner of the United States" (15), the Commission found that "the problems encountered by Spanish speaking persons and Native Americans in covered jurisdictions are not dissimilar from those encountered by Southern blacks" (16).

With the covered jurisdictions once again approaching the time when they could bail out of the special provisions, Congress again extended the act and this time considerably expanded it (VRA of 1965, amendments of 1975). The 1975 hearings included substantial testimony about discrimination against language minorities in education and voting. For example, purging of registration lists in Arizona eliminated large numbers of Indian voters from the rolls in Coconino and Apache counties. Counties notified affected voters via mail, but many Navajos, unable to read English, discarded the notices without understanding the impact of such actions (U.S. Commission on Civil Rights 1975, 85–6; included in U.S. Congress, House, 1975, *Hearings,* 1068–9). Congress recognized that issues of English literacy are very different for voluntary immigrants than for Spanish-heritage, American Indian, and Alaskan Native groups "living on territory suddenly annexed by the United States; in most cases their ancestors had been living on the same land for centuries" (U.S. Congress. Senate 1975, 38). After considering the impact of racially discriminatory educational systems and of state and local governments unresponsive to non-European immigrants, Congress ultimately defined "language minority groups" as persons of Asian American, American Indian, Alaskan Native, or Spanish heritage.

Existing provisions of the VRA were extended until 1982, long enough to ensure that redistricting following the 1980 census would be subject to preclearance in covered jurisdictions (Laney 2003, 27). The nationwide ban on literacy tests imposed in 1970 became permanent. The special provisions of Sections 4 through 9 – federal examiners, observers, and preclearance of changes – were imposed on all jurisdictions that had conducted the 1972 election with materials printed only in English where less than 50 percent of voting-age citizens had registered or voted in that election and where the Census Bureau determined that more than 5 percent of the voting-age citizens were of a single language minority. This formula in Section 4(f) resulted in coverage for Texas, Arizona, Alaska, and counties or other political subdivisions in California, Colorado, Florida, Michigan, New Mexico, New York, North Carolina, Oklahoma, and South Dakota (45 Fed. Register 44268, 46380, 47423, 1980).[2]

A final provision of the act codified the right of private parties to bring suit under the act and seek the same special remedies in any jurisdiction that were permitted automatically in jurisdictions covered under Section 4. The act also authorized payment of attorneys' fees to prevailing parties other than the United States, further encouraging private litigation to supplement cases brought by the Department of Justice.

Judicial Interpretations of the Voting Rights Act in the 1970s

During the 1970s, a number of issues about the VRA reached the judiciary. For example, in 1976, in *Beer v. United States*, the Supreme Court established "nonretrogression" as the standard for preclearance of proposed voting changes. In other words, the Justice Department and courts could object on the grounds of discriminatory effect only if changes made minority voters worse off than they had been before and not because changes established less equality than they could have.

The courts also addressed the scope of protection against vote dilution. The Supreme Court had acknowledged as early as 1965 that multimember election districts had the potential to "minimize or cancel out the voting strength of racial or political elements of the voting population," "designedly or otherwise" (*Fortson v. Dorsey* 1965, 439). In *Whitcomb v. Chavis* in 1971, the Court made it clear that simply losing elections was not sufficient proof of discrimination. Plaintiffs had to establish that they had "less opportunity than did other . . . residents . . . to participate in the political processes and to elect legislators of their choice" (149).

It was not until 1973, in a challenge to multimember legislative districts in Dallas and San Antonio, Texas, that the Supreme Court first upheld a vote dilution claim in *White v. Regester*. The case provided little guidance, however, because the Court simply found that the "totality of

[2] Covered jurisdictions and regulations for implementation of the provisions of the VRA regarding language minority groups are codified at 28 Code of Federal Regulations, Part 55.

the circumstances" demonstrated a constitutional violation, but it did not generalize or prioritize the factors. Lower courts moved into the vacuum and began to systematize the criteria. The most widely used ones were enunciated by the Fifth Circuit Court of Appeals in *Zimmer v. McKeithen* (1973), which did not include a showing of discriminatory purpose in the adoption of multimember districts.

Such litigation was necessarily jurisdiction-specific and required detailed, costly evidence of the jurisdiction's electoral history. Nonetheless, the Justice Department and private litigants initiated many cases and won some of them (McDonald 2003a, 158–63). Thus, they were stunned when the Supreme Court in 1980, in *City of Mobile v. Bolden*, cast doubt on whether the Fifteenth Amendment (and Section 2 of the VRA) protected against dilution of votes cast as well as mere access to the ballot. Moreover, the Court ruled that the Fifteenth Amendment and Section 2, like the Fourteenth Amendment, required a showing of intentional discrimination. Proving that a practice had a discriminatory effect on minorities would be insufficient to establish a violation of voting rights without also meeting the burden of proving that such effect was intended.

The 1982 Amendments

In response to this setback, voting rights advocates mounted a major lobbying effort to amend Section 2 to outlaw by statute electoral systems with discriminatory effects without the need to prove discriminatory intent. With the VRA Amendments of 1982, they succeeded. This change is especially important because Section 2 is permanent and nationwide in scope, opening the possibility of vote dilution cases anywhere in the country and against electoral systems that predate the passage of the 1965 act.

The 1982 amendments included other important changes as well. The special provisions were extended for another twenty-five years to 2007 but added a new approach to bailouts. Covered jurisdictions could petition the court for bailout before the end of this period by meeting several criteria, including rigorously following preclearance requirements, not having been assigned federal examiners, not losing a voting rights lawsuit, eliminating election rules that dilute or inhibit equal access, and making "constructive efforts" to equalize opportunities for an effective ballot (Hancock and Tredway 1985, 409–10, 417–21; Laney 2003, 36). Moreover, for the first time, individual political subdivisions could bail out, not just entire states, giving local governments an incentive to end past discriminatory practices.

Predictably, the expansion of Section 2 to cover discriminatory effects without the need to prove intent led to an increase in voting rights litigation and preemptive changes in electoral practices to avoid litigation. The average number of voting cases in federal courts grew from 150 per year before the 1982 amendments to 225 per year in the first years after passage; the number of jurisdictions preclearing changes in election methods with the Department of Justice more than doubled in the three years after 1982 compared to the three years before (McDonald 1992, 71). Many of these changes were shifts away from at-large electoral systems.

The Supreme Court's first interpretation of amended Section 2, *Thornburgh v. Gingles* (1986), addressed the use of at-large electoral districts and developed three criteria for when such districts constitute illegal vote dilution. These three "*Gingles* factors" have become the standard for such cases. Plaintiffs challenging at-large voting districts must first prove that:

1. The minority population is "sufficiently large and geographically compact" to make up a majority in one or more single-member districts;
2. The minority population is "politically cohesive"; and
3. The majority population usually votes as a bloc to defeat the minority's preferred candidate.

The first two conditions are essential because, "Unless minority voters possess the potential to elect representatives in the absence of the challenged structure or practice, they cannot claim to have been injured by the structure or practice" (*Gingles* 1986, 51, n. 17). Once these three preconditions are met, the court then determines from the "totality of circumstances" whether the minority population has been denied an equal opportunity to elect representatives of their choice. The Supreme Court relied upon the legislative history of the 1982 amendments (1982 U.S. Code Cong. & Adm. News 177, 206–7), which identified many important factors in Section 2 cases. These conditions came to be known as the "Senate factors":

1. The extent of any history of official discrimination in the state or political subdivision that touched the right of the members of the minority group to register, to vote, or otherwise to participate in the democratic process.
2. The extent to which voting in the elections of the state or political subdivision is racially polarized.

3. The extent to which the state or political subdivision has used unusually large election districts, majority vote requirements, anti–single-shot provisions, or other voting practices or procedures that may enhance the opportunity for discrimination against the minority group.
4. If there is a candidate slating process, and whether the members of the minority group have been denied access to that process.
5. The extent to which the members of the minority group in the state or political subdivision bear the effects of discrimination in such areas as education, employment, and health, which hinders their ability to participate effectively in the political process.
6. Whether the political campaigns have been characterized by overt or subtle racial appeals.
7. The extent to which members of the minority group have been elected to public office in the jurisdiction
8. Whether there is a significant lack of responsiveness on the part of election officials to the particular needs of the members of the minority group.
9. Whether the policy underlying the state or political subdivisions' use of such voting qualifications, prerequisites to voting, standards, practices, or procedures is tenuous.

Successful challenges of at-large electoral systems do not end all vote dilution controversies, of course. In the creation of new single-member districts or the reapportionment of existing ones, conflicts often arise over where the district boundaries are drawn. Manipulating boundaries of governmental units either to break up concentrations of minority voters ("cracking") or to isolate them in separate districts ("packing") is a long-standing tactic to dilute minority votes (Parker 1984). Redistricting following the decennial census tends to draw issues of racial fairness into combination with efforts to equalize district populations, achieve particular partisan distributions, and protect incumbent politicians in the process. Covered jurisdictions must get their reapportionment plans precleared by the Justice Department or the courts, and controversies often arise at that stage.

The Supreme Court Changes Course

Following the 1990 census, reapportionment issues dominated voting rights cases that came to the Supreme Court, and the Court made major changes in doctrine. In a series of cases starting with *Shaw v. Reno*

(1993) and including *Miller v. Johnson* (1995) and *Bush v. Vera* (1996), a closely divided Supreme Court checked the creation of districts in which racial minorities make up the majority of the population to increase their chances of electing a candidate of their choice (i.e., "majority-minority districts"). The Court compared such districts to other types of invidious racial segregation (*Miller* 1995, 911) and condemned "the offensive and demeaning assumption that voters of a particular race... will prefer the same candidates at the polls" (*Miller* 1995, 912). If districts are now challenged as racial gerrymanders, states must prove that they are necessary to meet a compelling interest, the highest standard imposed on governmental decisions. On the other hand, the Court accepted a majority-minority district justified for partisan political reasons in *Easley v. Cromartie* (2001).

At the same time, the Court made the standard for challenging a redistricting plan as discriminatory against racial minorities more difficult. In *Reno v. Bossier Parish School Board* (2000), the Court substantially narrowed the ability to challenge purposeful discrimination by ruling that Section 5 of the VRA permits preclearance of a redistricting plan even in the face of evidence of discriminatory purpose unless the purpose itself was retrogressive.

Controversies over racial considerations in reapportionment began again after the 2000 census. In *Georgia v. Ashcroft* (2003), the Supreme Court lent support in the context of Section 5 preclearance to arguments that minority voters' political influence could be enhanced by spreading them out over more districts at the cost of reducing the size of their majority and thus reducing the certainty of electing a minority candidate in other districts.[3]

The Supreme Court's voting rights jurisprudence has become extremely complex and contentious.[4] While the major cases have not emerged from Indian Country, they threaten the ability to address past discrimination through the creation of majority-minority districts generally. Pressure to address these issues arose as Congress considered reauthorization of the VRA before 2007, when all the special provisions would expire (see U.S.

[3] A growing empirical literature attempts to address this issue (see Cameron, Epstein, and O'Halloran 1996; Lublin 1998; Canon 1999; Epstein and O'Halloran 1999a, 1999b; Lublin and Voss 2000; Groffman, Handley, and Lublin 2001).

[4] A simple summary of several of these cases appears in Stephenson (2004, 264–74). One line of academic commentaries focuses on proper interpretation of the VRA and its interaction with the Court's interpretation of the Equal Protection Clause since *Shaw v. Reno* (see, e.g., Kousser 1999; Ely 2002; Karlan 2002; Pildes 2002; Issacharoff 2004). A second line of commentary addresses the continued constitutionality of Section 5 of the VRA for enforcing the Fifteenth Amendment (see, e.g., Pitts 2003; Rodriguez 2003).

Congress, House Committee on the Judiciary, 2005). On July 27, 2006, President Bush signed into law another 25-year extension of the special provisions, following overwhelmingly positive support in both houses of Congress (Fannie Lou Hamer, Rosa Parks, and Coretta Scott King Voting Rights Act Reauthorization and Amendments Act of 2006).

Changes to the law were few but important. Congress rejected the Supreme Court's holdings in *Reno v. Bossier Parish* and *Georgia v. Ashcroft*, restoring the broader definition of purposeful discrimination and the emphasis on the minority community's ability to elect candidates of their choice rather than have more amorphous purported "influence." Outdated provisions for appointing federal examiners were eliminated, but provisions for appointing federal observers were strengthened. Prevailing parties may now recover expert witness fees as well as attorney fees. Finally, the law also extends for another 25 years the important provisions discussed in the next section.

Bilingual Elections: Section 203

Also due to expire in 2007 was Section 203, which was part of the language minority amendments to the VRA in 1975. Less well known until the recent reauthorization debates than Sections 2 and 5, Section 203 bans English-only elections in jurisdictions where the language minority voting-age population is above 5 percent and the population has a literacy rate (defined as failure to complete the fifth grade) below the national average. Unlike Section 5, this section is not tied to voter registration and turnout data. The House Report explained the rationale for Section 203 as follows:

> Although in some areas language minority group citizens do not appear to suffer severe discrimination, they do experience high illiteracy in the English language, frequently as a result of unequal educational opportunities. The conduct of elections only in English in these jurisdictions, therefore, operates as an impediment to their access to the franchise. (U.S. Congress, House Committee on the Judiciary, 1975, 42)

This section requires bilingual ballots and election materials as well as assistance at the polls for language minorities, but jurisdictions covered only under this section are not subject to the special provisions. Initially, 369 political subdivisions (primarily counties) in thirty states were covered by these provisions (Laney 2003, 30; U.S. Congress, House, Committee on the Judiciary, 1992, Report, 7). Twenty different states included one or more jurisdictions covered for American Indian languages (plus Alaska for Native Alaskan languages).[5] Jurisdictions could bail out by proving to the local federal district court that the literacy rate of the language minority group in that district was, in fact, equal to or less than the national illiteracy rate for the group, but jurisdictions that sought bailout were largely unsuccessful (Hancock and Tredway 1985, 401, fn. 117).

The 1982 amendments to the act extended Section 203 for another ten years to 1992, but an important change was added, made possible by data collected for the first time in the 1980 census. The "Nickles amendment," sponsored by Senator Don Nickles, Republican, of Oklahoma, limited the count of voting-age citizens of a language minority to the "limited English proficient (LEP)," defined as those "who do not speak or understand English adequately enough [sic] to participate in the electoral process" (U.S. Congress, Senate, 1992, S. Rept. 9). Successful bailout suits from coverage under Section 4(f) by New Mexico in 1976 and Oklahoma in 1978 inspired this change. According to Hancock and Tredway, "virtually all of the persons who were members of the applicable language minority group were fluent in the English language and, thus, ... the English language election process did not discriminate against such persons" (1985, 403). Ironically, the Nickles amendment applies only to Section 203 and does not apply to the language minority provisions under Section 4(f), which covered a jurisdiction because of low electoral participation rates by language minority citizens rather than their literacy rate.

The 1992 Amendments

The Nickles amendment dramatically reduced the number of counties required to provide bilingual elections under Section 203 from 369 to 197 (U.S. Congress, House, 1992, 771). When Congress revisited the law in 1992, it retained the emphasis on LEP voters but fine-tuned the language minority requirement in other ways. In urban areas, large numbers of people who met the language criteria were not eligible for assistance because they did not constitute 5 percent of the county's voting-age population. In the 1992 amendments to the VRA, referred to as the Voting Rights Language Assistance Act, Congress responded by requiring election information in the language of any language minority group in a county if 10,000 or more such speakers were also LEP.

[5] These include Arizona, California, Colorado, Florida, Idaho, Maine, Michigan, Minnesota, Nebraska, Nevada, New Mexico, New York, Oklahoma, Oregon, South Dakota, Texas, Utah, Washington, Wisconsin, and Wyoming (45 Fed. Register 44268, July 1, 1980).

Other provisions were especially important for Indians. County boundary lines were often originally drawn without taking into consideration existing Indian reservations, resulting in reservations spanning two or three counties. As a consequence, it was very unlikely that the population otherwise eligible for bilingual election assistance would reach 5 percent of the population in each county. Congress responded with a new requirement for counties to provide minority language materials and assistance if 5 percent of a reservation's population is eligible, regardless of its proportion of the county population.

American Indian organizations, including the Native American Rights Fund (NARF), National Congress of American Indians (NCAI), International Native American Languages Institute, Oklahoma Native American Language Development Institute, the pueblos of Acoma and Zuni, and the nations or tribes of the Navajos, Cherokee, and Shoshone-Bannock lobbied extensively for this change and the law's extension. In their joint testimony, NARF and NCAI argued that strengthening and extending the VRA would further the federal government's commitment to preserve, promote, and protect Indian languages made in the Native American Languages Act of 1990 (U.S. Congress, Senate, 1992, *Hearing*, 336–7). Congress also found that the movement for English-only laws in many states threatened language assistance in voting (U.S. Congress, House, 1992, 771).[6]

When the Census Bureau makes new coverage determinations after each decennial census, the Voting Section contacts covered jurisdictions to inform or remind them of their obligations under the act. Justice Department officials provide information and answer questions as districts develop materials and establish training programs for translators.[7] Jurisdictions subject to language minority requirements under Section 203, but not under Section 4(f)4, do not have to preclear voting plans or submit to federally appointed election observers. Indeed, formal preclearance is not available from the attorney general, even if requested

[6] The statement by NARF and NCAI pointed out that U.S. English, one of the strongest advocates for English-only laws, acknowledges that Native American languages are "part of the heritage of the North American Continent," preservation of which "is an intellectual obligation we must assume" (U.S. Congress, Senate, 1992, *Hearings*, 339; quoting "US English Policy Position: Native American Languages," July 11, 1986). Although U.S. English takes a similar position today (www.usenglish.org/inc/legislation/other/native.asp, accessed January 3, 2005), both it and a similar group called English First nonetheless opposed the 1992 legislation (U.S. Congress, Senate, 1992, *Hearing*, 211–18, 299–301).

[7] The attorney general's Language Minority Guidelines appear in 28 C.F.R. Part 55 and on the department's website: www.usdoj.gov/crt/voting/28cfr/55/28cfr55.htm.

(28 C.F.R. Part 55.2(e)). To determine where formal enforcement is needed, Voting Section personnel informally monitor elections in covered jurisdictions through news reports, through complaints from local contacts, or by obtaining the jurisdiction's permission to send Department of Justice attorneys to observe. Occasionally, litigation is necessary to obtain compliance, as discussed in Chapter 3.

Both Section 203 and the special provisions in Sections 4 through 9 might have expired in 2007 if not for the extensive lobbying efforts of a broad coalition of civil rights organizations. Many of those organizations have been active in enforcing the Voting Rights Act in Indian Country and elsewhere for many years. We introduce in the next section the most important such groups for Indian voting litigation.

Principal Actors in Voting Rights Litigation on Behalf of Indians

The granting of rights in statutory and case law does not ensure that those rights will be formally invoked, much less protected. Charles Epp (1996; 1998) argues that a "legal support structure" is perhaps the most important influence on the sustained ability to "make rights matter." Extensive resources are needed, for example, to bring Section 2 vote dilution cases. Challenging at-large electoral systems or district boundaries requires expert historians and social scientists to establish historical patterns of discrimination and assess the extent of racially polarized voting (see Grofman 1992). Redistricting cases involve statistical analysis of census data to examine proposed district boundaries and develop possible majority-minority districts (Cunningham 2001, 32–4). Such expenses place vote dilution cases beyond the means of most private attorneys. Thus, there has been some organized group involvement in most of the American Indian vote dilution cases. This section describes the organizations mainly responsible for bringing Indian voting rights cases.

The two major sources of organizational support, financing, and legal expertise for voting rights cases on behalf of American Indians are the Voting Section of the Civil Rights Division of the U.S. Department of Justice, and the Voting Rights Project of the American Civil Liberties Union (ACLU). Both of these groups are very active in VRA cases on behalf of other racial and ethnic minorities as well. Other private organizations that have litigated voting rights for other minorities, such as the Lawyers' Committee for Civil Rights Under Law, the Mexican American Legal Defense and Educational Fund, and the NAACP Legal Defense and Educational Fund, have not been involved with Indian cases, however.[8] Moreover, some Indian organizations that once litigated voting rights cases have not done so in recent years.

The Voting Section of the Civil Rights Division of the Justice Department

The VRA explicitly gives the attorney general a litigative role in enforcing the law against jurisdictions that are not in compliance, especially under the nationally applicable Section 2. The Department of Justice also has an administrative role in appointing federal examiners and election observers under Sections 3, 6, 7, 8, and 9 and in preclearance actions under Section 5 (Landsberg 1997, 16). Within the Voting Section, some personnel specialize in one or the other of these two tasks, but there is some fluidity between them, especially when preclearance requests become especially numerous after the decennial census and the redistricting that follows (Cunningham 2001, 51).

By any formal measure, the Voting Section has the greatest legal resources for enforcing the VRA. According to data on the Department of Justice website, in fiscal year 2004 the section's budget was $4,131,000, with a staff of 105. The Civil Rights Division's attorneys are high caliber, mostly hired through an Honors Program the Department of Justice has sponsored since the mid-1950s (Landsberg 1997, 159).[9] The Department has had voting rights specialists since the organization of the Civil Rights Division changed from geographic to functional divisions in 1969 (Landsberg 1997, 108).[10] Voting discrimination is not the section's sole concern, however. It has responsibility for enforcing a number of statutes.[11]

From 1973 to 1980, the Civil Rights Division had an Office of Indian Rights. This office was charged with enforcing the 1968 Indian Civil

[8] This situation could change, as an attorney formerly with the Department of Justice had recently moved to the Lawyer's Committee at the time of the interviews. Indeed, the Lawyer's Committee joined the Arizona voter identification case filed in 2006 (*Intertribal Council of Arizona v. Brewer*).

[9] According to Toobin (2004), since 2002 politically appointed attorneys have taken responsibility for recruitment for the Honors Program away from the career attorneys.

[10] One attorney in the Voting Section in 2005 previously worked for the Voting Rights Project.

[11] The Voting Section is also responsible for enforcing the National Voter Registration Act of 1993, the Voting Accessibility for the Elderly and Handicapped Act, the Uniformed and Overseas Citizens Absentee Voting Act, and other statutory provisions, as well as the VRA. See the Section's website, www.usdoj.gov/crt/voting/overview.htm (accessed February 9, 2005).

Rights Act, which protects individuals against tribal governments, and with bringing discrimination cases on behalf of Indians. According to Department of Justice sources, the office had seven attorneys, a deputy, and a chief. Along with other types of cases, they filed at least eight voting rights lawsuits in five different states (see Table 3.1 in Chapter 3). The office was disbanded in 1980 on the premise that all lawyers in the Civil Rights Division would bring Indian cases.

The demise of the Office of Indian Rights may help explain the decline in the number of Indian voting rights cases initiated by the Department of Justice after 1980, but the level of activity fluctuated substantially in later periods as well. The Voting Section must respond if a jurisdiction applies for preclearance to either the attorney general or the court, but the Department of Justice has discretion over which enforcement actions it brings. According to former Civil Rights Division attorney Brian Landsberg, "The department relies on several obvious sources for its presuit investigations: complaints from individuals or organizations, news articles, statistics, and referrals from other federal agencies" (1997, 121). The department finds some complaints to be without merit and others not consistent with the department's priorities (Landsberg 1997, 122). Maintaining credibility for legal judgment and probity influences the division (118).

Choosing among the many potential cases that come to its attention is not simply a legal judgment, however. The Civil Rights Division operates in a very complex political environment, as Landsberg describes (1997):

> The core value of nondiscrimination should be and normally is the starting point. Prior division positions and case and statutory law strongly influence policy decisions. Litigants and their supporters lobby the attorney general, solicitor general, and assistant attorney general for civil rights, and sometimes even the president, to take positions favoring particular sides. They may be joined in that effort by members of Congress or by other federal agencies. The Civil Rights Commission writes reports on civil rights issues and recommends that various enforcement measures be taken. Overarching administration policies are articulated by presidents and their subordinates, and the division is expected to pay heed to them. Obviously the weight of each of these possible influences may vary from issue to issue and from one administration to the next. (117)

One of the most important internal influences on decision making is the relationship between career civil servants and political appointees. The attorney general, the solicitor general (who generally controls appellate litigation, especially at the Supreme Court), the assistant attorney general for civil rights, and most of the division's deputy assistant attorneys general are appointed by the president with the advice and consent of the Senate. The chiefs of the various civil rights sections and the rank-and-file attorneys are career attorneys.

Landsberg compares the function of combining appointees and civil servants in the executive branch to the role of bicameralism in the legislative branch – to bring different perspectives to bear on questions (1997, 156). He is quite optimistic about the balance that usually occurs between civil servants and political appointees but notes that this varies somewhat across administrations. He suggests that relations with the career attorneys were especially tense under the Reagan administration (1997, 168). Relations between civil servants and political appointees appear to be near an all-time low under the administration of President George W. Bush (Toobin 2004; Eggen 2005a, 2005b), with the influence of career attorneys reportedly diminishing (Eggen 2005c).

The number of Indian voting rights cases that the Justice Department filed certainly varies from one administration to the next. With the exception of the cases challenging at-large election of county commissioners and assistance for language minority voters in San Juan County, Utah, discussed in Chapter 4, the Department of Justice filed no cases of its own during the first Reagan administration and intervened in only two cases initially filed by private parties (*Shakopee Mdewakanton Sioux Community and the U.S. v. City of Prior Lake* 1985 and *Sanchez v. King* 1982). In the second Reagan term, it filed four language assistance cases under Section 203 or 4(f)(4) that had relatively minor Section 2 issues associated with them (*U.S. v. McKinley County* 1986a*, 1986b*; *U.S. v. Arizona* 1988*; *U.S. v. New Mexico* 1988*). During the administration of the first President George Bush, not a single Indian voting rights case was filed.

During the first Clinton administration, the Voting Section resumed filing language assistance cases under Section 203 but was also caught up in the Supreme Court's retrenchment on voting rights issues discussed previously. The Department of Justice received severe criticism from the Supreme Court (*Miller v. Johnson* 1995, 922–7) and some commentators (Cunningham 2001, esp. 128–35) for using its preclearance powers to push too hard for majority-minority districts. These majority-minority districts were in the South and not in Indian Country, but one decision narrowing preclearance standards did occur in a case involving Indians (*Arizona v. Reno* 1995).

During the second Clinton administration, the Department of Justice increased the number of cases it brought on behalf of Indians. For the first time since the Utah case in 1983, it began to challenge at-large, multimember electoral districts. Several cases were resolved by negotiations, but one against Blaine County, Montana, led to a full trial and appeal continuing on into the administration of President George W. Bush (*U.S. v. Blaine County* [2004]; see Chapter 5). Other than pursuing that case, the Department of Justice has been in a period of little activity on behalf of Indians under the Bush administration, commencing no new voting suits.[12] Preclearance activities in response to submissions from covered jurisdictions and administrative enforcement of language minority requirements continue during all administrations, but interpretation of preclearance standards also changes from one administration to another (Eggen 2005b, 2005c).

The Voting Rights Project of the American Civil Liberties Union

Despite the resources of the Department of Justice, enforcement of the VRA has depended much more on private litigation than government-plaintiff cases. According to court data, from 1977, when voting rights cases were first separately reported, through 2004, the number of government-plaintiff voting rights cases filed in U.S. district courts has totaled 248; the number of private cases filed during the same period is 5100.[13] The organization that has done more than any other for all minority groups, including Indians in recent years, is the Voting Rights Project of the ACLU. According to Gregory Caldeira, "The [Voting Rights] project did much of the day-to-day work of private enforcement of the Voting Rights Act, especially during the Nixon and Reagan administrations, years of conflict between the federal government and the civil rights movement" (1992, 240).

More recent periods continue to demonstrate the important role of private litigators when the current administration diminishes its own enforcement activity. Another distinction between private attorneys and those at the Department of Justice is that the former can function more exclusively as minority advocates. The Justice Department's "client" is the United States and its laws, not the voters whose rights have allegedly been infringed.

[12] In June 2002 the Civil Rights Division posted a publication entitled "Protecting the Civil Rights of American Indians and Alaska Natives," including some discussion of voting rights generally (www.usdoj.gov/crt/indian/broch.html, accessed August 17, 2003).

[13] These figures come from adding data in Table C-2 of the Annual Report of the Director of the Administrative Office of the United States Courts, 1977–2004.

Relative to its size, currently employing just four attorneys, the Voting Rights Project is by far the most active organization pursuing voting rights claims on behalf of American Indians. Indian voting cases are a relatively new emphasis for the Voting Rights Project, which is located in the Southern Regional Office of the ACLU in Atlanta. The Southern Regional Office was founded in 1964 to challenge discrimination in various institutions, including elections, but also juries and prisons (Walker 1999, 268–70). Samuel Walker, historian of the ACLU, calls the Voting Rights Project the "ACLU project with the greatest impact on civil rights," but "also probably the least well known" (1999, 356). The Voting Rights Project is "directly responsible for the election of countless black officials in the South and, as a result, has had a profound impact on local, state, and national politics" (Walker 1999, 356; see also McDonald 2003a).

With several other ACLU affiliates in the South now, the Regional Office focuses 95 percent of its efforts on voting rights cases (McDonald 2003b). About 75 percent of those cases concern racial discrimination, but the Voting Rights Project is also involved in cases concerning residency requirements, ballot access, and election technology reform.

Although the ACLU receives considerable revenue from individual memberships, it also depends on foundation funding, especially for its national projects. The low visibility but high impact of the Voting Rights Project's work, noted by Walker, has led to major funding from foundations including but not limited to the Field Foundation and the Ford Foundation (Walker 1999, 273; McDonald 2003b). With a current annual budget of the Southern Regional Office on the order of $1 million (McDonald 2003b), funding is sufficient for the Voting Rights Project to provide attorneys without charge and pay all litigation expenses when it accepts a case.[14] According to the director, the Voting Rights Project decides whether to accept a case on the basis of its legal merits, that is, the chances of ultimately winning in court. For example, it turned down one request because the prior success of an Indian candidate made meeting the criteria for proving discriminatory vote dilution unlikely (McDonald 2003b).

The Voting Rights Project also brings American Indian plaintiffs a wealth of expertise based on its extensive background litigating voting rights cases in the South, especially vote dilution cases. Of the cases challenging

[14] When successful, the Voting Rights Project seeks attorneys' fees from defendants. If recovered, such fees go to the national office of the ACLU, but the Voting Rights Project may draw on them (McDonald 2003b).

at-large electoral systems in Georgia cities and counties between 1974 and 1990, the Voting Rights Project provided representation in fifty-one of ninety-six cases – more than the Department of Justice, six other litigation groups, and civil rights attorneys in private practice together (McDonald 2003a, 195–6). Nationally, the Voting Rights Project filed approximately 157 suits in 180 jurisdictions by 1988 (Walker 1999, 356).

The Voting Rights Project acquires its cases in a variety of ways: through ACLU affiliates and other knowledgeable attorneys, word-of-mouth communication, and media coverage. The Voting Rights Project's first American Indian case was filed in 1980 in North Carolina, and included both African Americans and Lumbee Indians as plaintiffs (*Canady v. Lumberton City Board of Education* 1981).[15] Presumably the local legal services agency that sought the Voting Rights Project's help knew of its other work in North Carolina.

All of the Voting Rights Project's subsequent Indian cases were in western or midwestern states. Its first Indian case outside the South was *Windy Boy v. Big Horn County, Montana* (1986), filed in 1983. Two local attorneys with tribal connections planned to challenge at-large elections for the county commission and school board. One of the attorneys was married to the director of the Montana ACLU affiliate, who was aware of the ACLU's national projects and called the Voting Rights Project in Atlanta (McDonald 2003b). While the Voting Rights Project may initially come to an area via its affiliate, the Voting Rights Project staff makes acquaintances and gets media coverage in the course of a lawsuit, so people in the area are subsequently likely to call the Voting Rights Project directly (McDonald 2003b). The Voting Rights Project has been involved in four more Indian cases in Montana and one each in Colorado, Nebraska, and Wyoming.

Sometimes, as in South Dakota, the Voting Rights Project takes a more proactive role. As the work on at-large electoral systems in the South began to taper off by the mid-1990s, the Voting Rights Project started to take a closer look at voting discrimination in Indian Country. In the summer of 1997 or 1998, the director assigned an intern to do a study correlating census data and government jurisdictions in South Dakota to identify possible problems (Sells 2003). Subsequently, the director made a trip to the state, starting with a former U.S. senator he knew, to learn more about the local situation. One contact led to another, and the Voting Rights Project filed its first voting rights suit in South Dakota in 2000;

[15] The ACLU had also filed an amicus brief in *Harrison v. Laveen* in 1948 (see Chapter 1).

seven more cases in the state have followed. The director of the regional ACLU affiliate in South Dakota has continued to play a significant role (*Indian Country Today* 2002). Some civil rights controversies in which she has been involved, such as alleged discrimination in law enforcement, have evolved into voting rights suits (Sells 2003).

The Voting Rights Project staff is careful not to cross the line between educating people about their rights and encouraging litigation. The courts have resoundingly defended the right of groups such as the Voting Rights Project to bring litigation (see *In re Primus* 1978). Nevertheless, Voting Rights Project director Laughlin McDonald (2003b) has learned from many years of challenging racial discrimination in the South that trumped-up allegations of ethical violations are still used to interfere with attorneys' ability to defend people's rights.

Indian Organizations

In voting rights lawsuits on behalf of other ethnic and racial groups, private organizations besides the Voting Rights Project have been significant players. When Gregory Caldeira (1992) studied the "voting rights bar," he found the NAACP and NAACP Legal Defense and Education Fund, the Mexican American Legal Defense and Education Fund, and the Puerto Rican Legal Defense and Education Fund to be active participants. These ethnic organizations are still active in voting rights litigation or lobbying. In contrast, no organizations with a primary focus on Indians are currently very active in bringing voting rights cases. In fact, Caldeira's study missed two Indian organizations that were involved in voting rights litigation in the mid-1980s, neither of which is still actively litigating such cases.

The National Indian Youth Council (NIYC) was involved in at least ten voting rights cases between 1982 and 1989 (see Table 3.1 in Chapter 3). Founded in 1961, it is the second oldest national Indian organization after the NCAI (Wilkins 2002, 210). Thomas Cowger, a historian of the NCAI, describes the younger group: "Impatient with the pace of change and with the methods of the NCAI, the NIYC advocated greater militancy" and "brought a confrontational style to Indian politics," becoming known for "fish-ins" and other demonstrations to assert tribal fishing rights (1999, 140–1). By the 1980s, NIYC had turned more to litigation as a tactic. It was especially active challenging at-large elections in political subdivisions in New Mexico, its home state, but also got involved in cases in North and South Dakota and Arizona. Today, however, it no longer litigates voting rights cases, focusing more on job training and placement, voter registration, and environmental issues (Wilkins 2002, 210).

Another Indian organization that was actively involved in VRA litigation in the mid-1980s is NARF, the oldest and largest legal advocacy group for American Indians. With funding from the Ford Foundation in 1970, it arose from the California Indian Legal Services and moved to Boulder, Colorado, in 1971 to be more centrally located (Native American Rights Fund 2003). NARF brought cases in South Dakota in 1984 and 1986, challenging an at-large school board (*Buckanaga v. Sisseton Independent School District* 1986) and the location of polling places (*Black Bull v. Dupree School District* 1986*) (see *Sho-Ban News* 1986b, 15). In 1985 NARF also received funding from the Northwest Area Foundation of Minneapolis to conduct a study of voting returns and census data in Montana and the Dakotas to identify possible violations of the VRA (*Indian Country Today* [*Lakota Times*] 1985, 18). Today, however, their areas of litigation emphasize federal recognition; international rights of indigenous people; land and water issues; trust fund matters; cultural, economic, and education issues; and tribal sovereignty. NARF was actively involved in efforts to reauthorize the VRA (Native American Rights Fund 2005).

Another organization, the Indian Law Resource Center of Helena, Montana, joined the ACLU's Voting Rights Project in three lawsuits in the late 1990s: *Old Person v. Cooney* (2000, 2002), *Alden v. Board of Commissioners of Rosebud County* (1999*), and *Matt v. Ronan School District* (1999*) (see Indian Law Resource Center 1999). Voting rights are not a major focus, however, as the group states its purpose as "protection of indigenous people's human rights[,] cultures and traditional lands" (Indian Law Resource Center 2005). Although the Center's executive director, Robert T. Coulter, has written in support of the right of Indian individuals to "seek participation as voters, workers, entrepreneurs, and professionals when they deal with the world outside their reservations," he goes on to say that "it is as tribes or nations that Native Americans are most discriminated against" (2001).

For the Defendants: The Mountain States Legal Foundation

When Gregory Caldeira wrote about the voting rights bar, he noted: "No well-organized opposition has arisen to challenge the power of the voting rights bar" (1992, 241). Since that time, the Mountain States Legal Foundation (MSLF) has entered the field on the defendants' side in voting rights cases. The MSLF is one of the conservative litigation groups formed in the 1970s and 1980s to counter liberal successes in the courts (Epstein 1985).

Representing the defendants in *U.S. v. Blaine County, Montana* (2004), the MSLF argued unsuccessfully through the U.S. Court of Appeals that the 1982 amendments to Section 2 of the VRA are unconstitutional under the Tenth and Eleventh Amendments. MSLF then petitioned the Supreme Court, which declined the case.[16] The MSLF successfully represented the defendants in one VRA case concerning Hispanic voters, *U.S. v. Alamosa County, CO* (2004), but the court explicitly declined to reopen settled issues of constitutionality. In 2005 the MSLF took on the defense of Fremont County, Wyoming, when Indian voters and the ACLU challenged its at-large commission (*Large v. Fremont County*).

Like the Voting Rights Project, the MSLF provides all funding for the cases it selects. The group describes how it selects cases as follows:

> MSLF obtains its cases in a variety of ways including: (1) requests for assistance received from individuals who have heard of or been referred to MSLF; (2) recommendations by members of the Board of Directors or Board of Litigation; (3) identification of meritorious clients using information contained in various publications; and (4) internally on behalf of MSLF and its members in important matters of public interest. (Mountain States Legal Foundation 2004).

The MSLF website provides considerable information about the group's funding to make the point that it is a grassroots organization and is not funded solely by foundations and large corporations. The resources the MSLF provides are very important because the defendants in many of the American Indian voting rights cases are relatively small towns, school districts, or rural counties with limited legal budgets. The MSLF thus has the potential to be a formidable opponent of the advocates of voting rights enforcement.

Conclusion

In summary, while the VRA was originally written more with blacks than American Indians in mind, the amendments since 1975 have addressed problems of voting discrimination that the latter group faces as well. Advocates for voting rights for Indians have made steady use of the law since 1975, though the legal support structure for enforcement of the VRA for American Indians has fluctuated over the years, with different organizations being active in different periods. In Chapter 3 we look in more detail at the cases they have brought.

[16] Cert denied. 544 U.S. 992 (2005).

3

A Milestone on the Reservation

The Voting Rights Act Comes to Indian Country

The passage of the Voting Rights Act (VRA) in 1965 was the biggest legal milestone for the voting rights of U.S. citizens of color since the passage of the Fifteenth Amendment almost 100 years earlier. While they are not as numerous or as well known as those brought by African Americans, many cases have been brought by Indians alleging discrimination in the electoral process.

We have attempted to identify all voting rights cases brought by or on behalf of Indians under the VRA or the Fourteenth or Fifteenth Amendment since 1965 or cases brought under the VRA when Indian interests were at stake.[1] Such data facilitate comparisons of Indians' experience with the VRA with that of other minority groups, especially African Americans. We have found many similarities but also some differences.

The exact number is difficult to determine because many cases remain unpublished, but we have identified seventy-four to date. This number includes only cases filed in court and one Department of Justice "notice letter" of authorization to sue – a case that was settled without a complaint

[1] Most of the information in this chapter comes from legal documents submitted in the various cases. Documents other than published court opinions primarily come from the Voting Section of the Department of Justice, the Voting Rights Project of the ACLU, or the archives of the NIYC, held by the Center for Southwest Research at the University of New Mexico. Secondary sources, such as articles in scholarly journals or in newspapers (largely the Indian press), are cited where relied upon.

being filed.[2] These cases are displayed in Table 3.1 in chronological order of filing.[3] A few striking patterns appear.

Litigation has occurred in fifteen states. The geographical concentration is greater than this number might suggest. All but four cases (two in Wisconsin, one in Maine, and one in North Carolina) have occurred in the Intermountain West (Arizona, Colorado, Nevada, New Mexico, Utah, Wyoming) and the Great Plains states of Minnesota, Montana, Nebraska, North Dakota, Oklahoma, and South Dakota. The dubious distinction for having the most litigation belongs to New Mexico with nineteen cases, followed by South Dakota with eighteen. New Mexico's cases are largely concentrated in the 1980s and early 1990s, however, while South Dakota's span the whole period. Arizona has had eleven cases and Montana eight, with the other states having just three or fewer.

With very few exceptions, the cases have succeeded in winning at least some gains for Indian voting rights. As with most civil litigation, many of the successes have occurred through consent agreements among the parties rather than court-imposed applications of law. In only four of the seventy-four cases have the claims of Indian parties or their advocates been largely rebuffed – *Apache County v. U.S.* (1966); *Grinnell v. Sinner* (1992), *Old Person v. Cooney* (2002), and *Frank v. Forest County* (2003) – with partial success in *Stabler v. Thurston County* (1997) and *Arizona v. Reno* (1995).[4] This overall success in litigation demonstrates the importance of the VRA as a tool to address continuing discriminatory practices.

The cases fall into several major categories, which characterize the types of voting rights cases arising in Indian Country and serve as the organizing framework for this chapter (Table 3.2). Many cases raise more than one issue, so some cases are counted more than once in Table 3.2. In the first cases to be discussed, Indians' rights to register, vote, and run for office at all are in question. In these cases, defendants totally exclude Indians and sometimes explicitly argue against Indian voting rights. In most later cases exclusion is less explicit, but is accomplished through discriminatory

[2] Since 1991, Executive Order 12778 §1(a) has required the Justice Department and other federal agencies to send a "prefiling notice of complaint" to give prospective defendants an opportunity to settle before a suit is filed if they choose to do so. The seventy-four cases exclude Department of Justice objections to preclearance requests under Section 5 unless those objections resulted in litigation. In some contexts, Section 5 objections are an important administrative use of the VRA (Days, 1992), but they have not been very numerous in connection with American Indians because the state of Arizona and two counties in South Dakota are the only two covered jurisdictions in Indian Country.

[3] Within the same year, they are listed alphabetically by state.

[4] Uncontested bailout actions are not counted as defeats.

application of voting rules with respect to registration, polling locations, or voter identification.

The second set of cases concerns the inadequate provision of assistance for minority language voters in Indian Country, the affirmative requirement added to the VRA in 1975. In the third and largest category, twenty-six cases challenge vote dilution through at-large electoral systems. The fourth category contains cases about malapportioned districts and disputed boundaries, questions that tend to arise when Indians have not been considered as part of the voting population and after the decennial census.[5] Disputes about the relative population size of districts are typically resolved on straight Fourteenth Amendment Equal Protection clauses grounds and do not require reference to the VRA (see *Reynolds v. Sims* 1964; Phillips 1995).

Finally, some cases focus on the special provisions of the VRA, such as whether voting changes are subject to preclearance under Section 5 or whether jurisdictions qualify to bail out of coverage. For each category, we summarize the factual situations, legal issues, and legal outcomes to provide an overview of Indian voting rights cases. More detailed accounts of a few of the cases are presented in Chapters 4, 5, and 6.

The Right to Register, Vote, and Run for Office

States with large reservations, especially Arizona, South Dakota, and New Mexico, have had the most extensive history of conflicts over American Indians voting. In these states, Indians are sufficiently numerous to be a substantial political force if they participate fully in elections. The first major cases after the passage of the Voting Rights Act occurred in Apache County, Arizona. Apache County is located in the extreme northeastern corner of Arizona and is one of three adjoining counties containing large portions of the Navajo Reservation. In 1973 a private lawsuit (*Goodluck v. Apache County*), consolidated with one brought in 1974 by the Department of Justice (*U.S. v. Arizona*), challenged the apportionment of the three districts for the county board of supervisors. Reservation Indians had been excluded in calculating the population of the districts, resulting in almost ten times the number of people in one district than in another. In defense, the state and county argued that the Indian Citizenship Act was

[5] These questions also arise when at-large systems are replaced by single-member districts, but they are typically resolved in the remedial phase of those lawsuits rather than spawning separate cases.

TABLE 3.1. *Federal Voting Rights Cases Brought on Behalf of American Indians and/or Interpreting the Voting Rights Act re Indian Interests*

Case Name	Year Filed: Civil Action Number	Court Where Filed	Legal Issue	Major or Latest Court Opinion	Attorneys for Indians	Outcome
Klahr v. Williams (originally *Klahr v. Goddard*)	1965: 5112–PHX	USDC, Arizona	Do state House and Senate districts comport with the Fourteenth Amendment Equal Protection Clause in population size and treatment of Navajo Reservation?	339 F. Supp. 922 (D. Ariz. 1972)	n/a	In long-running redistricting dispute, court finds Navajo Reservation was intentionally divided to destroy electoral strength.
Apache County v. U.S.	1966: 292–66	USDC, District of Columbia	May Arizona and three counties bail out of VRA coverage under Sec. 4(a)? Navajos attempted to intervene and oppose.	256 F. Supp. 903 (D. D.C. 1966)	DOJ	Intervention denied. Bailout is permitted.
Goodluck v. Apache County Consolidated with *U.S. v. Arizona*	1973: 73–626 PCT 1974: 74–50 PCT	USDC, Arizona	Does a more than 10:1 disparity in population of county supervisor districts violate the Fifteenth Amendment and the VRA?	417 F. Supp. 13 (D. Ariz. 1975); aff'd 429 U.S. 876 (1976)	Legal Services DOJ	Indians are citizens and have the right to vote. The apportionment is invalid.
Little Thunder v. South Dakota	1974: 74–3033	USDC, South Dakota	Does a law preventing residents of unorganized counties from voting for county offices violate the Equal Protection Clause of the Fourteenth Amendment?	518 F.2d 1253 (8th Cir. 1975)	Legal Services	Yes, plaintiffs prevail.

Maine v. U.S.	1975: 75–2125	USDC, District of Columbia	Bailout action by nineteen Maine municipalities from VRA special provisions (Secs. 4–9)	Order and partial summary judgment, Sept. 17, 1976; stipulation July 5, 1977	DOJ	Eighteen municipalities are released from coverage, but Passamaquoddy Pleasant Point Reservation remains covered under Sec. 203.
Simenson v. Bell (originally Simenson v. Levi)	1976: 76–59-HG	USDC, Montana	Bailout action by Roosevelt County, MT, from coverage under Sec. 203	Memorandum and order, Jan. 24, 1978	DOJ	County fails to show that illiteracy rate of Indians in county is below national average.
New Mexico v. U.S.	1976: 76–0067	USDC, District of Columbia	Bailout action on behalf of three New Mexico counties from coverage under Sec. 4(f)(4)	Order, July 30, 1976	DOJ	Permitted: English-only elections were not discriminatory because language minority was also fluent in English.
Choctaw and McCurtain Counties v. U.S.	1976: 76–1250	USDC, District of Columbia	Bailout action on behalf of two Oklahoma counties from coverage under Sec. 4(f)(4)	Order, May 12, 1978	DOJ	Permitted: English-only elections were not discriminatory because language minority was also fluent in English.

(*continued*)

TABLE 3.1 *(continued)*

Case Name	Year Filed: Civil Action Number	Court Where Filed	Legal Issue	Major or Latest Court Opinion	Attorneys for Indians	Outcome
Independent School District of Tulsa v. Bell	1976: 76–C–573–B	USDC, Northern Oklahoma	Declaratory judgment action to establish that Cherokee language is unwritten, so plaintiff need not provide written election material in Cherokee.	Memorandum opinion, Dec. 7, 1977	DOJ	Summary judgment for plaintiff – DOJ did not object.
Apache County High School District v. U.S.	1977: 77–1815	USDC, District of Columbia	Was the school district obligated to get preclearance pursuant to Sec. 5 for procedural changes in a school bond election, and should preclearance be granted?	Memorandum opinion, June 12, 1980	DOJ	Summary judgment for U.S. – preclearance denied.
U.S. v. Town of Bartelme	1978: 78–C-101	USDC, Eastern Wisconsin	Does deannexation of a reservation from a town and exclusion of Indian voters violate the VRA?	Order, Feb. 17, 1978	DOJ	Plaintiffs win preliminary injunction.
U.S. v. Humboldt County	1978: R–78–0144	USDC, Nevada	Was voter registration of Indians inhibited in violation of Sec. 2?	Order, Sept. 7, 1978	DOJ	Plaintiffs win temporary restraining order.

U.S. v. Thurston County	1978: 78–0-380	USDC, Nebraska	Does an at-large election system for electing county supervisors dilute Indian votes under the Fourteenth and Fifteenth Amendments and Sec. 2?	Consent decree May 9, 1979	DOJ	County agrees to create seven single-member districts.
U.S. v. Tripp County	1978: 78–3045	USDC, South Dakota	Does reapportionment of Tripp and Todd Counties require Sec. 5 preclearance?	Order, Feb. 6, 1979	DOJ	State ordered to submit plan.
U.S. v. South Dakota	1978: 78–5018	USDC, South Dakota	Does law preventing residents of unorganized counties from voting for county offices violate the Equal Protection Clause of the Fourteenth Amendment, the Fifteenth Amendment, or Sec. 2 of the VRA?	636 F.2d. 241(8th Cir. 1980)	DOJ	Eighth Circuit Court reverses the district court and rules that exclusion does violate the Equal Protection Clause.
U.S. v. San Juan County	1979: 79–507-JB	USDC, New Mexico	Does at-large election of the county commission violate Sec. 2?	Stipulation, Apr. 8, 1980	DOJ	County agrees to change to single-member districts after 1980 census.
U.S. v. San Juan County	1979: 79–508-JB	USDC, New Mexico	Did elections comply with the bilingual election requirements of Sec. 203?	Stipulation, Apr. 8, 1980	DOJ	County agrees to expand Navajo voter registration, information, and assistance program.

(*continued*)

TABLE 3.1 (*continued*)

Case Name	Year Filed: Civil Action Number	Court Where Filed	Legal Issue	Major or Latest Court Opinion	Attorneys for Indians	Outcome
U.S. v. South Dakota	1979: 79–3039	USDC, South Dakota	Must state law revising system of organized and unorganized counties be precleared under Sec. 5 of the VRA?	Order, May 20, 1980	DOJ	Implementation of the law is enjoined.
Canady v. Lumberton City Board of Education	1980: 80–215-CIV-3	USDC, Eastern North Carolina	May elections proceed if annexation to district has not been precleared under Sec. 5?	454 U.S. 957 (1981)	ACLU; Lumbee River Legal Services	District court required preclearance, and Supreme Court enjoins election without it.
South Dakota v. U.S.	1980: 80–1976	USDC, District of Columbia	Declaratory judgment action to establish that the Unorganized Counties Act does not violate Sec. 5 of the VRA	Consent decree, Dec. 2, 1981	DOJ	Act is not precleared. New tax, contracting, and election provisions are agreed to.
Goddard v. Babbitt	1981: 81–1497-PHX-CAM	USDC, Arizona	Do legislative and congressional districts violate the Fourteenth and Fifteenth Amendments?	536 F. Supp. 538 (D. Ariz. 1982)	private	Districts struck down; stipulated revised plan places reservation in one district instead of three.

Sanchez v. King Consolidated with *Vargas v. Hooper*, *Yazzie v. Hooper*, *Olguin v. Hooper*, *Marsh v. King*	1982: 82–0067-M; 82–0084-C; 82–0180-C; 82–0219-JB; 82–0246-JB	USDC, New Mexico	Does legislative redistricting plan violate Equal Protection Clause, Fifteenth Amendment, and VRA, Sec. 2?	550 F. Supp. 13 (D. N.M. 1982); aff'd 459 U.S. 801 (1983); order on remand Aug. 8, 1984	NIYC, DOJ, several legal services agencies	Apportionment based on prior votes cast violates Equal Protection Clause. Subsequent plan dilutes votes in violation of Section 2.
Shakopee Mdewakanton Sioux Community and the U.S. v. City of Prior Lake	1983: 83–1059	USDC, Minnesota	Does city's exclusion of Indians from voting by deannexing reservation lands city had annexed eleven years earlier violate the VRA and Equal Protection Clause?	771 F.2d 1153 (8th Cir. 1985)	DOJ	Eighth Circuit Court upholds district court injunction and rules that deannexation is invalid, so Indians may vote.
Windy Boy v. Big Horn County	1983: 83–225-BLG	USDC, Montana	Does at-large election of county commissioners and the school district trustees violate Sec. 2 of the VRA and the Fourteenth and Fifteenth Amendments?	647 F. Supp 1002 (D. Mont. 1986)	ACLU	Court orders defendants to propose new plan with at least some members elected by district.
U.S. v. San Juan County	1983: C-83–1286W	USDC, Utah	Does at-large election of county commissioners dilute votes under Sec. 2 of the VRA?	Settlement and order, Apr. 4, 1984	DOJ	County agrees to change to three single-member districts.

(*continued*)

TABLE 3.1 (*continued*)

Case Name	Year Filed: Civil Action Number	Court Where Filed	Legal Issue	Major or Latest Court Opinion	Attorneys for Indians	Outcome
U.S. v. San Juan County	1983: C-83–1287	USDC, Utah	Did elections comply with the bilingual election requirements of Sec. 203 of the VRA?	Settlement and order, Jan. 11, 1983	DOJ	County agrees to improve assistance to Navajo voters.
Largo v. McKinley Consolidated School District	1984: 84–1751	USDC, New Mexico	Do at-large school board elections violate Sec. 2 of the VRA?	Consent decree, Mar. 21, 1988	NIYC	School district adopts single-member districts in November 1986.
Estevan v. Grants-Cibola County School District	1984: 84–1752-HB	USDC, New Mexico	Do at-large school board elections violate Sec. 2 of the VRA?	Order to enjoin election, Dec. 17, 1984	NIYC	Parties agree to postpone election to see if legislature mandates single districts, which it shortly does.
Buckanaga v. Sisseton School District	1984: 84–1025	USDC, South Dakota	Do at-large school board elections violate Sec. 2 of the VRA?	804 F.2d 469 (8th Cir. 1986); 15 Indian L.Rep. 3119 (D. S. D. 1988).	NARF	Court of appeals reverses district court and finds violation. The 1988 consent decree adopts cumulative voting for at-large seats.

American Horse v. Kundert	1984: 84–5159	USDC, South Dakota	Did county's rejection of cards from Indian voter registration drive violate Fourteenth and Fifteenth Amendments?	Order, Nov. 5, 1984	n/a	Court orders county to permit Indians to vote.
Felipe and Ascencio v. Cibola County Commission	1985: 85–0301	USDC, New Mexico	Does at-large election of county commissioners violate Sec. 2 of the VRA?	Consent decree, Feb. 18, 1987	NIYC	County adopts single-member districts for commissioner elections.
Tso v. Cuba Independent School District	1985: 85–1023-JB	USDC, New Mexico	Do at-large school board elections violate Sec. 2 of the VRA?	Consent decree, May 18, 1987	NIYC	Five single-member districts created, with new elections for all seats
Fiddler v. Sieker	1986: 86–3050	USDC, South Dakota	Did small number of voter application cards made available for Indian registration drive violate Sec. 2 of the VRA and First, Fourteenth, and Fifteenth Amendments?	Order, Oct. 22, 1986	NIYC	Court orders extended deadline for registration.
Black Bull v. Dupree School District	1986: 86–3012	USDC, South Dakota	Did county's failure to provide sufficient polling places on the reservation violate Sec. 2 of VRA and the First, Fourteenth, and Fifteenth Amendments?	Settlement, May 14, 1986	NARF and legal services	School district agrees to establish polling places on reservation, reschedule election, and do more publicity.

(*continued*)

TABLE 3.1 (*continued*)

Case Name	Year Filed: Civil Action Number	Court Where Filed	Legal Issue	Major or Latest Court Opinion	Attorneys for Indians	Outcome
Kirk v. San Juan College Board	1986: 86–1503	USDC, New Mexico	Do at-large elections for board of public junior college violate Sec. 2 of the VRA?	Order, Feb. 1987	NIYC	Court requires single-member districts.
U.S. v. McKinley County	1986: 86–0028M	USDC, New Mexico	Does county's provision of assistance to Navajo and Zuni voters satisfy Sec. 203 of the VRA?	941 F. Supp. 1062 (D. N.M. 1996)	DOJ	County agrees to improved assistance and federal examiners, but when U.S. wants to extend use of examiners for ten more years, court refuses. Parties settle in 1997 for extension until 2001.
U.S. v. McKinley County	1986: 86–0029C	USDC, New Mexico	Does county's configuration of precincts and polling places violate Sec. 2 of the VRA?	Consent decree, Jan. 13, 1986	DOJ	County agrees to restructure the precinct boundaries, increase the number of polling places from nineteen to twenty-five, and announce location of the new precincts to voters.

Casuse v. City of Gallup	1986: 86–1007	USDC, New Mexico	Does city's home-rule charter establishing at-large elections for city council violate Sec. 2 of the VRA and a 1985 state statute requiring cities with over 10,000 people to use single-member districts?	746 P.2d 1103 (N.M. 1987)	NIYC	Case certified to New Mexico Supreme Court, which rules that state law invalidates home rule charter.
Clark v. Holbrook Unified School District	1988: 88–0148-PTC-RGS	USDC, Arizona	Does at-large school board election dilute Indian votes in violation of Sec. 2 of the VRA?	703 F. Supp. 56 (D.C. Ariz. 1989)	NIYC	Judge orders hearing on plaintiffs' motion for a preliminary injunction.
U.S. v. Arizona	1988: 88–1989-PHX-EHC	USDC, Arizona	Do language assistance provided Navajo speakers and other voting access practices violate the standards of Section 4(f)(4) and Sec. 2 of the VRA?	Consent decrees, May 22, 1989, and Sept. 28, 1993; dismissed Dec. 14, 1995	DOJ	State agrees to create Navajo Election Information Program.
Bowannie v. Bernalillo School District	1988: 88–0212-JP	USDC, New Mexico	Do at-large school board elections violate Sec. 2 of the VRA?	Consent decree, Nov. 23, 1988	NIYC	District adopts single-member district elections.

(*continued*)

TABLE 3.1 (*continued*)

Case Name	Year Filed: Civil Action Number	Court Where Filed	Legal Issue	Major or Latest Court Opinion	Attorneys for Indians	Outcome
U.S. v. New Mexico	1988: 88–1457-SC	USDC, New Mexico	Do language assistance provided Navajo and Keres speakers and other voting access practices violate the standards of Sec. 203 and Sec. 2 of the VRA?	Settlement Mar. 28, 1990; consent orders in 1994 and 1997	DOJ	State agrees to create Native American Election Information Program; county fails to fully comply, then later consents to terms.
Cuthair v. Montezuma-Cortez, Colorado School District	1989: 89–S-964	USDC, Colorado	Does at-large election of school board members dilute Indian votes in violation of Sec. 2 of the VRA?	7 F. Supp. 2d 1152 (D. Col. 1998)	ACLU	At-large election for all seats does violate Sec. 2. Under consent decree, one majority-minority district is created, with other seats elected at-large.
Grinnell v. Sinner	1992: A1-92-066	USDC, North Dakota	Does at-large election of state legislators dilute Indian votes in violation of Sec. 2 of the VRA?	n/a	n/a	District Court dismisses for failure to meet first *Gingles* precondition.

Stabler v. Thurston County	1993: 93–00394	USDC, Nebraska	Under Section 2, does at-large election of school board and village trustees dilute Indian votes? Are Indians entitled to a third majority-minority district for county board of supervisors following redistricting?	129 F.3d 1015 (8th Cir. 1997); cert. denied 523 U.S. 1118 (1998)	ACLU	Court of appeals upholds district court requirement of third majority-minority district but finds that plaintiffs did not meet three *Gingles* preconditions for striking at-large school board and village elections.
U.S. v. Cibola County	1993: 93–1134-LH/LFG	USDC, New Mexico	Do county's language assistance to Navajo and Keres speakers, election practices, and polling locations violate the standards of Sec. 203 and Sec. 2 of the VRA and the Fourteenth and Fifteenth Amendments?	Joint stipulation Apr. 21, 1994; order Apr. 22, 2004	DOJ	County agrees to detailed Native American Election Information Program; after ten years, DOJ obtains two-year extension due to incomplete implementation.
U.S. v. Socorro County	1993: 93–1244-JP	USDC, New Mexico	Do county's language assistance to Navajo speakers and other voting access practices violate the standards of Sec. 203 and Sec. 2 of the VRA and the Fourteenth and Fifteenth Amendments?	Consent agreement, Apr. 11, 1994	DOJ	County agrees to detailed Native American Election Information Program.

(*continued*)

TABLE 3.1 (*continued*)

Case Name	Year Filed: Civil Action Number	Court Where Filed	Legal Issue	Major or Latest Court Opinion	Attorneys for Indians	Outcome
U.S. v. Arizona	1994: 94–1845-PHX-EHC	USDC, Arizona	May state proceed with judicial elections in the absence of preclearance under Sec. 5 of the VRA?	1994 U.S. Dist. LEXIS 17606	DOJ	Court enjoins judicial election until preclearance obtained.
Arizona v. Reno	1994: 94–2054	USDC, District of Columbia	What are the standards for preclearance under Sec. 5 of the VRA for adding judges who are elected countywide?	887 F. Supp. 318 (D. D.C. 1995); cert. granted but then dismissed pursuant to Rule 46, 516 U.S. 1155 (1996)	DOJ	Sec. 5 preclearance does not require meeting the Sec. 2 standard of nondiscriminatory effects, but U.S. is entitled to discovery for evidence of discriminatory purpose.
Old Person v. Brown (originally *Old Person v. Cooney*)	1996: S-96-04-GF-PMP	USDC, Montana	Do state House boundaries following redistricting dilute Indian votes in violation of Sec. 2 of the VRA?	230 F.3d 1113 (9th Cir. 2000); 182 F. Supp. 2d 1002 (D. Mont., 2002)	ACLU; Indian Law Resource Center	Ninth Circuit Court vacates finding of no dilution, but on remand district court again finds no dilution and, even if dilution exists, no available remedy, given imminence of post-2000 redistricting.

U.S. v. Parshall School District (unfiled)	Notice letter, Aug. 29, 1996	North Dakota	Does at-large election of school district members dilute Indian votes in violation of Sec. 2 of the VRA?	None	DOJ	Negotiations following notice letter led to election of Apr. 15, 1997, adopting district system for elections.
U.S. v. Bernalillo County	1998: 98–156BB	USDC, New Mexico	Do county's language assistance to Navajo speakers and other voting access practices violate the standards of Sec. 2 and Sec. 203 of the VRA and the Fourteenth and Fifteenth Amendments?	Consent decree, Apr. 27, 1998; stipulation July 1, 2003	DOJ	County agrees to provide numerous specific types of assistance to Navajo-speaking voters.
Matt v. Ronan School District	1999: 99–94-M-DWM	USDC, Montana	Does at-large election of school trustees dilute Indian votes in violation of Sec. 2 of the VRA and the Fourteenth and Fifteenth Amendments?	Stipulation, Jan. 13, 2000	ACLU; Indian Law Resource Center	School district agrees to create two multimember districts, one of which is majority-minority.
U.S. v. Blaine County	1999: 99–122-GF-PMP	USDC, Montana	Does at-large election of county commissioners dilute Indian votes in violation of Sec. 2 of the VRA?	363 F.3d 897 (9th Cir. 2004); cert. denied, 544 U.S. 992 (2005)	DOJ; (MSLF for def'ts)	Ninth Circuit Court upholds district court ruling that at-large elections do violate Sec. 2 and dismissing defendants' argument that Sec. 2 is unconstitutional.

(*continued*)

TABLE 3.1 (*continued*)

Case Name	Year Filed: Civil Action Number	Court Where Filed	Legal Issue	Major or Latest Court Opinion	Attorneys for Indians	Outcome
Alden v. Board of Commissioners of Rosebud County	1999: 99–148-BLG-DWM	USDC, Montana	Does at-large election of county commissioners dilute Indian votes in violation of Sec. 2 of the VRA and the Fourteenth and Fifteenth Amendments?	Order, May 10, 2000	ACLU; Indian Law Resource Center	Court orders creation of three single-member districts before redistricting based on 2000 census occurs.
U.S. v. Day County, Enemy Swim Sanitary District	1999: 99–1024	USDC, South Dakota	Does intentional exclusion of Indian residents and tribal lands from a proposed sanitary district violate Sec. 2 of the VRA and the Fourteenth and Fifteenth Amendments?	Consent decree with county, May 14, 1999; consent judgment and decree with sanitary district, June 16, 2000	DOJ	County defendants agree to approve incorporation of inclusive sanitary district; Enemy Swim District continues litigation but settles after motion for summary judgment is denied.
U.S. v. Roosevelt County	2000: 00-50-BLG-JDS	USDC, Montana	Does at-large election of county commission members dilute Indian votes in violation of Sec. 2 of the VRA?	Consent decree, Mar. 24, 2000	DOJ	County agrees to create three single-member districts.

U.S. v. Benson County	2000: A2-00-30	USDC, North Dakota	Does at-large election of county commission members dilute Indian votes in violation of Sec. 2 of the VRA?	Consent judgment and decree, Mar. 10, 2000	DOJ	County agrees to return to elections by single-member districts.
Emery v. Hunt Consolidated with: *U.S. v. South Dakota*	2000: 00–3008 00-3015	USDC, South Dakota	Does resumption of at-large elections in a legislative district formerly divided into two subdistricts, one of which had been majority-minority, dilute votes in violation of Sec. 2 of the VRA?	615 N.W.2d 590 (S.D. 2000) USDC order, Aug. 10, 2000 272 F.3d 1042 (8th Cir. 2001) (fees)	ACLU; DOJ	USDC certifies to state supreme court, which rules that redistricting is permitted only once a decade. Federal claims are mooted. Attorney fee issues later go to Eighth Circuit Court.
McConnell v. Blaine County	2002: 01–91-GF-RFC	USDC, Montana	Does at-large election of county commissioners dilute Indian votes in violation of Sec. 2 of the VRA?	Denial of intervention: 37 Fed. Appx. 276; 2002 U.S. App. LEXIS 10883 (9th Cir. 2002)	ACLU	Private suit filed when courts denied plaintiffs' intervention in *U.S. v. Blaine County*. Private parties later appear on appeal as plaintiff-intervenor-appellees in 363 F.3d 897.

(*continued*)

TABLE 3.1 (*continued*)

Case Name	Year Filed: Civil Action Number	Court Where Filed	Legal Issue	Major or Latest Court Opinion	Attorneys for Indians	Outcome
Vigil v. Lujan Consolidated with *Padilla v. Johnson*	2001: 01-1077BB/RLP; 01-1081 JC/LFG	USDC, New Mexico	Does the state court's plan for redistricting the state House of Representatives violate the Equal Protection Clause and the VRA?	191 F. Supp. 2d 1273 (D. N.M. 2001); dismissed as moot, Mar. 15. 2002	Tribal and private counsel	Federal court defers to state court.
Jepsen v. Vigil-Giron Consolidated with	2001: D0101 CV 2001-02177; -02178; -02179	New Mexico, 1st Judicial District	Does the state court's plan for redistricting the state House of Representatives violate the Equal Protection Clause and the VRA?	Findings and Conclusions, Jan. 24, 2002	Tribal and private counsel	State court amends legislative plan and creates six Indian-majority House districts
Bone Shirt v. Nelson (originally *Bone Shirt v. Hazeltine*)	2001: 01–3032	USDC, South Dakota	Must legislative district boundaries be precleared under Sec. 5 of the VRA even if only two counties are covered jurisdictions, and does districting dilute Indian votes in violation of Sec. 2 by packing Indian voters into a single district?	Preclearance: 200 F. Supp. 2d 1150 (D. S.D. 2002); Sec. 2: 2006 U.S. App. LEXIS 21409 (8th Cir. 2006)	ACLU	Legislative districts do require preclearance, and identified districts do violate Sec. 2.
Frank v. Forest County	2001: 01–C-847	USDC, Eastern Wisconsin	Does a districting plan for county supervisors dilute Indian votes in violation of Sec. 2 of the VRA and have too much deviation in population (18%) in violation of the Equal Protection Clause?	336 F.3d 570 (7th Cir. 2003)	Private counsel	Deviation in size is acceptable when district populations are so small. Plaintiffs fail to meet *Gingles* political cohesion criterion on Sec. 2 claim.

Quick Bear Quiver v. Nelson (originally *Quick Bear Quiver v. Hazeltine*)	2002: 02–5069	USDC, South Dakota	Do all voting changes in states that affect two covered counties have to be precleared under Sec. 5 of the VRA?	Consent order, Dec. 27, 2002; 387 F. Supp. 2d 1027 (2005).	ACLU	South Dakota agrees to seek preclearance of 600+ statutes and regulations since 1972 and refrain from implementing two specific statutes until preclearance is obtained.
Navajo Nation v. Arizona Independent Redistricting Commission (IRC) Consolidated with *Arizona IRC v. Bayless*	2002: 02–0807-PHX-ROS 2002:02-0799-PHX-ROS	USDC, Arizona	Do legislative district boundaries diminish the voting strength of minority voters in violation of Sec. 2 of the VRA and are the districts unequal in population in violation of the Equal Protection Clause?	230 F. Supp. 2d 998 (D. Ariz. 2002)	n/a	Indian plaintiffs withdrew from the case when the DOJ objected to preclearance because of districts in Hispanic but not Indian areas of the state.
Weddell v. Wagner Community School District	2002: 02–4056-KES	USDC, South Dakota	Do at-large elections of the school board, and polling locations and number of locations, violate Sec. 2 of the VRA?	Consent decree, Mar. 18, 2003	ACLU	School board members will continue to be elected at-large, but a cumulative voting system will be enacted. Polling place will be relocated.

(*continued*)

TABLE 3.1 (*continued*)

Case Name	Year Filed: Civil Action Number	Court Where Filed	Legal Issue	Major or Latest Court Opinion	Attorneys for Indians	Outcome
Cottier v. City of Martin (originally *Wilcox v. Martin*)	2002: 02–5021-KES	USDC, South Dakota	Does a plan distributing the Indian population across three two-member city council districts violate Sec. 2 of the VRA?	445 F.3d 1113 (8th Cir. 2006)	ACLU	Appellate court reverses holding that plaintiffs failed to prove white bloc voting sufficiently to meet third *Gingles* criterion and remands.
Kirkie v. Buffalo County	2003: 03–5024-CBK	USDC, South Dakota	Do county commission districts with over ten times greater population in an Indian district than a white district violate the Equal Protection Clause?	Consent decree, Feb. 10, 2004	ACLU	County agrees to new equal-sized districts and a special election.
ACLU of Minnesota v. Kiffmeyer	2004: 04–CV-4653 (JMR/FLN)	USDC, Minnesota	Do limits on acceptance of tribal ID card to establish identification for voting violate the Equal Protection Clause and the Help America Vote Act?	Temporary restraining order, 2004 U.S. Dist. LEXIS 22996 (D. Minn. 2004); consent judgment, Sept. 9, 2005	ACLU	State agrees to accept tribal ID cards on same basis as other ID cards.

Daschle v. Thune	2004: 04–4177	USDC, South Dakota	Does copying license plate numbers or following cars of Indian voters violate the Equal Protection Clause and the VRA?	Order, Nov. 2, 2004	n/a	Senator Tom Daschle won a temporary restraining order the night before the election.
Blackmoon v. Charles Mix County	2005: 05–4017	USDC, South Dakota	Do county commission districts that divide the Indian population and deviate over 19% in size violate Sec. 2 of the VRA and the Fourteenth and Fifteenth Amendments?	386 F. Supp. 2d 1108 (D. S.D. 2005); U.S. Dist. LEXIS 27551. 2005	ACLU	Malapportionment violates the Equal Protection Clause; existing districts enjoined; new districts pending.
Large v. Fremont County	2005: 05–CV-270-ABJ	USDC, Wyoming	Does at-large election of county commissioners violate Sec. 2 of the VRA and the Fourteenth and Fifteenth Amendments?	Filed Oct. 20, 2005	ACLU; (MSLF for defendants)	Pending
Intertribal Council of Arizona v. Brewer	2006: 3: 06-01362-JAT	USDC, Arizona	Does the Arizona Taxpayer and Citizen Protection Act violate the Fourteenth and 24th Amendments, the Civil Rights Act of 1964, Sec. 2 of the VRA, and the National Voter Registration Act?	Filed May 24, 2006	ACLU and others	Pending

DOJ, Department of Justice; USDC, U.S. District Court; VRA, Voting Rights Act.; ACLU, American Civil Liberties Union; MSLF, Mountain States Legal Foundation; NIYC, National Indian Youth Council; NARF, Native American Rights Fund.

TABLE 3.2. *American Indian Federal Voting Rights Cases by Type, 1965–2006*

Type of Case	No. of Cases
Denial of access to ballot	7
Discriminatory administration of election procedures	14
Enforcement of Section 203	8
Challenges to at-large elections	26
Disputes over redistricting	15
Disputes over Section 5 preclearance	9
Bailout actions	5
Other (Section 203 interpretation)	1

unconstitutional because Indians are immune from paying some taxes. A three-judge U.S. district court, affirmed by the U.S. Supreme Court, ruled in 1975 that Indians are indeed citizens under the Fourteenth Amendment and are entitled to the right to vote; further, the apportionment of the supervisor districts was unconstitutional (*Goodluck v. Apache County* 1975).[6]

The use of literacy tests and low voter turnout among Indians brought Apache County under the special provisions of the VRA since its passage in 1965.[7] Thus, when the Apache County High School District planned to have a bond election in 1976, it applied to the Justice Department for preclearance for changes related to the location of polling places, Spanish translation of election materials, and oral assistance for Spanish- and Navajo-speaking voters. The school district held the election before it received the preclearance, however, and then sought a declaratory judgment from the District Court for the District of Columbia when the Justice Department's objection blocked the implementation of the election results (*Apache County High School District v. U.S.* 1977*). The Justice Department's investigation had shown that the school district had consciously declined to publicize the election as much on the reservation as off it because the bond funds would be used to build high schools solely off the reservation, even though, as the judge later found, "over fifty percent

[6] A three-judge district court, made up of two district judges and one from a circuit court of appeals, is used in challenges to the constitutionality of statewide legislative or congressional districts and under several sections of the VRA, such as declaratory judgment actions by states for preclearance and actions to enjoin enforcement of state laws. At the time of *U.S. v. Arizona* (1975), three-judge courts were used for more types of actions, but their use was reduced by statute in 1976. See 28 U.S.C.S. §2284.

[7] Arizona had successfully bailed out of coverage after 1965 (*Apache County v. U.S.* 1966), but was included again by the updated formula in the 1970 amendments. See text.

of the [school district's] taxes come from the reservation" (Memorandum Opinion, June 12, 1980, 7).

The court ruled that the law covered school district elections and that the reduction in the number of polling places since the 1974 general election was a retrogression in the right to vote that brought the whole election plan under review. The Department of Justice objection stood. While the lawsuit was in progress, the school district had held another election to dissolve the existing district and break it up into separate ones. The Justice Department initially declined to preclear some of the procedures for this election as well but withdrew its objection after more information was provided (Days 1980).[8]

Apache County officials may have accepted the Indians' right to vote in county elections, but conflicts over equality of access to the ballot continued. In 1988 the Justice Department again sued Arizona (*U.S. v. Arizona* 1988*), alleging that officials in Apache County and adjoining Navajo County failed to furnish adequate information and assistance in the Navajo language, as required by the language minority provisions of the VRA, resulting in discriminatory procedures for registering voters, casting absentee ballots, and purging registration lists. The case was settled by consent decree on May 22, 1989, setting up a Navajo Language Election Information Program that remained under an annual reporting requirement until 1997 (Joint Motion and Order to Dismiss, December 13–14, 1995).

South Dakota has an even more complex history of legal conflict over the right of reservation Indians to vote. From the mid-1970s through the mid-1980s, a series of cases raised issues starting with complete exclusion from the ballot and continuing with various impediments to registration and voting.

The earlier cases concerned a peculiar distinction in South Dakota law between "organized" and "unorganized" counties dating back to the beginning of statehood. The unorganized Todd County encompassed the Rosebud Sioux Reservation. The adjoining organized county, Tripp County, performed most of the county government functions for Todd County. A similar relationship existed between organized Fall River County and unorganized Shannon County, which contains a large portion of the Pine Ridge Reservation.[9] State law provided a process for becoming

[8] For more background on the broader political context of these disputes, see McCool (1982), Phelps (1985, 1991), and Berman and Salant (1998).

[9] At the time of *Little Thunder v. South Dakota* (1975), unorganized Washabaugh County was also attached to organized Jackson County.

an organized county, but it required half of the voters to be "freeholders," which was extremely unlikely for Indians living on trust lands (*Little Thunder v. South Dakota* 1975, 1258, fn. 6). Residency requirements kept residents of unorganized counties from voting or running for office in elections for those officials in the organized counties who administered the same services for the adjoining unorganized counties.

In 1974 private plaintiffs supported by Legal Services attorneys brought the *Little Thunder v. South Dakota* case, challenging such total exclusion from voting as a violation of the Fourteenth Amendment.[10] The federal district court judge ruled for the defendants but the Eighth Circuit Court of Appeals reversed (1975), rejecting the state's argument that reservation Indians "do not share the same interest in county government as the residents of the organized counties" (1255).

The 1975 amendments to the VRA brought these South Dakota counties under the special provisions of the act. Nevertheless, officials failed to obtain preclearance before they held an election for county commissioners with newly apportioned districts, and the Justice Department sued to enforce the act in 1978 (*U.S. v. Tripp County*). The Justice Department found that the reapportionment plan was based on the voting population rather than the total population, resulting in the districts with large Indian populations being underrepresented. The court blocked certification of the election results and ordered officials to submit a new apportionment plan that could win approval from either the Justice Department or the District of Columbia court (Order, February 6, 1979).

Also in 1978, the Justice Department sued South Dakota and Fall River County because of the residency requirement that blocked an Indian resident of Shannon County from running for the county commission of Fall River County, which administered many of Shannon County's public services (*U.S. v. South Dakota* 1980). The defendants argued that nonresidents lacked an interest in county government, and again the same district judge found that the requirement was neither a violation of the Equal Protection Clause nor racially discriminatory under the Fifteenth Amendment or the VRA. Chiding the district judge for relitigating *Little Thunder*, the Eighth Circuit Court reversed and struck down the residency requirement for candidacy (1980).

[10] The U.S. Supreme Court had relied on the Equal Protection Clause of the Fourteenth Amendment in striking down restrictions limiting voters to property-holders or parents in *Kramer v. Union Free School District* (1969). In 1974, South Dakota was not yet covered by the special provisions of the VRA, and Section 2 of the act at that time required proof of intentional discrimination, as does the Fifteenth Amendment.

The South Dakota legislature responded to the litigation over the organized and unorganized counties by separating them administratively, but did not submit the new legislation for preclearance. The Justice Department then sued to enjoin implementation of the law until it had been precleared (*U.S. v. South Dakota* 1979*). When the state then submitted it, the Department objected because the law included provisions such as limiting the newly separate counties to contracting with the counties to which they had formerly been attached if they wanted to contract out for any governmental services. When negotiations with the Justice Department broke down, the state filed a declaratory judgment action instead (*South Dakota v. U.S.* 1980*). In 1981 the parties reached a consent agreement in which the state agreed not to implement the restrictions on the newly separate counties (Consent Decree, December 2, 1981).

A local effort to keep South Dakota Indians from voting at all appeared as recently as the late 1990s. White landowners formed the Enemy Swim Sanitary District that specifically excluded the Indian-owned lands in the vicinity. The Justice Department sued the county and the sanitary district, and, after taking extensive depositions, alleged that Indian-owned lands had been excluded out of fear that Indians would become a voting majority of the sanitary district (Plaintiffs' Required Statement of Material Facts, February 2, 2000, 24). Day County promptly settled, but the sanitary district did not settle until its motion for summary judgment was denied (*U.S. v. Day County, Enemy Swim Sanitary District* 1999*).[11]

The strategy of disenfranchising Indian voters through deannexations has occurred elsewhere in the upper Midwest. In 1978 the Justice Department won a preliminary injunction and the appointment of federal examiners for the Town of Bartelme and Shawanee County, Wisconsin, after the town deannexed land that was in the Stockbridge-Munsee Reservation, thus removing the Indians' right to vote in township elections (*U.S. v. Town of Bartelme* 1978*; see Wolfley 1991, 195 fn. 170). Similarly, the City of Prior Lake, Minnesota, annexed part of a Sioux community in 1972 but then attempted to deannex it in 1983, depriving the reservation residents of police and fire protection. The district court and the Eighth Circuit Court of Appeals ruled that the city could not disenfranchise the Indian voters or deny them municipal services (*Shakopee Mdewakanton Sioux Community and the U.S. v. City of Prior Lake* 1985).[11]

[11] Again in 2004, a suit arose in South Dakota from a review of Lake Andes city boundaries that resulted in excluding some Indian voters. Not included in Table 3.1 because filed

Many cases concerned not complete disenfranchisement, but discriminatory treatment in the application of general voting rules and procedures. In 1978 the Justice Department won a temporary restraining order against election officials in Humboldt County, Nevada, ensuring that residents of the Fort McDermitt Reservation would not be impeded from registering and voting. The district court ordered the appointment of a deputy registrar to register reservation residents and federal examiners for the elections (*U.S. v. Humboldt County* 1978*). In similar circumstances in South Dakota, the U.S. district court ordered county officials to accept voter applications they had rejected from an Indian voter registration drive (*American Horse v. Kundert* 1984*; see Wolfley 1991, 200–1). Attorneys with the National Indian Youth Council (NIYC) supported another South Dakota voter registration suit in 1986 (*Fiddler v. Sieker* 1986*), in which residents of the Cheyenne River Reservation alleged that election officials had impeded their registration drive by refusing to provide an adequate number of cards. The district court held in the plaintiffs' favor and extended the deadline for registration (see Wolfley 1991, 201).

Such informal efforts to discourage Indians from registering and voting continue into the present. In Charles Mix County in South Dakota in 2004, campaign workers for the Republican candidate for the U.S. Senate were systematically following Indian voters and writing down their license plate numbers (Rave 2004). The night before the election, a federal district judge found that "there was intimidation particularly targeted at Native American Voters" and issued a temporary restraining order (*Daschle v. Thune* 2004*, November 2, 2004, 2).

Other cases have alleged that Indians are denied an equal opportunity to vote because of the number and/or location of polling places. The Native American Rights Fund brought *Black Bull v. Dupree School District* (1986*) because Indians had to travel up to 150 miles to vote in school district elections (Wolfley 1991, 201). The case was settled when the school district agreed to establish more polling places on the Cheyenne River Reservation, reschedule the election, and broadly publicize the new date. In the same year, *U.S. v. McKinley County* (1986*) charged that a complicated precinct assignment process and a paucity of polling places resulted in rural Indians being erroneously assigned to precincts and required to travel great distances and around major geographic obstacles to vote for county commissioners. In a consent decree (January 13, 1986) the county

in state court under state election laws, the suit was dismissed on procedural grounds (*Zephier v. Cihak* 2004*; see Melmer 2004b).

agreed to reconfigure precinct boundaries, to establish more rural polling places, and to publicize these changes in English, Spanish, and Navajo.

The most recent source of conflict to emerge is voter identification requirements. Beginning with the 2004 elections, disputes over voter identification arose in several places in Indian Country. In Minnesota the issue was whether the state would accept tribally issued identification for Indians living off the reservation. The National Congress of American Indians (NCAI) and the Minnesota chapter of the American Civil Liberties Union (ACLU) filed a lawsuit in an attempt to force the state to accept valid tribal identification for all Indians (*NCAI News* 2004; Reynolds 2004a, 2004b). On the Friday before the election, a federal district judge ruled in favor of the Indian plaintiffs (*ACLU of Minnesota v. Kiffmeyer* 2004).

Disputes elsewhere over voter identification did not involve exclusion of tribal identification but may have nonetheless disproportionately affected Indians because significant numbers of them do not have a driver's license. In South Dakota a county auditor in Corson County (where a portion of the Standing Rock Reservation is located) issued written instructions that all voters must have photo identification – a clear violation of a new state law (Cohen 2004). This dispute was resolved without litigation. New Mexico had lawsuits in 2004 and 2005 in both state and federal courts over identification requirements (*Navajo Times* 2004; Associated Press 2005). They largely concerned disparate requirements for in-person versus mail or absentee registration and voting and were not brought specifically on behalf of American Indians, but the cases were followed with interest by the Indian press (*Navajo Times* 2004).[12] The Intertribal Council of Arizona and the Hopi Nation joined a coalition of plaintiffs challenging an Arizona voter identification law in 2006 (*Intertribal Council of Arizons v. Brewer*).

The Right to Language Assistance

Disputes like those just described about inadequate opportunities to register and vote have typically been brought under Section 2 of the VRA since the 1982 amendments were enacted. Such complaints often occur in the same case or a companion case with claims under Section 203 when

[12] Another area of litigation under the VRA with potential impact on American Indians but not pursued with their specific interests in mind are challenges to statutes disenfranchising persons convicted of felonies. *Farrakhan v. Washington* (2003) included one Native American among several plaintiffs challenging Washington state's statute. For background on this area of litigation, see Allen (2004).

election officials provide inadequate language assistance as well as make voting very inconvenient. Since the 1975 amendments were passed, Asian American, American Indian, Alaskan Native, and Spanish-speaking language minorities have the right under Section 203 to receive all election-related written materials and oral assistance at the polls in their own language if they make up 5 percent of the population of a jurisdiction or (since 1992) an Indian reservation. If this population also had a voting turnout of less than 50 percent in the 1972 presidential election, its right to such election assistance is ensured through all the "special provisions" of preclearance and, potentially, federal examiners and observers under Section 4(f), as in the 1988 case of *U.S. v. Arizona* (1988*) discussed earlier. The designated language minorities in many more jurisdictions are covered by Section 203, which is triggered not by voting turnout but by the rates of literacy and limited English proficiency.

Section 203 is a relatively little-known part of the VRA because it is largely implemented administratively. The Justice Department will file a lawsuit if a jurisdiction refuses to comply, but not one single case under Section 203 has reached a full trial on the merits. All cases have been resolved with consent agreements.

Decennial census data determine which jurisdictions are covered by Section 203 and Section 4(f). According to Justice Department officials, each covered jurisdiction receives a letter from the Voting Section reminding them of their obligations under the law. Newly covered jurisdictions receive a personal visit from a Justice Department official to explain the law. In general, jurisdictions must provide more than ballots in the languages for which they are covered; whatever information they provide in English about any aspect of election procedures must also be provided in the other language(s), such as explanatory information about candidates, ballot issues, and procedures for absentee voting and for registering and purging voters.

The Section 203 cases taken to court by the Justice Department on behalf of American Indians have largely occurred in New Mexico, with six such cases filed between 1979 and 1998 in the U.S. District Court for the District of New Mexico (*U.S. v. San Juan County* 1979b*; *U.S. v. McKinley County* 1986a*; *U.S. v. New Mexico* 1988*; *U.S. v. Cibola County* 1993*; *U.S. v. Socorro County* 1993*; *U.S. v. Bernalillo County* 1998*). New Mexico has a history of exclusion of Indians from the ballot similar to that of Arizona, and also has numerous minority language communities with limited English proficiency (LEP) and some continuing racial tension. There has been one case involving Navajos in Utah (*U.S. v. San Juan*

County, Utah 1983b*; see Chapter 4) and a Section 4(f) case involving Apache and Navajo Counties in Arizona (*U.S. v. Arizona* 1988*).

These cases concern language assistance to speakers of Navajo, Zuni, Keres, and other pueblo languages. These languages are historically unwritten and thus trigger the law's requirement for oral assistance. These cases typically end with detailed consent agreements in which the jurisdictions agree to establish a comprehensive program of language assistance, specifying numbers and training of bilingual outreach workers, registrars, and/or poll workers; radio and newspaper advertising of election information; locations for voter services; and voter education programs. The Justice Department monitors compliance, and the litigants sometimes return to court for extensions of the consent agreements, reporting requirements, and judicial supervision.

At-Large Electoral Systems

The largest category of voting rights cases in Indian Country consists of challenges to jurisdictions where candidates are elected at-large in multimember districts. At-large systems in Indian Country have had impacts similar to those on African Americans in the South (McDonald 2003a, 131–2, 193).

> At-large representation was another tactic utilized by whites seeking to maintain their political control. Many local governments such as city councils, school boards, and county commissions elect multi-member bodies. When those representatives are chosen at large, the white majority within a community can utilize racial bloc voting to elect all of the members of the board. Insulated minorities can be frozen out. (Phelps 1991, 77)

School boards and county commissions are especially important levels of local government to rural Indians because they control public services that directly affect reservation residents (Berman and Salant 1998). Most of the lawsuits have challenged at-large elections for these types of governmental bodies, and a few have targeted municipal governments.

The Supreme Court ruled as early as 1969 that the VRA applies to such vote dilution as well as to outright exclusion from the ballot (*Allen v. State Board of Elections*). With smaller single-member districts, some can be majority-minority districts in which minority voters stand a much better chance of electing candidates of their choice. The American Indian cases seeking such a change fall into three periods that track the ups and downs of vote dilution case law at the national level – the mid-1970s to 1982, 1982–93, and 1993 to the present.

The Justice Department brought two cases on behalf of American Indians during the first period, when the Supreme Court's "totality of the circumstances" approach in *White v. Regester* (1973) guided litigation over at-large elections. In Nebraska the parties in *U.S. v. Thurston County* (1978*) entered into a consent decree in 1979 that created seven single-member districts for the county board of supervisors, two of which would be majority-minority (see Wolfley 1991, 195, fn. 170). Also in 1979 the Justice Department successfully brought a similar suit over county commission elections in San Juan County, New Mexico (*U.S. v. San Juan County* 1979a*).

The U.S. Supreme Court's decision in *City of Mobile v. Bolden* (1980), discussed in Chapter 2, dealt a huge blow to vote dilution cases, and no new Indian cases were filed until after the passage of the 1982 amendments to the VRA. By revising Section 2 to outlaw discriminatory effects of voting practices, as well as intentional discrimination, Congress provided clear statutory grounds for challenging at-large elections in areas not covered by the special provisions or that predated 1965 in the covered jurisdictions.

In Indian Country, as nationally (McDonald 1992, 71), challenges to at-large elections increased dramatically. We have identified twelve such cases during the 1980s. With the exception of *U.S. v. San Juan County* (1983a*), Utah (discussed at length in chapter 4), the cases were all brought by private counsel rather than the Justice Department.

The ACLU's Voting Rights Project brought the first and last at-large election cases of the decade for Indian plaintiffs: *Windy Boy v. Big Horn County*, in Montana (1986), filed in 1983, and *Cuthair v. Montezuma-Cortez, Colorado School District* (1998), filed in 1989. The Voting Rights Project was primarily focused on at-large cases in the South at this time, but it got involved in the *Windy Boy* case through the Montana ACLU affiliate (McDonald 2003b). After a trial in federal district court, the judge, sitting by designation from the federal court in Los Angeles when the Montana judge declined to hear the case (Shaw 1986, A-4), found evidence of "official discrimination that has hampered the ability of Indians to participate in the political process," such as irregularities in voter registration procedures, Indian names dropped from voting lists, and failure to appoint Indians to county boards and commissions (*Windy Boy v. Big Horn County* 1986, 1008-09). Applying the analysis from *Zimmer v. McKeithen* (1973), the judge ordered the county to dismiss the at-large election system for county commission and school board members.

The *Cuthair* case, which also challenged at-large school board elections, was more procedurally complex. Again, a local attorney brought in the ACLU (McDonald 2003b). The case was originally filed in 1989, and a consent decree was entered the following year. The plan established did not result in the election of an Indian member, and the parties eventually returned to court. Following a full trial, the court found "a history of discrimination in both the electoral process and in life in general which has only recently begun to improve" (*Cuthair v. Montezuma-Cortez, Colorado School District* 1998, 1169). Applying the *Gingles* test established in 1986, the court ruled that the at-large system violated Section 2. The parties then agreed on a system in which the portion of the school district encompassing the Ute Mountain Ute Reservation would elect one of the seven directors and the other six would continue to be elected at-large by voters in the remainder of the school district.

The most active organization bringing at-large election cases for Indians during the 1980s was the NIYC. Attorneys associated with NIYC brought successful challenges in federal district court to at-large elections in numerous jurisdictions in New Mexico, where it was headquartered. These included several school districts (*Largo v. McKinley Consolidated School District* 1984*, *Estevan v. Grants-Cibola County School District* 1984*, *Tso v. Cuba Independent School District* 1985*, *Bowannie v. Bernalillo School District* 1988*); a county commission (*Felipe and Ascencio v. Cibola County Commission* 1985*); a community college board (*Kirk v. San Juan College Board* 1986*); and a city council (*Casuse v. City of Gallup* 1987) (see Wolfley 1991, 199, fn. 203).

Several of these cases were settled when the state passed legislation in 1985 that required by-district elections in school districts larger than 16,000, in counties larger than 13,000, and in cities larger than 10,000 (Act of April 4, 1985).[13] When the city of Gallup resisted the legislation, the VRA case filed against the city in federal district court was certified to the New Mexico Supreme Court to determine a question of state law. The latter court ruled in *Casuse v. City of Gallup* (1987) that the city's home rule charter calling for city council members to be elected at-large

[13] Various secondary sources reported these population sizes differently, but the session laws confirm that they have not changed. See Act of April 4, 1985, ch. 202, 1985 N.M. Laws 1238 (school boards); ch. 203, 1985 N.M. Laws 1239 (municipalities), and ch. 204, 1985 N.M. Laws 1242 (counties).

did not immunize the city from the state legislation. After prevailing in these battles, the NIYC went on to bring successful suits in 1986 against a community college board (*Kirk v. San Juan College Board* 1986*; see *Sho-Ban News* 1986a, 1987) and in 1988 against a school district smaller than the size mandated by legislation to change (*Bowannie v. Bernalillo School District* 1988*).

NIYC occasionally worked outside of New Mexico as well. After succeeding in New Mexico, NIYC joined a suit in 1988 to challenge at-large elections for school boards in Arizona (*Clark v. Holbrook Unified School District* 1989). Arizona law at that time did not allow single-member districts for school boards (Trahant and Pitzl 1988, A1), so the plaintiffs sought to invalidate the law under Section 2 of the federal Voting Rights Act. Forty-two percent of the Holbrook district, adjoining the Navajo Reservation, was Navajo, yet no Navajo had ever been elected (Trahant and Pitzl 1988, A9). The federal judge denied the defendants' motion to dismiss and ordered a hearing for a preliminary injunction (1989). This eventually led to a settlement and a change to single-member districts. Finally, NIYC also considered but ultimately did not file an at-large challenge in North Dakota (Henderson 1985).

One final lawsuit over at-large school board elections in the 1980s was unique in two respects. *Buckanaga v. Sisseton School District* (1986) was the only at-large election challenge brought by the Native American Rights Fund (NARF), and it concluded with an unusual remedy. Filed in 1984, the case was lost in the federal district court of South Dakota but was appealed to the Eighth Circuit Court of Appeals. Applying the new *Gingles* test from the Supreme Court, the appellate court reversed the district court and remanded the case for specific findings on the facts needed to establish a violation (1986).

The parties settled by consent decree in 1988 and agreed to a cumulative voting system in which voters could cast the same number of votes as there were positions to be filled in that election – three votes for different candidates, two votes for one and one for another, or all three votes for a single candidate (1988). Some scholars (e.g., Guinier 1997) have advocated cumulative voting as an alternative to majority-minority districts when minority voters are geographically dispersed. Judges are unlikely to impose this remedy, however, and one court of appeals struck down such a judicial order in a case in Tennessee (*Cousin v. Sundquist* 1998).

Thus, in the absence of a consent agreement, geographical dispersion can make it difficult for Indian plaintiffs to win. A 1992 case in North Dakota challenged the state's redistricting plan because at-large election of state legislators diluted the voting strength of voters on or near the Fort Berthold Indian Reservation (*Grinnell v. Sinner* 1992*). The federal district court dismissed the case for failure to meet the first prong of the *Gingles* test ("ACLU Pushing Plans to Increase Odds of Indian in State House," *Native American Law Digest* 2001, 11–12).

Litigation activity against at-large elections in Indian Country encountered greater uncertainty in the 1990s because of the Supreme Court's series of cases beginning with *Shaw v. Reno* (1993), summarized in Chapter 2. These cases arose in the context of decennial redistricting in the South, but have had implications for the use of majority-minority districts as remedies for vote-diluting at-large elections as well. According to ACLU attorneys, defendants routinely raise the *Shaw–Miller* defense in vote dilution cases (McDonald 2005a).

Voting rights cases concerning reservation Indians are less likely than cases concerning African Americans in the South to trigger *Shaw–Miller* problems. Reservations almost by definition are relatively geographically compact areas with high concentrations of minority voters, in contrast to the elongated shapes of the North Carolina and Georgia districts in question in *Shaw* and *Miller*. Nevertheless, the *Shaw–Miller* line of cases was significant in at least a couple of American Indian voting rights cases.

For example, the South Dakota legislature cited *Shaw* and *Miller* in 1996 when it voted to reverse an action it had taken earlier. In 1991 the legislature had divided one state House of Representatives district into two single-member districts to create a majority-minority district for residents of the Cheyenne River Sioux and Standing Rock Sioux Reservations. Other House districts had two members elected at-large. When the legislature restored the two-member district, the ACLU and the Justice Department both brought suit under the VRA, but the ACLU ultimately won in the South Dakota Supreme Court under a state statute construed to permit redistricting only once after each decennial census (*Emery v. Hunt* [*In re Certification of a Question of Law*] 2000).[14] Two of the five state justices, however, saw the legislature's action as justified under *Shaw* and *Miller*.

Indian plaintiffs suffered a partial loss on *Shaw–Miller* grounds in one case. In 1993 the ACLU returned to Thurston County, Nebraska, which had settled a case with the Justice Department in the late 1970s by

[14] Federal opinions arising out of *Emery v. Hunt* and the companion case, *U.S. v. South Dakota* (2001), address only issues of attorneys' fees: 272 F.3d 1042 (8th Cir. 2001), 236 F. Supp. 2d 1033 (D. S.D 2002), and 132 F. Supp. 803 (D. S.D. 2001).

changing from an at-large county commission. Filing in federal district court, the plaintiffs alleged that the county had failed to keep up with the growing Indian population and should have created a third majority-minority district in the redistricting after the 1990 census. The plaintiffs also challenged continuing at-large elections for trustees of the Village of Walthill and the Thurston County school board. The district court sustained the plaintiffs with respect to the county commission districts but rejected their challenge to the municipal and school elections. Upholding the district court, the Eighth Circuit Court of Appeals ruled in *Stabler v. Thurston County* (1997) that the plaintiffs had failed to meet the three criteria of the *Gingles* test and that the plaintiffs' proposed districts would be racial gerrymanders in violation of the standards of *Shaw* and *Miller*. The Supreme Court declined to take the appeal.

In contrast, the ACLU, in cooperation with attorneys from the Indian Law Resource Center in Helena, successfully brought two at-large cases in Montana in the late 1990s without running afoul of *Shaw–Miller*. Both cases were settled without trial when the defendants conceded that the three *Gingles* factors necessary to prove vote dilution were present (*Matt v. Ronan School District* 1999*, Order January 13, 2000, and *Alden v. Rosebud County* 1999*, Order, December 29, 1999). The defendants in the *Ronan School District* case, which had had many conflicts over the education of Indian students (Bick 2001), agreed to subdivide the district into two multimember districts, with Indian voters comprising a clear majority in one of the two. The defendants in the *Rosebud County* case agreed to change from a three-member county commission elected at-large to three single-member districts, one being majority Indian, but sought unsuccessfully to postpone the change until after 2000 census data were available (Order, May 9, 2000).

After an absence of more than ten years, the Justice Department returned to the issue of at-large elections in Indian Country in the second half of the 1990s. The Department successfully challenged at-large county commission elections in Benson County, North Dakota (*U.S. v. Benson County* 2000*), and at-large school board elections in Parshall, North Dakota; the latter case was settled after a notice letter without a complaint and consent decree ever being filed. Benson County had changed from district to at-large elections after the first Native American commissioner was elected in 1988 (U.S. Department of Justice 2000). In the Parshall district, some Indian parents felt that the climate for their children had been so bad that they sent their children instead to a government school forty miles away (Porterfield 1997).

In 1999 and 2000, respectively, the Justice Department also brought challenges to at-large commission elections in Blaine County and Roosevelt County, Montana. Roosevelt County settled quickly and agreed to institute single-member districts, reportedly to save the expense of litigation (*U.S. v. Roosevelt County* 2000*; Greene 2000, 4A). The Blaine County case, in contrast, was fought at great length when the Mountain States Legal Foundation came to the defense of the county and even contested the constitutionality of the VRA. The ACLU filed its own case when denied the right to intervene (*McConnell v. Blaine County* 2002). Eventually the Justice Department prevailed in both the district court and the Ninth Circuit Court of Appeals (*U.S. v. Blaine County* 2004). This case is discussed in detail in Chapter 5.

One of the latest challenges to at-large elections in Indian Country, brought by the ACLU in 2002, resulted in adoption of a cumulative voting system rather than single-member districts (Cavanagh 2002). *Wedell v. Wagner Community School District* (2002*) is the second Indian case in South Dakota (after the *Buckanaga* case in the 1980s) in which the parties agreed to this resolution.

Finally, in 2005, the ACLU and two local attorneys, on behalf of five residents of the Wind River Reservation, brought the first Indian voting rights case in Wyoming (*Large v. Fremont County* 2005*). Still pending, the suit alleges that the at-large election of county commissioners has both a discriminatory purpose and intent and violates Section 2 of the VRA and the Fourteenth and Fifteenth Amendments. Like virtually all the other at-large election lawsuits in the past twenty years, this one claims that local circumstances meet the *Gingles* test and Senate factors and asks the federal district court to enjoin elections under the existing system.

Redistricting

Although single-member districts may generally be more advantageous to minority voters than at-large districts, they open the door for further disputes about where to draw district lines. The governing principle of one person–one vote results in disputes about exactly how equal in population districts have to be and where the boundaries should be located in creating equal-population districts. Disputes and litigation under the Equal Protection Clause predictably arise over these matters after decennial censuses because partisan advantages and incumbents' interests are at stake. Thus, when issues of racial equality are also raised, they become part of extremely complex political battles.

One early such battle arose in Arizona. When the U.S. Supreme Court in *Reynolds v. Sims* (1964) first required all upper and lower houses of state legislatures to be apportioned on the one-person–one-vote principle, Arizona's attempt to redistrict resulted in litigation driven by partisan interests filed in 1965 (*Klahr v. Goddard*). Several years later, the boundaries were still in contention when the Navajo tribe alleged that its reservation had been divided for the purpose of weakening the tribe's political strength. The three-judge federal district court agreed in *Klahr v. Williams* (1972) and imposed its own districting plan for the upcoming 1972 elections. In its next session, the legislature slightly modified the court's plan vis-à-vis the Navajo Reservation to create districts that left 90 percent of the Navajos in one district and better satisfied the Hopi and White Mountain Apache tribes. The court accepted this plan (*Klahr v. Williams* 1974), finally ending the long-running reapportionment battle until the next census (see *Goddard v. Babbitt* 1982 later).

Indians were again involved in major lawsuits over redistricting after the 1980, 1990, and 2000 censuses. Aided by attorneys from the NIYC, the Justice Department, and several legal services agencies, Indian and Hispanic plaintiffs challenged New Mexico's 1982 reapportionment statute because it used votes cast rather than total population data to determine the districts (Schermerhorn and Stoto 1984). A three-judge district court declared this a violation of equal protection, and the U.S. Supreme Court affirmed the decision (*Sanchez v. King* 1982). Now using total population data, the legislature developed a new redistricting plan, and the plaintiffs challenged nineteen of seventy new districts as violating Section 2 of the VRA and the Fourteenth and Fifteenth Amendments. The district court found no intentional discrimination but applied the factors from *White v. Regester* (1973) and *Zimmer v. McKeithen* (1973), concluding that minority voting strength was diluted, and imposed its own redistricting plan (Findings of Fact and Conclusions of Law, August 8, 1984).

Also after the 1980 census, the San Carlos Apache tribe intervened in a new Arizona redistricting lawsuit with complex partisan alignments, because its reservation had been divided among three different legislative districts and congressional districts. The Justice Department had declined to preclear the legislative districts under Section 5. At the trial, legislators of both parties testified that the reservation should not have been divided. The parties to the suit stipulated to a new plan that placed the whole reservation in one legislative and congressional district (*Goddard v. Babbitt* 1982).

After the 1990 census, Indian plaintiffs aided by the ACLU unsuccessfully challenged eight Montana House districts created in 1992. The suit was filed in 1996 and went to trial in 1998. After the district court ruled for the defendants, the Ninth Circuit Court of Appeals reversed and remanded because the district court had erred in its interpretation of two components of the totality of circumstances test when it found white bloc voting insignificant and Indians already proportionally represented (*Old Person v. Cooney* 2000). Nevertheless, a new district judge held a second trial and then ruled that the districts did not dilute Indian voting strength (*Old Person v. Brown* 2002). The judge reached this conclusion in part because, by this time, the state's redistricting commission was already working on new districts using 2000 census data.[15]

Following the 2000 census, a major lawsuit again arose over Arizona's state legislative redistricting. Although the case is known as *Navajo Nation v. Arizona Independent Redistricting Commission* (2002), the Navajo and San Carlos Apache plaintiffs were relatively minor players in a complex battle in both state and federal courts initiated by a group representing Hispanic voters. The Indian parties withdrew from the case when it became clear that the Justice Department's denial of preclearance was because of problems with districts in which Indian interests were not at stake (230 F. Supp. 2d 1004). The suit continued with the remaining parties until they agreed on a plan that they argued met the Department of Justice's objections, and the court ruled that this consensus plan complied with federal law.

The Navajo and Jicarilla Apache Nations joined redistricting litigation in New Mexico following the 2000 census and succeeded in state court in obtaining six Indian-majority state House districts (*Jepsen v. Vigil-Giron* 2001*). Republican challengers of the state court's plan attempted to invoke Indian interests in their efforts to get federal court review of the plan (*Vigil v. Lujan* 2001). In response, the tribes intervened and rejected these "groundless Voting Rights Act and Equal Protection arguments" (Response of the Jicarilla Apache Nation, February 8, 2002, 24) and challenged those parties' standing to bring claims on behalf of communities to which they do not belong (Response of the Navajo Nation, February 8,

[15] Another case in the 1990s alleged that redistricting had fragmented two Minnesota reservations, but the case turned entirely on vote dilution allegations by urban minorities, largely African Americans (*Emison v. Growe* 1992, 440, fn. 39). Because of the small role of Indian interests and the apparent absence of tribal involvement, we omit it from Table 3.1, even though it resulted in an important U.S. Supreme Court decision on the VRA in 1993.

2002). The three-judge district court ultimately dismissed the Republicans' challenge, and the state court's plan stood (Order, March 15, 2002, and Defendants Speaker Lujan and President Pro Tempore Romero's Motion to Dismiss Consolidated Cases..., February 8, 2002).

The ACLU successfully sued South Dakota after its 2001 legislative reapportionment. *Bone Shirt v. Hazeltine* is a complex case combining issues of preclearance standards (2002) and vote dilution (2006*) by controlling district boundaries, electing at-large representatives for House districts, and "packing" Indian voters excessively into one district instead of creating two majority-minority districts. The preclearance issue is discussed in the next section of this chapter, and the Section 2 vote dilution issues are discussed at length in Chapter 6.

Not all redistricting cases are challenges to statewide legislative plans. Working with local counsel, the Potawatami Community of Forest County, Wisconsin, sued in 2001 over the redistricting plan for the county board of supervisors. The plaintiffs argued that the deviation in population across the districts violated Section 2 of the VRA and the Equal Protection Clause. The district court ruled in *Frank v. Forest County* (2002) that the plaintiffs' proposed plan failed to meet the political cohesion criterion of *Gingles* and that the amount of population deviation (18.03 percent) in the county's plan was barely within that allowable under the U.S. Constitution. The Seventh Circuit Court of Appeals affirmed (2003).

Since the 2000 census, the ACLU has brought three local redistricting suits in South Dakota's federal district court under the Equal Protection Clause and the VRA. In *Cottier v. City of Martin* (2006), Indian plaintiffs initially challenged a deviation across city council districts of at least 21.4 percent. The malapportionment was corrected, but the 36 percent Indian voting-age population was distributed across three two-member districts such that they were not a majority in any district. After the trial, the judge ruled that the plaintiffs had failed to meet the *Gingles* requirement to prove white bloc voting, but the Eighth Circuit Court of Appeals reversed on this point and remanded the case for further proceedings (2006).

The second case was successful with much less effort. In *Kirkie v. Buffalo County* (2003*), the one county commission district with almost all Indian voters had over ten times the population of an all-white commission district. The case ended with a consent decree adopting new districts and agreeing on precincts and polling places for a special election under the new districts (Consent Decree, February 10, 2004).

In *Blackmoon v. Charles Mix County* (2005a), Indian plaintiffs sued after the county commission voted to make no boundary changes despite a total deviation in district size exceeding 19 percent and boundaries that divided the Yankton Sioux tribal members across three districts (Melmer 2005c, 2005d). The county obtained emergency legislation from the state allowing it to redistrict before a court so ordered, but the plaintiffs temporarily blocked the legislation because it had not been precleared by the Justice Department, as required by *Quick Bear Quiver v. Nelson* (2005). The plaintiffs won on a summary judgment with respect to the unequal population size, and the Justice Department approved the legislation when it was finally submitted for preclearance. Litigation is continuing on the configuration of the new districts (2005b).[16]

Section 5 and Bailouts

As noted in Chapter 2, the most unusual feature of the VRA is Section 5, which requires covered jurisdictions to seek preclearance for all changes in voting laws and practices from either the U.S. attorney general or the U.S. District Court for the District of Columbia. This requirement was intended to keep districts with a history of discrimination from devising new discriminatory laws as old ones were eliminated. Although relatively few parts of Indian Country are covered by Section 5 (the state of Arizona and two counties in South Dakota), the preclearance process has led to greater consideration of Indian interests in several cases.

After the U.S. Supreme Court ruled in a Louisiana case that the VRA covers judicial elections (*Clark v. Roemer* 1993), the state of Arizona submitted for Justice Department preclearance a plan to add four judgeships to the trial courts in two counties covered by Section 5. The Department denied preclearance on the grounds that the at-large election of these judges violated Section 2 by diluting Indian votes and sought to enjoin the election for these new judgeships when the state continued to qualify candidates for the election (*U.S. v. Arizona* 1994). The three-judge district court of Arizona ruled for the United States but issued only a preliminary

[16] A lawsuit challenging the redistricting of Minneapolis City Council wards alleged that Native American influence in one ward had been diluted, but the case was primarily about African American and partisan interests (*Johnson-Lee v. Minneapolis* 2004). The case is omitted from 3.1 because the judge found that the new plan had intentionally kept intact an Indian housing community (43, fn. 11), and because the incumbent Native American city council member did not join the suit and was indeed subsequently reelected in the redrawn district (Lonetree 2005).

injunction because the state filed for a declaratory judgment with the U.S. District Court of the District of Columbia. In *Arizona v. Reno* (1995), that court ruled that the addition of judgeships is not retrogressive and a jurisdiction does not have to prove that a voting change would survive a Section 2 challenge before it can be precleared. Preclearance can be denied for a discriminatory intent, however, and the court permitted discovery on the question of the purpose of the plan.[17] In this case, *Apache County High School District* (1977), and *Navajo Nation* (2002), Department of Justice preclearance objections increased Indian voters' opportunity to have their concerns heard.

ACLU litigation following the 2001 legislative redistricting in South Dakota also clearly demonstrated the importance of the preclearance requirement. The first issue in *Bone Shirt v. Hazeltine* (2002) was whether the state had to preclear its reapportionment plan even though only two South Dakota counties were covered jurisdictions. When a three-judge district court ruled in 2002 that it did, the ACLU promptly sued to require the state to seek retroactive preclearance of more than 600 laws changing voting rules and procedures passed in the state since those two counties first came under Section 5 coverage in the 1970s (*Quick Bear Quiver v. Hazeltine* [later *Quick Bear Quiver v. Nelson* 2005]). The state settled that case within a few months, agreeing to work with a federal magistrate to develop a process for preclearing the plans, to allow the plaintiffs to monitor the process, and to refrain from implementing two statutes prior to preclearance that the plaintiffs deemed to be especially harmful to the interests of American Indians in the state (Dakota-Lakota-Nakota Human Rights Advocacy Coalition 2002; *Washington Post* 2002; McDonald 2004). As of June 2006, the Justice Department had precleared all statutes the state had submitted since that time (U.S. Department of Justice 2006), but the plaintiffs can invoke the court's continuing jurisdiction in *Quick Bear Quiver* when needed, as they did in the *Blackmoon* case described earlier.

Congress acknowledged the unusual leverage that Section 5 creates over covered jurisdictions by including the bailout provisions in Section 4. These provisions enable jurisdictions covered through application of the criteria in that section to go to the District of Columbia's U.S. district court and prove that they did not use tests or devices in a discriminatory fashion (Hancock and Tredway 1985, 389–92). The very first use of the Section 4 bailout provisions was a case concerning American Indians.

[17] The Supreme Court accepted the state's request for review but later dismissed it when the parties settled (516 U.S. 1155, 1996).

Because of their use of literacy tests and their low voter registration and turn-out rates, the three northeastern counties of Arizona including the Navajo and Hopi Reservations became covered jurisdictions in 1965. Following the Section 4 procedures, the state and the three countries filed for a declaratory judgment, and the United States, following an investigation by the Department of Justice, consented to the bailout. The Navajo tribe and numerous members of its tribal council attempted to intervene, citing the use of a literacy test in a 1964 election to turn away registered Indian voters, the general deterrent effect of the literacy test, and the Justice Department's failure to interview enough Navajos before supporting the bailout. Nevertheless, the District of Columbia's U.S. district court ruled that their evidence of discrimination and of inadequate investigation was insufficient to support their intervention or to support denial of the requested bailout (*Apache County v. U.S.* 1966).

Turning to lobbying, the chairman of the Navajo Tribal Council submitted a statement supporting a nationwide ban on literacy tests to the hearings on the 1970 amendments (U.S. Congress, Senate 1970, 678–9). He argued that such tests have deterred Arizona Navajos from voting even if they are not discriminatorily applied. This and others' lobbying was successful, and the nationwide ban was included in the 1970 amendments. Moreover, the same three Arizona counties fell under the special provisions again when the coverage formula was updated and based on the 1968 elections. This time, according to Hancock and Tredway (1985, 396), the state did not file a bailout action.

The 1975 amendments covering language minorities also included bailout procedures. Jurisdictions covered under Section 4(f)(4) could prove to the District Court of the District of Columbia that English-only elections had not had the purpose or effect of denying or abridging the right to vote. Jurisdictions could bail out from Section 203 by proving to the local federal district court that the illiteracy rate for the applicable language minority group was equal to or less than the national illiteracy rate (42 USC §1973aa-1a(d)). After these provisions went into effect, the United States consented to bailouts of counties in New Mexico in 1976 (*New Mexico v. U.S.*) and Oklahoma in 1978 (*Choctaw and McCurtain Counties v. U.S.*) that had been covered for Indian languages under Section 4(f)(4). Hancock and Tredway report (1985, 403) that Justice Department investigations showed an absence of discrimination. Maine similarly bailed out without objection for all of its municipalities, except that the Passamaquoddy Pleasant Point Indian Reservation remained covered under Section 203 (*Maine v. U.S.* 1975*, Stipulation of Dismissal Without Prejudice, July 5, 1977).

A contested and unsuccessful bailout action under Section 203 concerning American Indians was brought in 1976 by Roosevelt County, Montana, which twenty years later was subject to litigation over its at-large elections. In *Simenson v. Bell* (1976*), the county clerk/recorder sought bailout on the grounds that nobody had responded to public notices that sought to identify voting-age Indians who could not read English. While the Montana judge sympathized with a rural county facing "egalitarian legislation directed principally at the heavily populated urban areas of the country," he concluded that the evidence presented did not prove that the illiteracy rate of the county's Indians was below the national average rather than above it, as census data had determined (Memorandum and Order, January 24, 1978, 1).

While it was not a full bailout case, an Oklahoma school district filed suit in 1976 for a declaratory judgment that the Cherokee language is unwritten and therefore that the state is not required to provide written election materials in that language. The court granted summary judgment to the plaintiff to guarantee that the current attorney general's assurance of this interpretation could not be reversed later by a new attorney general (*Independent School District of Tulsa v. Bell* 1976). This case may have arisen because Section 203 does not have a preclearance procedure, as does Section 4(f)(4), and the attorney general explicitly declines to preclear jurisdictions' proposals for compliance with Section 203 (28 CFR §55.2(e)).

Although the 1982 amendments included provisions intended to facilitate bailouts from coverage under the special provisions of Sections 4 through 9 (Hancock and Tredway 1985, 409–10), they have not been used often.[18] No jurisdictions in Indian Country have sought bailout under these revised provisions.

Conclusion

American Indians have made active use of the VRA, especially in the western states, where their numbers are large enough in some areas to have potential political influence. They have challenged total exclusions from the ballot box, attempts to discourage their participation, and electoral

[18] Lexis reports no bailout actions at all filed in the District Court for the District of Columbia since that time. The Department of Justice web page for Section 5 coverage (www.usdoj.gov/crt/voting/sec_5/covered.htm, accessed June 24, 2006) reports that eleven political subdivisions in Virginia have bailed out with Department of Justice consent.

systems that make their participation fruitless. They are also one of the principal intended beneficiaries of Section 203 as they attempt to preserve their cultures through their native languages and still participate in the U.S. electoral process. In the overwhelming majority of cases, they have won settlements or judicial decrees that improve their ability to participate in electoral politics. The continuing emergence of new cases suggests that voting rights problems in Indian Country are still common and that Congress was wise in 2006 to continue preclearance requirements for some jurisdictions.

Litigation, however, is complex, time-consuming, and heavily dependent on access to sophisticated counsel. The case studies in the following chapters clearly illustrate the complexity and difficulty of bringing VRA cases to trial and implementing the results. The first case study focuses on implementation of one of the earliest VRA cases in Indian Country. The second and third case studies focus on the intricacies of recent VRA trials and illustrate the many facets of a Section 2 case. Taking full advantage of these victories requires continuing political mobilization. The last two chapters go beyond the courthouse to examine the litigation's immediate consequences and their larger political impact.

4

It's Our Turn

Indian Voting in San Juan County, Utah

The most basic right of self-governance, the right to vote, eluded American Indians well after passage of the 1924 Citizenship Act. As late as 1938, seven states still refused to allow Indians the right to vote (Peterson 1957, 121). Among those states was Utah. A Utah statute, adopted in 1897, shortly after statehood, required all voters to be both residents of the state and citizens of the United States but excluded, as residents, Indians living on reservations:

> Any person living upon any Indian or military reservation shall not be a resident of Utah, within the meaning of this chapter, unless such a person had acquired a residence in some county prior to taking up his residence upon such Indian or military reservation. (An Act Providing for Elections 1897, 172)

The state's two-pronged test created a difficult hurdle for American Indians. Although Indians were granted citizenship in 1924, those living on reservations still failed to meet Utah's residency requirement. The prohibition remained law until 1957, leaving Utah with the distinction of being the last state to enfranchise American Indians living on reservations.

The right to vote is only the first step in effective political participation (Grofman, Handley, and Niemi 1992, 23). Additional barriers, described in previous chapters, erode effective opportunities for equal participation. This chapter explores the barriers that prevented Navajo voters living in San Juan County, Utah, from having an equal opportunity to participate in the election process and elect candidates of their choice. San Juan County relied upon an at-large system for electing its three-person commission. Although 46 percent of San Juan County's population was

American Indian in 1980, no Indian had ever been elected to the commission or any other county office. In 1983, the Department of Justice filed two complaints alleging voting rights violations in San Juan County. In the first complaint, the Justice Department alleged that the at-large system for electing county commissioners diluted the voting strength of Navajos in violation of Section 2 of the Voting Rights Act (VRA). In the second complaint, the Justice Department claimed that the county violated Section 203 of the VRA by failing to provide bilingual materials to Navajo voters.

The first section of this chapter examines the historical context of Indian–white relations in the county. This provides an important background for understanding the current political, social, and economic factors, which are essential components of proving vote dilution. We begin this section with the Navajo War of 1863, a definitive event in Navajo–white relations, and continue through the early 1980s. The second section covers voting rights law and litigation in Utah. This section examines the challenge to Utah's voting law, which resulted in the enfranchisement of American Indians in 1957. The next section focuses on two voting rights cases filed by the Justice Department in 1983 (*U.S. v. San Juan County, Utah* 1983a*; *U.S. v. San Juan County, Utah* 1983b*). Both cases were settled within months of the original complaints. In the first settlement, San Juan County agreed to dismantle its at-large system and replace it with a single-member district system for electing commissioners. In the second case, San Juan County agreed to develop a voter outreach program and provide bilingual assistance to Navajo citizens. While it is useful to understand the outcome of voting rights litigation in terms of changes to electoral processes or structures, it is equally important to understand the effects of these changes. More than twenty years have passed since the two cases were settled. The final section assesses the impact of these cases on registration and turnout among Navajos in the county, on the success rate of Indian candidates, and on policy outcomes.

Historical Context

American Indians across the nation have a long history of conflict with federal, state, and local governments. Such is the case in San Juan County, as reflected in the history of Navajos in southeastern Utah since the mid-nineteenth century.

The federal government's relationship with the Navajo people deteriorated rapidly in the mid-nineteenth century when the U.S. government fought one of the "most violent and decisive military campaigns ever waged against a major North American tribe," known as the Navajo War (Bailey and Bailey 1986, 9). General James Carleton's interests in removing the Navajos went far beyond maintaining peace and order in the Southwest. His correspondence indicates an interest in opening the Navajo lands to mining (Young 1968, 39). On the eve of the war, Carleton wrote to Captain J. G. Walker of Walker Mines to inform him that the surveyor general was en route "to visit your new gold regions" (quoted in Young 1968, 39–40). In 1863 General Carleton declared "open season" on the Navajo people. More than 700 volunteers under the command of Colonel Kit Carson attacked the Navajo camps, burned their hogans, destroyed their crops, and seized their livestock (Young 1968). The first part of General Carleton's plan to end the "Navajo problem" was a success (Young 1968).

The second stage of the plan called for the relocation and imprisonment of the Navajo people. Nearly 8,500 Navajos endured the "Long Walk" to Fort Sumner, also known as Bosque Redondo, in New Mexico (Bailey and Bailey 1986, 10). The U.S. government intended to "civilize" the Navajo people by turning them into self-supporting farmers (Young 1968, 43; Bailey and Bailey 1986, 25–6). However, the expense of maintaining the Navajos became overwhelming for the federal government, and within a few years a plan emerged to create a new reservation (Bailey and Bailey 1986, 25). The Treaty of 1868, known in the Navajo language as "naalt-soos sani" or the Old Paper, established a 3.5-million-acre reservation in Arizona and New Mexico. The original reservation encompassed one-fifth of the land that the tribe had previously used (Young 1968, 42). Subsequent additions to the reservation were made in the late nineteenth and early twentieth centuries. In 1884, land south of the San Juan River in Utah was added to the reservation (McPherson 2001, 16). Additions in 1905, 1933, and 1958 further expanded the reservation into Utah's San Juan County (Thompson 1983, 67; McPherson 2001, 18, 20).

The U.S. government's assimilation policy, coupled with the increasing number of settlers in the Southwest, created new challenges for the Navajo people (Thompson 1983; Bailiey and Bailey 1986, 62). The federal government instituted its "civilization" programs to suppress "objectionable" aspects of Navajo culture (Bailey and Bailey 1986, 106). The programs concentrated on the education of Indian children, missionary activities to convert Indians to Christianity, and Indian housing and dress (Bailey and Bailey 1986, 62). A key component of the assimilation process was the education of Navajo children in missionary and government boarding schools. The first school for Navajo children was established at Fort Defiance in 1869 by the Presbyterian minister Reverend James Roberts and his wife. At the time, the Navajo population residing near Fort Defiance was large, but as Navajo herds increased, families moved away. By 1879, U.S. Indian Agent Eastman determined that attempts to educate the Navajos had failed because of low enrollment. Only three students could read McGuffy's first reader, and only ten could sign their names. He recommended building a boarding school at Fort Defiance, which was completed in 1882, to increase the number of students (Bailey and Bailey 1986, 63–5). Additional boarding schools for Navajo children were established in the late 1880s in Grand Junction, Colorado, Phoenix, Arizona, Sante Fe, New Mexico, and elsewhere. The Blue Canyon Day School was the only school built on the reservation (Bailey and Bailey 1986, 168). Initially, few Navajo children attended the schools. By 1890, only 89 Navajo children were enrolled in school out of a school-age population of 6,090 (Bailey and Bailey 1986, 168).

Early experiences in the boarding schools were at the very least unpleasant and in some instances dangerous (Young 1968). Parents voiced their concerns at an 1892 council meeting. Their criticism was aimed at the superintendent of the Fort Defiance boarding school (Young 1968, 51). One mother complained that her son had been handcuffed and confined. Another parent said, "When I brought my son to school he had two eyes. The next time I saw him he only had one" (quoted in Young 1968, 52). Other parents were concerned that the schooling policy would destroy Navajo culture (Bailey and Bailey 1986, 65). In an act of defiance, Ba'illilli, a prominent Navajo, and his followers shot at tree stumps, pretending that their targets were federal agents who took their children to the boarding school in Shiprock, New Mexico. The incident prompted William H. Shelton, the Indian superintendent, to arrest Ba'illilli and the others. The arrest came after a brief fight that left two Navajos dead. Ba'illilli and seven others were jailed without a trial (Benally et al. 1983, 170–3). They were released in 1909 after two years of confinement when the Arizona Supreme Court found the detention unlawful (*In re By-a-lil-le* 1909).

Assimilation policies were only one source of conflict between whites and Navajos in the late nineteenth century. Land use, accelerated by growing Indian and white populations, was a second source of tension. Between 1868 and 1892, the Navajo population doubled from 9,000 to 18,000. The non-Indian population also experienced substantial growth in the Southwest, increasing from 83,000 to 200,000 (Bailey and Bailey 1986, 73). The right to use public lands became a central issue as more settlers moved to the Southwest. The underlying assumption among cattlemen in San Juan County, Utah, was that "Indians did not have the same right to the public lands as the white man" (McPherson 1995, 164). There were calls from whites for the allotment of all Navajo reservation lands, with the "surplus land" to be sold to the settlers (Young 1968, 58).

Historian Robert W. Young wrote that the Navajo people are "the product of the centuries that preceded, during the course of which their destiny was shaped by a wide variety of influences, some of which affected them only indirectly" (Young 1968, 1). Certainly the events of the nineteenth century, including the Navajo War, the Long Walk, incarceration at Fort Sumner, assimilation policies, and conflicts over land, directly influenced the Navajo people. In the twentieth century, the U.S. government's livestock reduction program was a "sudden, radical change in their way of life ... a change that would reach deeply into Navajo culture" (Young 1968, 69). In 1928, a study by the Indian Service concluded that the number of livestock on the Navajo reservation had to be reduced in order to restore the range. Congressional hearings in 1931 also called for a reduction of livestock on the reservation. However, no action was taken until John Collier was appointed commissioner of Indian affairs in 1933 (Bailey and Bailey 1986, 184–6). Commissioner Collier defined four objectives for the Navajo livestock reduction program: the reduction of livestock on the reservation and a program of erosion control; the creation of public works programs to minimize the economic impact of the reduction; congressional legislation to expand reservation boundaries and consolidate off-reservation landholdings; and the consolidation of Navajo administration into a single agency and the restructuring of tribal government (Bailey and Bailey 1986, 185).

Livestock was the most important means of financial support for the Navajo people in the early twentieth century (Bailey and Bailey 1986, 124). The stock reduction program was an "economic war of attrition and destruction, symbolically comparable in tribal memory to the events seventy years before – the roundup of Navajos for the Long Walk to Fort Sumner" (McPherson 1995, 202). In 1933, the Navajos and Hopis were grazing a total of 999,725 sheep units. By 1944, the reservation had only 548,000 sheep units (Bailey and Bailey 1986, 201). Herds continued to decline in the 1940s. Between 1944 and 1947 the number of sheep and goats on the reservations declined by almost 30 percent (Bailey and Bailey 1986, 220). In 1975, the total number of sheep units for the reservation was 845,142, a figure below the prestock reduction number of 999,725 sheep units (Bailey and Bailey 1986, 302).

Although the program devastated the Navajo economy, the ramifications for the Navajo people went far beyond financial loss (McPherson 2001, 117). The Navajo people viewed sheep as central to their lives. Charlie Blueeyes equated livestock with life itself: "Livestock is what life is about, so people ask for this blessing through *dzitleezh*. From the sheep and cattle, life renews itself" (quoted in McPherson 2001, 105). The destruction of the traditional Navajo economy produced intense anger toward the federal government (McPherson 2001, 110) and psychological devastation (McPherson 2001, 118). Navajos continue to talk about the reduction program, equating it with the Long Walk to Fort Sumner (McPherson 2001, 119).

The economic opportunities for Navajos following the significant reduction of their herds in the 1930s were relatively minor, with a few exceptions. The growth of the mining industry, including oil and gas production on the Utah portion of the Navajo Reservation, spurred substantial economic growth in the 1960s and early 1970s. The oil fields in the Aneth area yielded $34.5 million in royalties for the Navajo tribe in 1956 (McPherson 1995, 209). Production peaked in 1960, only to fall dramatically in the 1970s. By 1972, Aneth oil production had dropped 74 percent (McPherson 2001, 183). The royalties from oil and gas production were split between the tribe and the state of Utah. Utah received 37.5 percent of the royalties to be used for education, road construction, and the general benefit of the Navajo people (McPherson 2001, 181). Several accusations regarding misuse of funds by the state of Utah were made in the 1970s and later. In 1991, an audit conducted by the state of Utah found that the trust fund monies had been mismanaged and misused by the Utah Division of Indian Affairs. Some of the funds were used to construct buildings and roads off the reservation (McPherson 2001, 221).

Voting Rights in Utah

Before the VRA litigation in the 1980s, there had been two major legal battles in Utah brought by or on behalf of American Indians to ensure their right to participate fully in the electoral process. The first case, in 1956, challenged Utah's electoral law that prohibited American Indians living on reservations from voting. The second challenge, in 1972, was brought when two Navajos were denied the right to run for the county commission in San Juan County.

Utah law since statehood had prohibited Indians who resided on a reservation from voting, using the justification that they were not residents for purposes of registration and voting (An Act Providing for Elections 1897, 172). In 1940, Joseph Chez, the attorney general of Utah, issued an opinion indicating that the statute barring Indians from voting was no longer applicable because "the attitude of the Government towards the Indians themselves with relation to voting privileges has changed materially since the Utah statute in question was created" (Opinion of the Attorney General of Utah, October 25, 1940). Indians residing on the Uintah and Ouray Reservation in Duchesne County were permitted to vote from 1940 until 1956, when a second, and contradictory, opinion was issued (Allen 1956). The second opinion, issued by Attorney General E. R. Callister, upheld the statute prohibiting Indians who resided on a reservation from voting. The opinion simply stated: "Indians who live on the reservations are not entitled to vote in Utah... Indians living off the reservation may, of course, register and vote in the voting district in which they reside, the same as any other citizen" (Opinion of the Attorney General of Utah, March 23, 1956).

In 1956, Preston Allen, an American Indian living on the Uintah and Ouray Reservation, challenged the law after his application for an absentee ballot was refused because he had not established residency off the reservation. Mr. Allen challenged the statute in the Utah Supreme Court as violating the Fourteenth and Fifteenth Amendments of the U.S. Constitution. However, the court ruled against Allen, distinguishing reservation Indians from other state citizens (Allen 1956; *Allen v. Merrell* 1956). The court relied on three arguments for upholding the statute. First, reservation Indians are members of tribes "which have a considerable degree of sovereignty independent of state government." Second, the federal government remains largely responsible for the welfare of reservation Indians and maintains a high degree of "control over them." And finally, reservation Indians are "much less concerned with paying taxes and otherwise being involved with state government and its local units, and are much less interested in it than are citizens generally" (*Allen v. Merrell* 1956, 492). The court described Indians who reside on reservations as "extremely limited in their contact with state government and its units, and for this reason also, have much less interest in it or concern with it than do other citizens" (494). The court attributed the lack of interest in government in part to the fact that reservation Indians were not subject to most of the taxes that support state and local governments. In the final portion of its ruling, the Utah Supreme Court opposed allowing nontaxpaying citizens to vote: "... allowing them to vote might place substantial control of the county government and the expenditures of its funds in a group of citizens who, as a class, had an extremely limited interest in its function and very little responsibility in providing the financial support thereof" (495). Allen appealed his case to the U.S. Supreme Court. However, before the Court could act, the Utah legislature removed the prohibitory language from the State Code and the case became moot (*Allen v. Merrell* 1956, 1957).

The change in Utah's electoral law did not solve all of the problems. In 1972, two Navajo Indians living in San Juan County filed to run for county commission seats. After filing their declaration forms, they were informed by the county clerk that they needed fifty signatures. However, the county clerk failed to inform the two Indians that the signatures had to be notarized. The unnotarized signatures were turned in five days late, and the clerk refused to place the two men on the November ballot. The men filed suit in federal court, arguing that the statute created an arbitrary and unreasonable barrier to political participation. The Federal District Court for Utah agreed and ruled that the San Juan County clerk had violated the Fourteenth Amendment by failing to place the two candidates on the ballot for the commission (*Yanito v. Barber* 1972). The court found that the plaintiffs were "unfairly treated," as they had made numerous attempts to file their candidacy correctly but were not fully informed of all the requirements by county officers. When the defendant was asked why she did not inform the plaintiffs of the requirement to file a petition with fifty notarized signatures, she responded that she did not consider it her duty to advise them of the legal requirements. The court ruling made special note of the relationship between Indians and government, stating that "there has been a history of intentional discrimination, first, on the part of the Federal Government and, in more recent times, on the part of the state." The county was required to place the Indians' names on the ballot as candidates for the county commission. Neither individual was elected.

The Voting Rights Act in San Juan County, Utah

In the 1970s and early 1980s, the Department of Justice was involved in numerous voting rights cases in the Southwest. While working in the area, Justice Department attorneys became aware of possible voting rights violations in San Juan County, Utah, and began an investigation (Schermerhorn, 2004). Following the investigation, the Justice Department filed two voting rights cases against San Juan County in the fall of 1983. In the first complaint, it alleged that the county provided inadequate assistance for Navajo-speaking voters in violation of Section 203 of the VRA. The second complaint addressed the system for electing county commissioners. The Justice Department argued that the at-large system of electing county commissioners diluted the votes of American Indians in violation of Section 2 of the VRA.

The Bilingual Voting Rights Case in San Juan County

In 1975, Congress amended the VRA after determining that language minorities faced unique difficulties in registering and voting. Difficulties included inadequate numbers of minority registrars, uncooperative registrars, failure to locate voters' names on precinct lists, and purging of registration lists. Voters faced intimidation at polling places, inconvenient polling places, and hostility. There was also an underrepresentation of minorities as poll workers. Unavailable or inadequate assistance to illiterate voters and a lack of bilingual voting materials also hindered the ability of language minorities to participate (*Congressional Quarterly Almanac* 1975, 528–9).

The 1975 amendment included several provisions that gave the VRA real enforcement power in Indian Country. The first is the preclearance requirement, discussed in Chapter 2. The second provision of the 1975 amendment that affected San Juan County is the bilingual requirement. Bilingual ballots and election materials, as well as assistance for language minorities, were required if the minority population was above 5 percent of the total population and had a literacy rate below the national average. (Congress defined illiteracy as the failure to complete fifth grade.) In addition to San Juan County, three additional counties in Utah were covered under this section of the VRA. Uintah County, home to a large population of American Indians with illiteracy rates above the national average, was covered under this section of the act; and Carbon County and Tooele County, were covered based on their Spanish-speaking populations. In 1982, Congress again addressed the bilingual provisions by requiring political subdivisions to provide oral instructions to voters whose "predominant language is historically unwritten" (42 U.S.C. 1973 b[f][4] [1982]). These actions created the potential for American Indians to have an equal opportunity to vote and a meaningful voice in government.

The vast majority of the Indian population in San Juan County was Navajo in 1980; other Indian tribes in the area include Utes and Piutes. At the time, a large proportion of the Navajo population was unable to speak, write, or read the English language and instead spoke the Navajo language (*U.S. v. San Juan County, Utah* 1983b*, Agreed Settlement and Order, Jan. 11, 1984, 2).

The Department of Justice filed a lawsuit in the fall of 1983, claiming that San Juan County violated Section 203 of the VRA by failing to provide an effective number of bilingual interpreters, failing to ensure effective translation of the ballot into Navajo, and failing to post notices of the polling places in Navajo. The county also allegedly failed to provide effective oral instructions, assistance, and information in the Navajo language concerning the voter registration process, candidate nominations and filing procedures, the absentee voting process, registration forms, registration and voting notices, and voter purging processes (*U.S. v. San Juan County, Utah, 1983b**, Complaint, November 22, 1983).

The parties agreed to a settlement of the lawsuit on January 11, 1984, that required San Juan County to provide bilingual assistance and materials for American Indian voters (*U.S. v. San Juan County, Utah* 1983b*, Agreed Settlement and Order, Jan. 11, 1984). The settlement required the county to establish a bilingual voter registration program. The program included the establishment of one or more registration sites on or near the reservation for the 1984 and 1986 elections and at least one bilingual worker at each site. Announcements of registration deadlines and election dates were to be made in English and Navajo on Navajo radio stations, in the local newspaper, and at tribal chapter meetings. The county agreed to provide training on the bilingual voting requirements for poll workers and county employees involved in elections. The county hired an election coordinator to assist with the bilingual voter registration program. The coordinator, a Navajo, was hired on contract from 1984 to 1990. His duties included informing Navajos of registration deadlines and elections.

In 1990, the county and the Department of Justice entered into an amended settlement and order that provided for "additional measures to ensure that the election process in San Juan County is fully and effectively accessible to Indian citizens" (*U.S. v. San Juan County, Utah* 1983b*, First Amended Settlement and Order, October 11, 1990, 1). The amended order required San Juan County to employ one full-time bilingual voting coordinator for twelve months of each general election year to coordinate the Navajo Language Election Information Program. The full-time coordinator was hired in 1990 and is retained as an employee of the County Clerk's Office. The election coordinator's duties include attending Navajo Nation chapter meetings, conducting voter education programs, registering voters, and providing information on registration deadlines and elections. The coordinator also conducts or assists with voter registration drives (Tapaha 2004).

In 1995, the parties jointly moved to terminate the provisions of the First Amended Settlement and Order. The county acknowledged that "its obligation to comply with Section 203 of the Voting Rights Act continues" (*U.S. v. San Juan County, Utah* 1983b*, Joint Motion for Termination of Consent Decree and Entry of Order, July 19, 1995, 2). The parties also agreed to extend the use of federal examiners to oversee elections until December 31, 1998. On December 30, 1998, the U.S. District Court ordered the extension of the federal observers until December 31, 2002 (*U.S. v. San Juan County, Utah* 1983b*, Order, December 21, 1998).

Vote Dilution in San Juan County

In the second complaint filed against San Juan County in 1983, the Justice Department claimed that the at-large system for electing county commissioners violated Section 2 of the VRA. The at-large system, the Department claimed, caused "irreparable injury" because it diluted the votes of American Indians and denied them an equal opportunity to participate in county elections and elect candidates of their choice to the commission (*U.S. v. San Juan County, Utah* 1983a*, Complaint, November 22, 1983, 5). Although Indians comprised 46 percent of the county population, no Indian had ever been elected to the three-person commission.

Although the case was settled without trial, the Justice Department would likely have prevailed at trial because the conditions were present to satisfy the *Gingles* test and the Senate factors.[1] As described in Chapter 2, the courts rely on two sets of criteria, the *Gingles* test and the Senate factors, to determine whether vote dilution has occurred. The first *Gingles* test requires the minority population to be sufficiently numerous and geographically compact to constitute a majority in a single-member district. The Navajos were heavily concentrated on the Navajo Reservation, and they were sufficiently numerous and compact to constitute a single-member district. In 1980, San Juan County's population was 12,253. Indians comprised 5,600, approximately 46 percent of the county population. The 1980 census estimated that 4,539 Indians in the county lived on the Navajo Reservation, meeting the criterion of the first *Gingles* test. The second *Gingles* test requires that the minority population to be politically cohesive. The third *Gingles* test requires proof that the majority population votes as a bloc to defeat the minority's preferred candidate.

[1] The case was filed well before the *Gingles* factors were established by the U.S. Supreme Court. However, these factors had long been evidence required by trial courts.

Once these three conditions are met, the court then determines whether the minority population was denied an equal opportunity to elect representatives of their choice based on the totality of circumstances. The legislative history of the 1982 amendment to the VRA recognized nine criteria that are often relied on by the federal courts to make this determination. These nine criteria, generally referred to as the "Senate factors," will now be described.

The first factor is the extent of any history of official discrimination in the state or subdivision that impedes the right of the minority group to register, vote, or otherwise participate in the democratic process. Both state law and the practices in San Juan County prevented American Indians from participating fully and equally in the electoral process. Prior to 1957, as we have seen, Indians who resided on a reservation were prohibited from voting by statute. The statute was removed from law in 1957 while the case was on appeal to the U.S. Supreme Court. More recently, a second incident of voting discrimination against American Indians occurred in 1972, when the San Juan County clerk denied the right of two Navajos to run for the San Juan County Commission. San Juan County was found to be in violation of the Fourteenth Amendment (*Yanito v. Barber* 1972). The lack of bilingual materials for Navajo voters also qualified as discrimination that prevented Navajos from participating equally in the democratic process in San Jan County.

The second Senate factor is whether voting in state elections or elections in its political subdivisions is racially polarized. The complaint filed by the Department of Justice stated that "white voters generally do not vote for Indian candidates or for issues identified with the Indian community. As a consequence, Indian candidates receive support from the Indian community, but not from the non-Indian communities" (*U.S. v. San Juan County*, Complaint, 1983a, 4). Sources have confirmed that racial bloc voting influenced other elections. White candidates viewed as pro-Indian by the white community had difficulty winning elections. In the early 1980s, a white man running for county attorney who was viewed as pro-Indian lost the election. The candidate believes that many whites did not vote for him because he was pro-Indian and married to an Indian woman (Swenson 2004b). Polarization, according to some, remains in San Juan County. Former Commissioner Lynn Stevens noted that in a recent election for sheriff, whites voted for the white candidate and Navajos voted for the Navajo candidate (Stevens 2004). Commissioner Manuel Morgan agreed that racial polarization remains, although the situation is slowly improving (Morgan 2004).

The extent to which the state or its political subdivisions have unusually large election districts, majority vote requirements, anti–single shot provisions, or other voting practices or procedures that enhance the opportunity for discrimination against the minority group is the third Senate factor. San Juan County's at-large election procedure for selecting county commissioners met this criterion.

The fourth Senate factor is whether a candidate slating process exists and whether the members of the minority community have been denied access to that process. From our study, it appears that candidate slating did not exist in San Juan County.

The fifth factor is the extent to which the members of the minority group in the state or its subdivisions bear the effect of discrimination in such areas as education, employment, and health, which hinder their ability to participate effectively in the political process. American Indians in San Juan County indeed suffered the effects of such discrimination. The economic situation for the Navajo people living in the county in the 1980s was dire. The 1980 census revealed that 58.4 percent of the Navajo population fell below the poverty level, compared to 12.5 percent of the white population living in the county (U.S. Census 1980b, Table 10, 81; US Census 1980a, Table P-5). The median income of whites ($16,858) was more than double that of Indians ($8,406) (U.S. Census 1980a, Table P-5). Navajos living on the reservation were even further below the poverty level. The median income for Navajo families living on the Utah portion of the reservation was $7,307 in 1979 (U.S. Census 1980b, Table 10, 81). According to the 1980 census, 24 percent of Navajos living on the reservation were unemployed (U.S. Census 1980b, Table 9, 72).

Evidence also suggested a disparity between whites and Navajos in San Juan County in health care. No health care facility existed on the Utah portion of the Navajo Reservation until the 1960s (McPherson 1995, 278). In 1970, 33 percent of deaths among Navajos living in San Juan County were preventable compared with only 18 percent for the entire state of Utah (Bork 1973, 10–11). This was probably due to geographic isolation, polluted and inadequate water supplies, lack of sanitation facilities, and poor nutrition (Bork 1973). The housing situation was also grim. Sixty-five percent of homes on the Navajo Reservation lacked complete plumbing, more than 60 percent were without a refrigerator, and 82 percent had no central heating system. More than half of the homes on the reservation had no electric lighting, nearly all homes (93.5 percent) lacked a telephone, and 64 percent of homes had an outhouse or privy (U.S. Census 1980b, Table 11, 90).

Inequity within the public school system in San Juan County in the 1970s and 1980s was also evident. Educational opportunities for American Indian children in the San Juan School District began in the mid-1930s following passage of the Johnson O'Malley Act in 1934, which provided federal funds for the education of Indian children. However, attempts to integrate the countywide public school system met fierce opposition. Community members argued that integration would cause "discipline, scholarship, and pupil morale to deteriorate" (Black 1983, 350). By 1958, only 120 students in the district were Indian, 4.4 percent of the student population (*Sinajini v. Board of Education of the San Juan School District* 1975).

Over the next decade, the picture did not improve for Navajo children. They dropped out of school at significantly higher rates than whites. In 1970, approximately 28 percent of Navajo males and 31 percent of Navajo females terminated their education in elementary school (Bork 1973, 28). In 1970, the median number of years of school completed for Navajo males (twenty-five years of age or older) was 5.5 compared to 12.6 for the Utah male population. Educational attainment was only slightly higher for Navajo females, who completed an average of only 6.9 years of formal schooling, significantly below the state average of 12.4 years (Bork 1973, 13–15).

Numerous obstacles made attaining an education difficult for Indian children in San Juan County. Language barriers were a major challenge for Indian students entering the San Juan School District. A majority of them were from homes in which the predominant spoken language was Navajo. A significant number of students spoke little or no English when they entered public school in San Juan District (*Sinajini v. Board of Education of the San Juan School District* 1975). Their limited language proficiency was coupled with an additional obstacle: the long distance between Indian homes and the public schools. Students living on the reservation were bussed to school, some traveling up to 166 miles each day, which resulted in a 1974 lawsuit (*Sinajini v. Board of Education of the San Juan School District* 1975). At the time, the only two high schools in the district were located in the northern portion of the county, off the reservation. The parents of Indian children sued the San Juan School District, claiming that the distance reduced the quality of education for Indian children. The parties agreed to a settlement in 1975 that included the construction of two high schools on the Navajo Reservation, both of which would be completed by 1978 (Deyhle 1995, 417). The high school in Montezuma Creek did open in 1978, but construction of the school in Monument

Valley took eight years (McPherson 1995, 288). In addition to constructing two high schools on the reservation, the school district agreed to create and implement a bilingual and bicultural education program (*Sinajini v. Board of Education of the San Juan School District* 1975).

Testimony provided at a hearing before the U.S. Commission on Civil Rights in 1973 noted areas of educational inequality in addition to the bussing problem and language barriers addressed in the *Sinajini* case. Children in the southern portion of the county, generally Navajo children, had limited extracurricular activities compared to children in the northern part of the county. Children in the southern area had no band program and few athletics. The curriculum was also unequal. Students in southern schools had few art classes and limited physical education, and science labs were "almost totally lacking" in comparison to the situation in schools in the northern portion of the county (Hennessey 1973, 245–52).

A description of the political and cultural climate at the time of the two voting rights cases may also support the extent of discrimination faced by American Indians in San Juan County. Accounts of such discrimination are well documented; this section notes only a few examples. In the 1970s, a restaurant window featured the sign "No Dogs or Indians Allowed." The Blanding Cemetery was segregated as late as the 1970s. The well-manicured areas of the cemetery were reserved for whites, and Indians were buried in the weeds and sagebrush. Indians had difficulty renting properties off the reservation. Rude or nasty comments aimed at American Indians were also common. Indian parents recall their daughters being called "squaws" by white classmates in the 1970s and 1980s (Swenson 2004b).

The sixth Senate factor is whether political campaigns have been characterized by overt or subtle racial appeals. A white candidate who ran for office in the county believes that there has always been a racist undercurrent in campaigns (Swenson 2004b). Others disagree (Redd 2004).

The seventh Senate factor is the extent to which members of a minority group have been elected to public office in the jurisdiction. Navajos ran as candidates for the San Juan County Commission in 1972, 1976, and 1980. No Navajo won (Dalton 1983). The eighth Senate factor is whether elected officials ignore the particular needs of the minority community. One example is the disparity in spending between the reservation and nonreservation areas of the county. A study by the accounting firm Arthur Young found that the county received $28.5 million in revenue from the reservation between 1978 and 1987, mostly from oil and gas companies, but spent only $7.2 million on services for reservation residents (Miniclier 1990).

The final Senate factor is whether the policy underlying the state's or subdivision's use of such voting qualifications, prerequisites to voting, standards, practices, or procedure is tenuous. Certain requirements, such as at-large elections, may be tenuous if the policy is uncommon in the state or does not adhere to state policy. However, at-large elections were used in San Juan County, as well as in all other counties in the state of Utah in 1984, to elect commissioners; thus, San Juan County's at-large elections did not meet the tenuous standard.

The county and the Justice Department settled the Section 2 case in 1984 and dismantled the at-large system for electing county commissioners, replacing it with three single-member districts (*U.S. v. San Juan County, Utah* 1983a*, Agreed Settlement and Order, April 4, 1984). District 1 includes the northern portion of the county and a small section of the Navajo Reservation, District 2 is almost entirely outside of the Navajo Reservation but includes the small Ute Reservation of White Mesa. District 3 lies in the southeastern portion of the county and is almost entirely within the Navajo Reservation. The new plan for electing county commissioners was approved by San Juan County voters in November 1984. Sixty-four percent of the voters approved the plan; 36 percent opposed it. The four-year terms of the commissioners are staggered, and the first election for the single-member seats occurred in November 1986. Replacement of the at-large electoral system enabled American Indians living in District 3 to elect Mark Maryboy as the first Navajo commissioner in San Juan County in 1986. Upon Maryboy's retirement in 2002, Manuel Morgan, also a Navajo, was elected.

The Impact of the Voting Rights Cases in San Juan County

What impact has the VRA and litigation had on Navajos in San Juan County? This research question can be divided into four successive stages or generations (Davidson and Grofman 1994, 14–16). The first generation addresses minority enfranchisement. The second deals with vote dilution and the success of minority candidates. The third examines the "extent to which minority elected officials become an integral part of the political process" (Davidson and Grofman 1994, 14). The fourth explores the substantive policy outputs that minority officeholders get and the impact of these policies on the minority community. Incorporating Grofman and Davison's model, we examine Navajo voter registration and voting rates, the success of Navajo candidates, and the effect of Navajo elected officials on policies affecting the Navajo community in San Juan County.

Following the settlements in 1984, voting rates among Native Americans in San Juan County increased substantially. An analysis of registered voters and turnout in five precincts within the Navajo Reservation indicates a significant increase in both the number of registered voters and voter turnout since 1984. The number of registered voters in these five predominantly Indian precincts rose from 1,719 in 1984 to 3,358 in 2004, an increase of more than 95 percent. In addition, turnout in these precincts increased from 1,000 in 1984 to 1,480 by 2004, an increase of 48 percent. The highest turnout recorded was 1,531 in 1990, when an entire slate of Indian candidates ran for every county office.[2]

The increase in registration and turnout among Native Americans in San Juan County can be attributed to many factors. Many believe it is largely due to the activity of the election coordinator (N. Johnson 2004a; Stevens 2004; Tapaha 2004). In addition, Native Americans in San Juan County may be more familiar with the electoral process than they had been in the past (Swenson 2004a; Tapaha 2004; Maryboy 2005). A third factor that may contribute to increased rates of participation is that Indians feel more welcome to participate (Stevens 2004; Swenson 2004b; Tapaha 2004). Commissioner Lynn Stevens noted that the county has made significant efforts to encourage Indians to register and create a more welcoming atmosphere. A fourth factor that may have increased participation is holding tribal elections and county elections on the same day (Swenson 2004a; Ellingson 2005). A fifth factor is the belief among Native Americans that their vote counts and that someone will listen to their concerns (Morgan 2004; Tapaha 2004).

The final factor is an intense campaign to mobilize voters and candidates (Ellingson 2005). In 1990, an intensive nonpartisan registration drive took place to register voters on the reservation. Student volunteers from the University of Utah, private attorneys, and others registered 2,300

[2] The five precincts selected for analysis, are located in the Utah portion of the Navajo Reservation. Precincts 2, 3, 13, 14, and 16, all except Precinct 2, are located wholly on the reservation. Only a small portion of Precinct 2 is off the Reservation. Precincts 1, 12, and 17 are only partially on the Navajo Reservation and were excluded from the analysis. The total Indian population in San Juan County grew from 5,622 in 1980 to 8,157 in 2000. This figure includes Indians other than Navajos and areas outside of the five precincts selected for analysis; we are unable to determine exact Navajo populations for those five precincts.

Navajo people (Sisco 1990a, B1). The registration drive coincided with an all-Indian slate of candidates running for six county offices.

These efforts generated a white backlash. Many locals were unhappy with the "outsiders" coming to San Juan County (Flagg 1990, B1). The campaign slogan for the slate of Indian candidates was "Niha Whol Zhiizh," which means "It's our turn." It was perceived as radical by some whites living in San Juan County. Many "whites feared that the Indian peoples were about to take over and all hell would then let loose. But, the slogan merely meant that justice was due" (Sleight 1998, 18). The all-Indian campaign also illuminated concerns within the white community about nontaxpayers being elected and setting the tax rates. Blanding resident Howard Ranall stated, "It looks crooked to me to have someone getting a job that's paid by the taxpayers and not having to pay taxes yourself" (quoted in Tobar 1990). Melvin Dalton, father of the San Juan county clerk, expressed a similar opinion: "They should make citizens out of the Indians. Now they are super-citizens." He also stated: "I wouldn't feel so bad about them running if they made them citizens. But they don't even pay property taxes" and "We've gotten along fine until this" (Sisco 1990b, B1).

Navajo voters have faced official obstacles as well. Approximately a week prior to the 1990 election, the San Juan county clerk refused to place about 500 Navajos on the registration lists. She claimed that the names were duplicates; however, after meeting with representatives from the state attorney general's office and the lieutenant governor's office, she added the names to the registration rolls. Purging of the lists occurred again in 1995. A list of the purged names was maintained by the county clerk's office, and those names were returned to the official voter rolls before the 1998 election by the county clerk. No purging has occurred since (N. Johnson 2004b, 2005).

The second-generation research question concerns the success of Indian candidates. Although Indians ran for six county offices in 1990, only Mark Maryboy won. He was elected under the court-imposed district system, while all other county offices were won in at-large elections. Currently, one of three commissioners is Navajo. However, Indian candidates have continued to be unsuccessful in running for countywide offices. They had the greatest opportunity for success in 1990, when the record number of Indian candidates, combined with the registration drive, boosted turnout among Navajos to its highest level ever. However, only Maryboy was successful, clearly demonstrating the advantages of district elections to Indian candidates.

Third- and fourth-generation research examines the impact of minority elected officials on policy outcomes. Previous research found that "increased minority office holding associated with single member districts has also been associated with a substantial shift in responsiveness to minority interests and the inclusion of minorities in decisionmaking" (McDonald 1989, 1277). Our study of San Juan County supports this finding. Mark Maryboy, the first Navajo commissioner in San Juan County, believes that he was able to bring attention to issues of importance to the Navajo community. Although he was often outvoted 2 to 1 by the other commissioners, he was still able to raise awareness and get issues on the table for discussion (Maryboy 2005). He also believes that he was able to increase the number of services provided by the county to reservation residents during his tenure. For example, the funding provided to the reservation, based on oil and gas revenues, increased during Maryboy's tenure (Maryboy 2005). Others argue that services on the reservation, particularly the maintenance of roads, were better addressed following Maryboy's election (Morgan 2004; Ellingson 2005; Maryboy 2005). Commissioner Ty Lewis stated that in the last ten to fifteen years, the county has done more on the reservation, such as build new roads and pave roads, than it had done previously (Lewis 2004). Maryboy attributed the shift in county responsiveness to conducting his own research on issues, bringing issues to the table, and being vocal in commission meetings (Maryboy 2005). The current commissioner from District 3, Manuel Morgan, also believes he has a voice on the county commission. However, he also notes that the votes of two commissioners are required to get the county to work on issues that address the needs of Navajos residents. Some issues that still need to be addressed, according to Commissioner Morgan, include economic development, health care, and education for Navajos in the county (Morgan 2004). Overall, having an Indian on the commission provides better representation for the Navajos in San Juan County, and county policies reflect this (Morgan 2004; Stevens 2004; Swenson 2004a; Tapaha 2004; Maryboy 2005).

The election of Maryboy and Morgan to the commission has also created a new way for Navajos to be involved in the political process. Navajos living both inside 3 and outside District 3, contact the Navajo commissioner with their concerns (Morgan 2004; Stevens 2004; Maryboy 2005). Commissioner Lynn Stevens believes that Navajos are more comfortable talking with the Navajo commissioner than with a white commissioner (Stevens 2004). Furthermore, Indians now vote at a higher rate and thus exercise more political influence. Every candidate must remember that Navajos will vote (Stevens 2004).

Despite Navajo successes at the polls, the evidence indicates that there continues to be a disparity between whites and American Indians in the county. The 2000 census estimated that the median family income in 1999 for American Indian families in San Juan County was $18,438 compared to $42,152 for white families. The census also estimated that 3,809 Indians in San Juan County lived below the poverty level in 1999 compared to only 530 whites (U.S. Census 2000, Summary File 3).

Allegations of discrimination against American Indians in the county continue. Recent allegations include discrimination in the selection of juries and discrimination in the schools. In 1993, a Navajo filed a case alleging jury discrimination (*Crank v. Utah Judicial Council* 2001). The plaintiff argued that jury pools, created using tax rolls and voter registration, result in the underrepresentation of Indians on juries. The suit contended that no American Indian had shown up on a jury pool list from 1932 to 1970 (Thompson 1998, B1). A 1996 consent decree requires that jury pools accurately reflect the demographics of the county. They must be within 5 percent of the county's adult Native American population. Since the decree, "there are significant numbers of Navajos on juries" in San Juan County (Swenson 2004b).

In the early 1990s a new education case emerged – *Meyers v. Board of Education of the San Juan School District* (1995). It concerned the right of Navajos living on the reservation to a free public education and who is responsible for providing it. The court determined in 1995 that the Bureau of Indian Affairs, the state of Utah, and the San Juan School District are obligated to provide a free education to Indians living on the reservation. The plaintiffs originally brought the case to compel the district to provide a high school and improve the quality of elementary education at Navajo Mountain.

The *Meyers* case was not the only discrimination case filed against the school district in the 1990s. Evidence that the school district had failed to meet the bilingual and bicultural requirements of the 1975 court order sent the *Sinajini* case back to court. During the seventeen years since this case was settled, the success rate for Indian students remained below that of white students in the San Juan County School District. Indian students in the district had lower reading levels, were consistently behind in mathematics, and had a higher dropout rate than white students. At the high school level, Indian students were five grade levels behind their white peers in reading (Deyhle 1993, 12), and they had made "no real gains in reading scores since 1977" (9). Lower reading levels are the result of few courses in reading and English as a second language and a lack of bilingual teachers. The district also failed to implement a uniform bilingual/bicultural education program (Deyhle 1993). The parties agreed in 1997 that the district would implement such a program monitored by a six-person committee (*Sinajini v. Board of Education of the San Juan School District* 1997).

The evidence in this case supports the finding that the successful voting rights cases increased the participation of Navajo citizens, increased the success of Navajo candidates, and increased the responsiveness of county government to Navajo interests. Success, however, was limited. Significant disparities remain between Navajos and whites in San Juan County.

Conclusion

In the twenty years since the two voting rights cases in San Juan County were settled, the cases have had positive effects on the Indian community. First, since 1984, both voter registration and voter turnout rates among Navajos have increased significantly. There are many reasons, including a higher level of efficacy among Navajos, more interest, more knowledge about the election process, and the feeling that one's vote counts. Some of these factors, including increased knowledge of the election process, can be attributed to the county's efforts to inform voters through the election coordinator. Second, two Navajos' election to the county commission indicate the positive effect of the single-member district system. Their election is associated with a shift in government responsiveness to the needs of the Navajo citizens and the inclusion of Navajos in the political process. These elections provided a new way for Indians in San Juan County to access government services. Navajo elected officials provide an essential link between Navajos and county government. Navajos, both inside and outside District 3, contact the Navajo commissioner with concerns. Navajo elected officials also force the county to address issues important to the Indian community. Although the Navajo commissioner is only one of three, and thus can be overruled, he is able to bring issues to the table. This role is important and should not be underestimated. A final sign of success is the increased number of Navajo candidates for political office. These are indicators of the impact of the VRA in Indian Country.

5

Going to Court for a Seat at the Table

Fort Belknap versus Blaine County

The Fort Belknap Indian Reservation in central Montana is home to two tribes: the Assiniboine and the Gros Ventre. The 675,000-acre reservation consists primarily of rolling prairie, with bottomlands along the Milk River, which forms the northern border of the reservation. The Little Rocky Mountains cover the southern quarter of the reservation. It is a sparse, hardscrabble landscape where rainfall is unpredictable, and the wind blows furnace-hot in the summer and has an arctic bent in the winter. It is a difficult place to support a modern economy but perfect country for buffalo, which is what drew the Assiniboine and Gros Ventre to this region.

Nearly all of the Fort Belknap Reservation is in Blaine County, which was organized in 1912. Approximately a third of the county's residents are Indians. Unlike the Blackfeet farther west or the Sioux to the east, these two tribes never engaged in warfare with the incoming settlers. Early on they decided to try to get along with the newcomers rather than fight them, perhaps in the hope of receiving better treatment.

Since 1927, Blaine County had used an at-large voting system to elect three commissioners; each commissioner represented a residential district but was elected at-large by all voters in the county. The commissioners served six-year terms, which were staggered so that only one commissioner was chosen every two years. Until the *U.S. v. Blaine County* case was litigated, no Indian had ever been elected to the county commission.

In 1999, on behalf of the Indians living in Blaine County, the Justice Department filed a Voting Rights Act (VRA) suit in federal district court against the county, arguing that the county's Indian citizens had "less opportunity than white citizens to participate in the political process and to elect representatives of their choice in violation of Section 2 of the Voting Rights Act." The suit requested the court to declare the at-large staggered election system a violation of the law. The complaint closely followed the *Gingles* factors in describing the political situation in Blaine County, arguing that the Indian population was sufficiently numerous and geographically compact to constitute a majority in one single-member district. The complaint also alleged that elections were racially polarized into Indian and white voting blocs, and that poverty and a history of discrimination had a detrimental effect on Indians' ability to participate in the electoral process (*U.S. v. Blaine County*, Complaint, November 16, 1999, 3–5).

The Mountain States Legal Foundation (MSLF) agreed to serve as pro bono legal counsel for the county. In their response to the complaint, they argued that the *Gingles* factors were not present:

> The various American Indian peoples residing in Blaine County, Montana are not homogeneous, politically, in elections, or otherwise, but are rather heterogeneous and no generalizations may be made about the "Indian vote." Rather, on information and belief, the American Indian peoples in Blaine County, Montana, do not engage in polarized voting along racial lines, but, rather, should any such polarized voting exist, it is along tribal, political and economic lines. One may not opine concerning "Indian candidates of choice," but, rather, must address "tribal candidates of choice." (*U.S. v. Blaine County*, Defendants' Answer to Complaint, January 3, 2000, 4)

But perhaps of even greater importance, the county argued that the VRA, "as Plaintiff seeks to apply it in this case, is unconstitutional" (3). Thus, the MSLF was clearly setting up the Blaine County case as a test of the constitutionality of Section 2 of the VRA, and its application to American Indians.

This chapter takes a close look at the Blaine County case, with special emphasis on the contextual factors present at the time of the case and the arguments presented by each side. The first section provides the historical background. The second section briefly summarizes information regarding socioeconomic disparities, racial discrimination, and bloc voting – all important factors in a Section 2 case. The third section summarizes the positions taken by the parties at trial, the evidence offered by expert witnesses, arguments concerning summary judgment, and the proposed finding of facts. The final section explains the outcome of the case and its significance.

The Historical Context

The history of the Gros Ventre and Assiniboine people follows a fairly typical pattern of conquest, gradual loss of land, cultural and political conflict, economic hardship, and ultimately a struggle over political power (Weber 1989, 111). However, the protagonists in this case disagreed vehemently on whether this history constituted "invidious discrimination" and who was to blame for the unfortunate circumstances of the Indians.

Although the two tribes at Fort Belknap are culturally distinct, they had intermixed considerably by the time of white settlement in the area. In 1855 the two tribes, along with the Blackfeet Tribe, signed one of the many treaties negotiated by Isaac Stevens. The Stevens Treaty granted to these three tribes a reservation that included virtually all the land between the Missouri River and the Canadian border. But, like many "permanent" homelands, this reservation was greatly reduced in size when settlers starting moving into the area. In 1888 the U.S. Congress passed a law that broke up the northern Montana reservation into three much smaller reservations – a loss of 17.5 million acres for the Indians; eighty years later, the Indian Claims Commission called that act "unconscionable on its face" (*Blackfeet and Gros Ventre Tribes v. U.S.* 1967, 286). Fort Belknap was one of the three reservations (Fort Peck and Blackfeet were the other two). In 1896 the Fort Belknap Reservation was further reduced when the tribes, under tremendous pressure, sold 40,000 acres in the Little Rocky Mountains to the U.S. government. Gold had been discovered in that area, and the government wanted to open it to mining. The tribes received $9 per acre for the land.

Fort Belknap suffered no further land losses after 1896, but local whites made repeated efforts to obtain more Indian land and water. The landmark Indian water rights case, *Winters v. U.S.* (1908), was fought over water for the Fort Belknap irrigation project. In that prolonged legal struggle, the Indians won the court decision but had great difficulty forcing upstream non-Indians to abide by it. Seven years after the case was decided by the Supreme Court, the superintendent of the Bureau of Indian Affairs at Fort Belknap wired Washington "[a]bout entire flow [of] Milk River being diverted by white appropriators above our diversion point." Twenty years after the decision, the Indians were still experiencing problems, and the Bureau again asked the Justice Department to stop the "interference by white people with Indian water rights" (McCool 1987, 64). During the same era, efforts were made to transfer reservation lands to local non-Indians. A petition drawn up by tribal leaders in 1911 declared,

"There are a lot of white men around this reservation who want to take away our land" (Hoxie 2000, 26).

Given the long history of conflict over land and water rights, it is not surprising that Montana was not receptive to the idea of Indians voting. The first territorial legislature limited suffrage to "white male citizens" (First Montana Assembly 1866), but the Fifteenth Amendment soon rendered that law unconstitutional. In 1868 the Territorial Assembly limited jury service to white male citizens who paid taxes (General Laws 1868, 70). This was soon followed by laws that forbade anyone under guardianship from voting (General Laws 1871, 460, 471). In 1876 the Territorial Assembly made it illegal to establish an election precinct on an Indian reservation (Laws, Memorials 1876, 87).

Montana became a state in 1889 and continued limiting the right of Indians to vote, usually on the basis of taxpaying status. The state's Enabling Act withheld suffrage from Indians not taxed (Montana Enabling Act 1889). In 1897 the state's attorney general rendered an opinion that no resident of an Indian reservation could vote unless he owned property off the reservation (Biennial Report of the Attorney General 1897, 38). In 1901 voting in school district elections was restricted to taxpayers (Laws, Regulations 1901, 29). Six years later, the same limitation was placed on elections for road and water districts (Laws, Regulations 1907, 140). In 1932 the state legislature reiterated this policy and required that only taxpayers vote in any referendum concerning debts, taxes, and liabilities (Laws, Regulations 1932, 551).

Montana law made it nearly impossible for an Indian to maintain his or her tribal identity, live on the reservation, and still vote. The state attorney general in 1912 ruled that anyone receiving tribal funding or participating in tribal affairs is ineligible to vote (Biennial Report of the Attorney General 1912, 240). In 1919 the Montana legislature prohibited the creation of an election district within any Indian reservation (Laws, Regulations 1919, 115), effectively making it impossible for Indians to vote without moving off the reservation and severing tribal relations. When Indians were granted citizenship in 1924, the leading newspaper in Blaine County objected, editorializing that "The addition of a large body of ignorant, uninformed voters, who have no conception of what the process of voting means, who are unable to a large extent to even read the ballots, is certainly a mistake" (quoted in Hoxie 2000, 33).

By the 1960s, most of the laws restricting Indian suffrage in Montana had been removed but significant hurdles remained. In *Old Person* v. *Cooney* the Ninth Circuit Court found that there was a "history of discrimination by the federal government and the State of Montana from the 1860s until as recently as 1971" (2000, 1129). In addition, there was still great economic disparity between whites and Indians, and tensions between the two groups had an impact on electoral outcomes.

The Contemporary Context

There is no distinct dividing line between the past and the present, especially for American Indians, whose culture places so much emphasis on tradition and family heritage. In addition, much of what constitutes the contemporary context at Fort Belknap was part of the controversy in *U.S. v. Blaine County*. However, to adequately understand the case, it is necessary to describe some basic indices of the contemporary political, economic, and cultural environment in Blaine County.

One important factor in Section 2 cases is the relative economic well-being of the parties. It is widely recognized that poverty, joblessness, and poor education suppress voting and other forms of political behavior (Brady, Verba, and Schlozman 1995; Wolfinger and Rosenstone 1980). Poverty on the Fort Belknap Reservation is not a recent phenomenon. After being forced to settle on a reservation that was a small remnant of their traditional use lands, the Assiniboine and Gros Ventre people became dependent on the federal government for sustenance. These provisions, guaranteed by treaty, were never sufficient. After the wild buffalo herds were exterminated by white hunters, the Indians became destitute. The Indian agent at Fort Belknap in 1884 described the tribal members as a "horde of half-fed women and children" and implored the government to "alleviate their suffering" (quoted in Hoxie 2000, 9). When federal agents came to the reservation in 1910 to arrange the purchase of land in the Little Rockies, they were informed by tribal leaders that the people were in a desperate condition: "we are dying off nearly every day, and the cause of it is that we are starving to death" (quoted in McCool 1987, 65).

More recent data from the 1980 and 1990 censuses indicate a significant income disparity between Indians and non-Indians in Blaine County.[1] In 1980, the median family income for non-Indians in the county was $16,588; compared to $9,120 for Indians. By 1990 this gap had narrowed

[1] The 1990 census provided the most recent data available for the trial. Thus, both sides relied upon 1990 data but used population figures from the 2000 census in their proposed findings, and the district court relied upon those later figures in rendering its decision.

only slightly; for non-Indians the median family income was $24,627, and for Indians it was $14,176. This income disparity was reflected in the percentage of families living in poverty in Blaine County: 14 percent of non-Indian families versus 41 percent of Indian families.

An associated socioeconomic factor is the impact of education. The 1990 census showed that 32 percent of whites and 24 percent of Indians were high school graduates. Bachelor's degrees were held by 14 percent of whites and 5 percent of Indians. Graduate degrees were held by 4 percent of whites and 1 percent of Indians. Still another socioeconomic factor is the level of unemployment. Again, census data indicated a significant disparity. Indian unemployment actually increased from 1980 to 1990, escalating from 10 percent to 26 percent. For the non-Indians of Blaine County the unemployment rate changed from only 2 percent to 3.6 percent.

Other important elements in a Section 2 case are the presence of racially charged elections and a history of discrimination. The history of Montana, like that of other western states, has elements of racism regarding Indians. When an Indian reservation was proposed in eastern Montana in 1867, the territorial assembly reacted angrily: "[This reservation] would be valueless to the barbarian excepting in so far as it would enable him to glut his vengeance upon the pioneers of the border settlements and arrest the tide of empire...." (quoted in Hoxie 2000, 12). This "tide of empire" attitude was reflected in official policy for many years; the parties in the Blaine County lawsuit disagreed as to whether it was federal policy only, or also attributable to official state policy. Official acts of discrimination gradually disappeared, but unofficial or social racism lingered on in some individuals. At times this racism was overt, as when Indians were referred to as "copper-colored banditti" (Hoxie 2000, 11). When it was proposed in 1930 to allow Indian children to attend the public school in Harlem – just across the Milk River from the Fort Belknap Reservation – angry white parents objected, arguing that "Indian children were filthy with disease and the entrance of the Indian children would endanger the health, even the life of the white pupils in the public schools" (quoted in Hoxie 2000, 38–9). However, whether this constituted an official state policy of discrimination, or simply the isolated prejudices of a few individuals, was one of the questions addressed by the lawsuit.

In recent years, social discrimination has typically been expressed in more subtle terms, especially as society in general has become less accepting of overt racism. Still, accusations of discrimination have occurred consistently throughout the years. In 1973 Indians accused the local sheriff of mistreating Indian prisoners (*Harlem News* November 8, 1973, 1). The following year there were accusations of police brutality *(Harlem News* May 23, 1974, n.p.). In 1981 Indians filed a lawsuit against the Harlem police chief for allegedly assaulting Indians and making racist remarks (*Harlem News* July 1, 1981, n.p.). At the trial, witnesses for the plaintiffs alleged that discrimination still occurred. The question in the trial was whether these alleged behaviors constituted invidious discrimination by the county or were merely unrepresentative attitudes expressed by a few individuals.

Ill feelings between Indians and non-Indians have resulted in a number of disagreements over the Harlem school district.[2] In 1984 and 1985, discussions over the condition and location of the high school polarized the community (*Harlem News* December 5, 1984, 1). The school had previously been declared unsafe by a unanimous vote of the school board in 1976. The local press made references to "tense" encounters and a "total breakdown of communication" between whites and Indians (*Harlem News* January 30, 1985, 2; *Harlem News* July 24, 1985, 1).

Another school issue has been disagreements over federal "impact aid" that the school district receives to pay for the education of Indian students and the input Indian parents have on school administration (*Harlem News* March 6, 1985, 2). This issue became so contentious that it resulted in an investigation by the U.S. Department of Education, which concluded that the "efforts by the Tribal leaders and parents of Indian children were rebuffed and ignored" and the school district was guilty of "dismal past performance" (*Harlem News* November 13, 1985, 1; U.S. Department of Education 1985, 15, 21). In 1985, the Montana Advisory Committee to the U.S. Civil Rights Commission held a public forum in Harlem to discuss the Indian–white conflict over school issues (*Harlem News* August 21, 1985, 1; August 28, 1985, n.p.; September 25, 1985, 1). One of the issues was that school board elections had been polarized, with "Harlem residents voting to a great degree for Harlem-based candidates and Fort Belknap residents voting for candidates who reside there" (*Harlem News* September 25, 1985, 1). The lead speaker from the reservation said that the purpose of the forum was to examine "what we perceive to be civil rights violations against us as an Indian people by School District #12 [Harlem]"

[2] It is worth noting that at one point in the mid-1980s, Indian leaders began calling for a district plan of electing school board members because they could not overcome their numerical disadvantage in the at-large electoral system. This idea was abandoned when Indians voted in sufficient numbers to win some at-large contests. See *Harlem News*, January 23, 1985, 1; February 6, 1985, 1.

(Plumage 1985). A survey of teachers and administrators completed at about that time revealed that 78.5 percent of the respondents thought that racial discrimination occurred in the school (Huff 1997).

Anti-reservation sentiment, opposition to Indians' local tax exemptions, and resentment over special programs for Indians have become an organized political movement in Montana. Groups such as Montanans Opposing Discrimination[3] and Totally Equal Americans advocate the unilateral abrogation of treaty rights. A recent report by the Montana Human Rights Network claimed that the objective of these groups is "a systematic effort to deny legally established rights to a group of people who are identified on the basis of their shared culture, history, religion and tradition" (Montana Human Rights Network 2000). There is disagreement as to whether these groups are racist or merely opposed to current federal Indian policy. However, their presence has drawn attention to the animosities between Indians and whites and has heightened political tension. These tensions have been expressed by Indian candidates for office:

- "Right now I know there is distrust on both sides." Judith Gray, Indian school board candidate (*Harlem News* March 26, 1985, 13).
- "Each government [Blaine County, Fort Belknap, state of Montana] has resources the others do not. Instead of sitting across the table from each other like adversaries, we should concentrate on working together...." Christine Main, Indian county commission candidate (*Harlem News* May 7, 1986,1).
- "For too long, a polarization has separated us not only politically but also socially and economically." Judith Gray, Indian school board candidate (*Harlem News* April 1, 1987, n.p.).

Allegations of political polarization have played a role in the administration of the Harlem school district. The Fort Belknap Community Council disapproved of the school district's failure to use its federal impact funds to maintain the school building (it was declared unsafe), and they opposed a federal grant to the school, writing that "The Indian and white communit[ies] in School District #12 are completely polarized" (Fort Belknap Community Council 1985). This polarization was reflected in votes for taxes to support the school at that time; a majority of Harlem voters rejected the mill levy, but a majority of Fort Belknap voters supported it (Fort Belknap Community Council 1985, 4–5).

[3] The North Montana branch of this organization has been in existence since at least 1977. See *Chinook Opinion*, April 6, 1977, 2.

Allegations of polarized politics also concerned campaigns for county commissioner. For example, a race in 1985 was described as follows in the *Harlem News*: "... the recent election had racial overtones in that whites voted for whites and Indians for Indians" (April 10, 1985, 1). Similar allegations were made regarding school board races. For example, when two Indian candidates ran for the school board in 1985, the local newspaper reported that they "got strong support from the reservation as the vote count split strongly along the river dividing that community from Harlem" (*Harlem News* April 3, 1985, 1).

These examples provide anecdotal evidence that at least some elections may have been characterized by racial bloc voting. The extent and frequency of racial bloc voting can be measured statistically. Thus, both plaintiffs and defendants relied upon statistical analyses, performed by expert witnesses, to assess the extent to which racial bloc voting occurred. Their reports are discussed in the next section.

The Trial

A bench trial was conducted in Great Falls, Montana, in October 2001 before Judge Philip Pro. Both sides relied upon expert and lay witnesses. For the plaintiffs, Professor Fredrick Hoxie, a historian, investigated the history of the Fort Belknap Reservation and concluded that "Since the founding of Blaine County there has been a history of discrimination that has defined the terms for Indian–white contact in the area surrounding the Fort Belknap Reservation in the modern period" (Hoxie 2000, 65). Professor Daniel McCool, a political scientist, also appeared for the plaintiffs and submitted a qualitative analysis of the *Gingles* and Senate factors, concluding: "The long history of discrimination, ill feelings regarding taxes, their socio-economic level, their minority status, and bloc voting have combined to create a disadvantage for the Blaine County Indians in the at-large elections for the county board of commissioners" (McCool 2000, 20).[4]

The third expert witness to appear on behalf of the plaintiffs was Professor Theodore Arrington, a political scientist trained in the statistical analyses that are used to estimate racial bloc voting and political cohesion – ecological regression analysis, correlation analysis, and

[4] Parts of the second section of this chapter were based on McCool's expert witness report in this case.

homogeneous precinct analysis.[5] He concluded that "Indian citizens in Blaine County do not participate equally in the political process of that county, and do not have an equal opportunity to elect representatives of their choice for County Commissioner" (Arrington 2000, 29). The statistical expert hired by the defendants, political science Professor Ronald Weber, arrived at a different conclusion. Although he agreed that American Indian voters "are usually cohesive," he found "no usual pattern of polarization in voting." As a result, "... whatever polarization in voting exists does not end up being politically or legally consequential, in that the candidates of choice of Native American voters are not usually defeated due to non-Native American bloc voting ..." (Weber 2000, 8–9). Thus, "Native American vote dilution does not occur in Blaine County ..." (95).

The conflicting conclusions reached by Arrington and Weber with respect to white bloc voting can be partially explained by two important factors that concern which electoral contests are the most probative, meaning which elections reveal more about the factors important in a Section 2 case. The outcome of the statistical analyses measuring cohesiveness and racial bloc voting can be largely determined, in some cases, by the weight given to these factors.

The first factor is whether the statistical analysis gives additional weight to contests that pit a non-Indian against an Indian. The plaintiffs argued that "Minority v. white contests are considered more probative than contests involving only nonminority candidates because by analyzing contests with different racial choices, a court can clearly see how the electorate responds to race" (United States' Proposed Findings of Act and Conclusions of Law, January 10, 2002, 58). The defendants, on the other hand, argued that "only slight additional weight should be accorded primary [and general] elections in which American Indians were candidates" (Defendants' Findings of Fact and Conclusions of Law, January 10, 2002, 23).

These positions are reflected in the methodology of the respective statistical experts. Arrington placed much greater emphasis on white-versus-Indian races, but Weber ignored the race of the contestants, giving each election equal weight. Both experts agreed that Indians vote cohesively. The biggest point of contention was in regard to the measure of racial bloc voting; does a bloc of cohesive white voters usually defeat the Indian

[5] King's ecological inference is the fourth method often used to estimate racial bloc voting.

candidate? The answer turned on the question of whether race should be a factor in determining which elections are most probative. Dr. Arrington argued:

> What is the "acid test" of the ability of a minority group to participate equally in the political process and elect representatives of *their* choice? In jurisdictions where there have been minority candidates whose votes can be analyzed, the "acid test" is whether the minority voters can elect a candidate of their own race, ethnic, or language group *when such minority candidates are their choice*. If they cannot do so, they are not able to participate equally with whites. (Rebuttal Declaration of Theodore S. Arrington, 2001, 24–5)

The rebuttal report filed by the defendant's expert, Dr. Weber, did not address specifically the question of whether additional weight should be placed on Indian-versus-white elections, but argued that Dr. Arrington's approach "assumes that voters know who the Native American and non-Native American candidates are. The ballot does not carry any labels as to the group background of the candidates..." (Weber, A Rebuttal Report on Liability Issues for Hearing in *U.S. v. Blaine County*, 2001, 24).

The second factor concerns the difference between endogenous and exogenous elections. An endogenous election is a race for the office that is being contested – the county commission races in this case. An exogenous election is one with significant overlap in the electorates but different jurisdictions. Thus, an exogenous election may or may not include most or all of the voters in the jurisdiction being sued. In this case, an example would be contests for the Harlem school board; all of the voters in such elections live in Blaine County.

Regarding exogenous elections, the plaintiffs argued that "exogenous minority v. white elections are also highly probative" (United States' Proposed Findings of Fact and Conclusions of Law, January 10, 2002, 60). Most of these elections were school board races, which played a prominent role in Dr. Arrington's analysis; he found that "racial polarization is evident in 19 out of the 20 Harlem School Board elections held over the last 20 years" (Arrington 2000, 22). The defendants argued that these "exogenous elections for school board are irrelevant for determining whether legally significant, racially polarized voting exists in Blaine County." That is, because they involved only three of the twenty-six precincts in the county, they were "structurally different" and focused on different issues (Defendants' Findings, January 10, 2002, 21; also see Weber 2000, 8–9).

Ultimately, it is up to the court to decide how to weight white-versus-Indian elections in comparison with other races and endogenous-versus-exogenous elections. But before this case went to trial, the defendants, as they had indicated in their answer to the original complaint, filed a motion for summary judgment based on the claim that Section 2 of the VRA, as amended in 1982, was "beyond the power of Congress and facially unconstitutional"; furthermore, they alleged, it was never intended to apply to Indians (Defendants' Motion for Summary Judgment, January 31, 2001, 1).[6] Their motion focused on the difference between requiring plaintiffs to prove the *intent* to discriminate and merely proving that the challenged action *resulted* in discrimination. When Section 2 was amended, a clear objective of the bill's authors was to replace the intent test with the results test. The complaint in the Blaine County case was based on the latter, which is all that is required under the amended Section 2.

The defendants argued that Congress, in passing the 1982 amendments to Section 2 of the VRA, rendered it unconstitutional. They argued that the U.S. Supreme Court, in a series of five cases, had prohibited such legislation and established a stringent test – congruence and proportionality – to limit Congress when it engaged in "prophylactic legislation to enforce the Fourteenth Amendment or Fifteenth Amendment...."[7] According to the defendants' motion, "Section 2 of the Voting Rights Act, as amended in 1982, does not meet this stringent test. There is no factual predicate at all in the legislative history of the 1982 amendments and certainly not any of the sort required before Congress may impinge on the sovereignty of the state by prohibiting [its] constitutional utilization of at large elections" (Memorandum in Support of Defendants' Motion for Summary Judgment, January 31, 2001, 26–7).

Furthermore, the defendants argued, Section 2 did not apply to Montana and Blaine County because Congress

> had no evidence before it that there existed intentional unconstitutional discrimination by Montana....From 1965 through the present, the only "evidence" before Congress of voting discrimination against American Indians concerned the Navaho [sic] in Arizona and one incident each in Wisconsin, Nevada, Nebraska, New Mexico, and South Dakota. In all of those instances lawsuit [sic] were brought and successfully prosecuted, or consent decrees were obtained, based

[6] A motion for summary judgment can be granted if the judge decides that there is no genuine issue of material fact. This terminates the case without further action.

[7] See *City of Boerne v. Flores* (1997) and Hasen (2005).

on allegations of unconstitutional, intentional discrimination. (Memorandum in Support of Defendants' Motion for Summary Judgment, January 31, 2001, 28–9)

Blaine County's motion for summary judgment provoked a vigorous forty-two page response from the Justice Department arguing that Section 2 "is an appropriate enforcement legislation because it is predicated on a pervasive history of unconstitutional conduct by the States, which continues to infect contemporary government decision-making, and because the legislation is reasonably designed to remedy and prevent those constitutional violations." And, the Department of Justice pointed out, every court that had addressed the constitutionality of Section 2 had upheld it (United States Response to the Memorandum in Support of Defendants' Motion for Summary Judgment, January 28, 2001, 6). Justice also argued that "Congress examined an overwhelming amount of evidence documenting a long history of racial discrimination against American Indians prior to both the 1975 and 1982 amendments to the VRA" (13).

The American Civil Liberties Union (ACLU) also submitted a brief opposing the defendants' motion, arguing that Congress amended Section 2 in 1982 to "make clear that proof of racial purpose was not required for a statutory violation" (Brief in Opposition to Defendants' Motion for Summary Judgment, January 27, 2001, 2). They pointed out that the Supreme Court had expressly affirmed the constitutionality of Section 2 and quoted Justice Sandra Day O'Connor: "It would be irresponsible for a State to disregard the Section 2 results test" (7). And, like the Justice Department, the ACLU argued that Congress clearly intended to apply Section 2 to Indians because the high court had before it "ample evidence of the discriminatory purpose and effect on minorities generally of a whole host of voting practices and procedures" (35).

The defendants responded by arguing that, at the time of the passage of the Section 2 amendments, Congress had no evidence of a "systematic, nationwide pattern of intentional and unconstitutional use, by legislative bodies, of at-large elections to dilute the voting strength of American Indians" (Reply to the United States' Response to Blaine County's Motion for Summary Judgment, March 14, 2001, 4). The defendants then made an argument that focused on who is to blame for the long history of discrimination and mistreatment of Indians:

...the United States sets forth its own sorry record regarding Native Americans. That record details the history of conquest of American Indians, as

> sovereign tribes, by the United States in its westward expansion, citing the dispossession of tribes from their lands and the removal of their people to reservations.... American Indians still suffer from education and economic deficiencies, all caused by the United States and its policies. (5)

In essence, Blaine County was saying: the discrimination is not our fault, so do not interfere with our county voting system.

In all, the parties involved produced 133 pages of briefs regarding the motion for summary judgment. It was quite apparent that this case over a remote county in northern Montana had suddenly grown very important; it had the potential to significantly alter the voting rights case law. Judge Pro issued a ten-page decision in July 2001. It was a succinct and unequivocal denial of the motion for summary judgment. He noted that the VRA "has been unsuccessfully challenged many times, both before and after the 1982 amendments" (*U.S. v. Blaine County* 2001, 1149). And it was applicable to Indians: "The fact that the Act was primarily intended to remedy discrimination against African Americans in the southern states in the 1960s does not make it any less proper to use as a remedy for discrimination against Native Americans today. There is ample evidence that American Indians have historically been the subject of discrimination in the area of voting" (1152). So, *U.S. v. Blaine County* was back to being simply an Indian voting rights case again.

The parties submitted their proposed findings of fact in September 2001. The plaintiffs noted that "no Indian has ever been elected or appointed to the County Commission. Although the 2000 Census of Population shows that 38.6% of the Blaine County voting age population is Native American, no person generally known by the residents of Blaine County to have Indian ancestry has ever held a countywide office..." (United States' Proposed Findings of Fact and Conclusions of Law, January 10, 2002, 16).[8] The plaintiffs offered extensive discussion of the political, economic, and social segregation of Indians and whites in Blaine County, as well qualitative and quantitative evidence regarding Indian cohesion and racial bloc voting. In addition, the plaintiffs pointed to three "structural barriers" that "enhance Indian vote dilution" (42). These included the staggered terms for county commissioners, which prevented Indians from using a single-shot strategy, the fact that the current residency districts in the county split the reservation, and the geographical size of the county, which made it difficult to campaign

[8] There was disagreement between the parties concerning the racial identity of one county officeholder, hence the phrase "generally known by the residents."

countywide (43). The brief then proceeded through the three prongs of *Gingles* and the Senate criteria. Their brief concluded: "Plaintiffs have shown the three *Gingles* factors, as well as most of the other Senate factors, and, therefore the totality of the circumstances establish that Blaine County's existing at-large method of electing county commissioners has a racially discriminatory result in violation of Section 2 of the Voting Rights Act" (83).

The defendants' proposed findings offered a starkly different view of Indian history, the requirements of Section 2, and the impact of the at-large system on Indian voters, beginning with the claim that "there is no distinct American Indian interest that could be furthered by electing an American Indian candidate to the Blaine County Board of Commissioners" (Defendants' Findings of Fact, January 10, 2002, 5).

The defendants then addressed the extent of political cohesion among Indians and argued that the Indians were not politically cohesive for two reasons. First, they lacked interest in county government: "American Indians are not and cannot be politically cohesive for want of distinct political interests that could be furthered by the Blaine County Board of Commissioners" (6). This is because "the Tribe [sic] provides all the services that might typically be provided by county government" (26). Second, Indians have a low rate of turnout, especially in the Democratic Party primaries: "... American Indians in Blaine County are not politically cohesive. Obviously this is so; 80% to 90% of American Indians in Blaine County simply do not turn out to vote in primary elections" (13). After a review of election returns and Dr. Weber's analysis, the brief encouraged the court to find that "legally significant racially polarized voting does not exist in Blaine County and that most American Indian candidates of choice were not defeated by non-Indian bloc voting, irrespective of whether American Indian candidates were running ..." (38).

Another central argument made by the defendants was that the Indians' losses at the polls and other misfortunes were due to reasons other than racial discrimination by the majority electorate in the county. They offered three arguments. First, the alleged racial discrimination of the federal government was merely "benign neglect, which does not equate to invidious discrimination" (51). Federal government Indian policy was simply part of Manifest Destiny, and "great migrations in history have always come at the cost of those in the way ..." (52). The brief then summarized the various stages of federal government Indian policy, noting their serious deficiencies, and then stated that "for better or for worse, American Indians have a unique status in America. The question before this Court thus becomes determining the impact of that unique status on the Court's analysis of the alleged violation of the VRA" (57). The brief answered this question by failing to find evidence of discrimination: "The United States has introduced no competent evidence to suggest that Congress acted out of racial bias toward American Indians or in an invidiously discriminatory manner based on their race, color, or language, and there is no such evidence.... To the contrary, the policy of the United States Government toward American Indians has been one that seeks to ensure equality, not to discriminate invidiously" (58).

The second argument was that the laws and policies of Montana, alleged to be discriminatory, were in fact not based on race, but on other reasonable factors. For example, early laws limiting suffrage had no impact on Indians because they were not yet citizens; limiting voters to those who paid taxes "was common across the nation" and was not specific to Indians (61). Laws that were specific to Indians or reservations were simply a recognition that reservations were under federal government jurisdiction:

> A 1912 Montana Attorney General's opinion provided that anyone who takes part in tribal affairs and receives tribal funds may not vote at a general or school election. There is no evidence that this opinion was aimed at American Indians on account of their race. Rather, it was yet another outgrowth of the reservation system and the status of American Indians as citizens of independent sovereigns with a trust relationship with the United States. Not surprisingly, therefore, the Attorney General believed that any non-Indian on the payroll of a sovereign nation could have a conflict of interest in voting in the affairs of another state or nation. (64)

Thus, Montana's laws were simply a reasonable response to the federal government's Indian policy.

The third argument recognized that there are serious problems on the reservation, but attributed those to federal government policy and not the alleged racism of local non-Indians:

> To the degree that any animus exists [between whites and Indians in Blaine County], it exists because of the reservation system, tribal sovereignty, and dual citizenship, all of which have been imposed on American Indians and on Blaine County by the United States Government, as well as the economic and political consequences that flow therefrom. The animus to which the United States refers is not directed toward or related in any way to race. (81)

The defendants ended their brief with a plea to leave the at-large system intact in Blaine County.

The Decision

Judge Pro's decision, rendered in March 2002, carefully listed the *Gingles* factors and the Senate factors. The defendants conceded that the Indians met the first *Gingles* test, so it was not an issue. The second *Gingles* test, political cohesiveness, was also relatively straightforward since experts for both sides had found a significant degree of Indian cohesiveness in actual voting. The judge rejected the defendants' argument that low turnout was an indication of low cohesion and that the Indians had no special interest in county government (Findings of Fact and Conclusions of Law and Order, March 21, 2002, 9).

The third *Gingles* test, white bloc voting, required the judge to assess the probative value of various election contests and, in effect, select between the methodologies employed by the statistical experts. The judge chose to give special weight to white-versus-Indian races: "The record establishes a total of seven American Indian versus white elections were held in Blaine County.... The Court finds [that] these seven elections represent strong evidence of legally significant polarized voting in Blaine County" (13). The court also pointed to nonstatistical evidence, such as newspaper accounts and interviews, to support its conclusion. Thus, the plaintiffs satisfied all three *Gingles* criteria.

Judge Pro then turned to the Senate factors. The first one, a history of discrimination, had been hotly disputed throughout the case, as evidenced by the previous discussion. The judge relied on two sources to make his decision. First, he noted that in *Old Person* v. *Cooney*, the district judge had "chronicled in detail" the history of discrimination by both the United States and Montana (15). Second, he noted that the plaintiffs had "presented extensive testimony at trial relating to the history of official discrimination..." (15) and concluded that the first Senate criterion had been met.

The second Senate factor, in regard to racially polarized elections, overlaps with the second and third *Gingles* factors and thus had already been approved. The third factor, concerning procedures that enhance discrimination, was also present because the "at-large system has consistently resulted in the inability of American Indians to elect candidates of their choice" (16). The fourth factor, regarding candidate slating, was inapplicable.

The fifth, regarding differences in education, employment, and health, required the court to decide if the "effects of discrimination," such as lower education and employment levels, have hindered minority group political activity. After noting that Blaine County is the poorest in Montana, Judge Pro decided that the plaintiffs had adequately demonstrated the ill effects of past discrimination. However, there was insufficient evidence to support the sixth factor – the use of racial appeals in campaigns.

The seventh factor is in many ways the most important; while the other criteria focus on procedural characteristics, this one focuses on the actual outcome: have Indians won county offices? The judge noted that the absence of any electoral victories is "a highly probative indication of impermissible vote dilution." In Blaine County, "no American Indian has ever been elected or appointed to any of the 13 elective offices...." (17). The judge contrasted this situation with the electoral success that Indians had experienced in school board elections, where "a fair chance of being elected exists" (18).

The eighth factor concerns the lack of responsiveness of local officials to the needs of the Indians. Judge Pro found little evidence of this but dismissed defendants' argument that the at-large system made county government more responsive to the needs of the entire county (18). And finally, the judge noted that the plaintiffs need not prove intent to discriminate when the at-large system was adopted, but only the discriminatory effects of this system (19–20).

The judge found in favor of the plaintiffs and ordered the county to produce "an election plan" that remedied the Section 2 violations (22). To no one's surprise, the MSLF appealed the case to the Ninth Circuit Court of Appeals. They did not take issue with the remedy imposed on Blaine County. Rather, they again raised the constitutional issues that had been the focus of their motion for summary judgment and contended that Congress had exceeded its enforcement powers when it amended Section 2 in 1982. Their position was based on two arguments: that there is no widespread evidence of purposeful voting discrimination, which means that the amended Section 2 is out of proportion to the alleged harm, and that the Fifteenth Amendment only prohibits intentional discrimination, not discriminatory results. The court of appeals rejected these arguments and upheld the district court's decision.

In responding to the first argument, the appellate court noted that Section 2 cases require a very difficult burden of proof: "plaintiffs must usually present the testimony of a wide variety of witnesses – political scientists, historians, local politicians, lay witnesses – and sift through records going back more than a century.... Plaintiffs must not only prove compactness, cohesion, and white bloc voting, but also satisfy the totality-of-the-circumstances test." Thus self-limiting, "nationwide application of this provision is undoubtedly constitutional" (*U.S. v. Blaine County* 2004, 906). Such widespread application was necessary, reasoned the court (907).

The appellate court then dealt with the second argument: "Congress thoroughly considered the practical and constitutional implications of the results test, and reasonably concluded that an intent test would not effectively prevent purposeful voting discrimination" (908).

The court also took issue with the defendants' claim that the Indians had no distinct political interest in county government, pointing out that both the Supreme Court and the Ninth Circuit Court of Appeals had ruled that "it is actual voting patterns, not subjective interpretations of a minority group's political interests, that informs the political cohesiveness analysis.... The County ... essentially asks us to deny the validity of American Indian voter's self-professed interests. Were we to do so, we would be answering what is inherently a political question, best left to the voters and their elected representatives" (910). The three appellate judges then went through a litany of what the defendants claimed were errors committed by Judge Pro and ruled that he had made no factual or legal errors. They then affirmed the district court's decision, including the constitutionality of Section 2 (916).

In the appellate court's decision, the judges offered a lengthy explanation of why the amendments to Section 2 were necessary and how they fit into the constitutional fabric of the Fifteenth Amendment. In doing so, they quoted Justice Sandra Day O'Connor: "[It is] the sad reality that there still are some communities in our Nation where racial politics do dominate the electoral process" (907).

In December 2004, the defendants filed a writ of certiorari to the U.S. Supreme Court, which was denied in April 2005. In the meantime, the county had adopted a single-member district plan, including a district that is Indian majority. A tribal member, Delores Plumage, was elected commissioner for that district in 2002. After the Supreme Court rejected the county's appeal, one of the non-Indian commissioners told a reporter: "It's over with. We're going to go forward from here and treat everybody alike and patch up the wounds" (Hewes 2005).

Conclusion

The Blaine County case is a textbook example of a successful Section 2 litigation that resulted in the election of a minority group person to the newly altered political jurisdiction. It is true that Bull Connor is dead, but old biases sometimes live on in the form of certain electoral procedures. Upon taking office, Delores Plumage made history just as surely as the first blacks who won elections following the early VRA cases in the 1960s and 1970s.

Blaine County is also important because the MSLF hoped to use it as a test case to challenge the constitutionality of the VRA, especially as it applied to Indians. In denying certiorari, the high court put an end to that effort, at least for the time being. The Roberts court may take a different position when and if the issue arises again.

And finally, it is important to consider the plaintiff's victory within the broader social and political context. While the case was on appeal, the town of Havre, situated between the Fort Belknap Reservation and the Rocky Boys Reservation, was the subject of an in-depth article regarding racist attitudes. The article created so much controversy that federal mediators came to town in an effort to calm the unrest (Miller 2005). A *Denver Post* story described the commotion: "...a series of events in Havre – a newspaper article, the distribution of racially charged leaflets and the intervention of a Justice Department mediator – have combined to transform this town tucked between two reservations into an emblem of racial strife" (Riley 2005). The article that initiated such attention quoted a local non-Indian man as saying, "Native Americans here are like the blacks in the south" (Pettinger 2005).

6

Lakotas in the Legislature

The Bone Shirt Case

American Indians and the state of South Dakota have a complex and difficult history. Unlike the Assiniboine and Gros Ventre of Fort Belknap, the Sioux of the northern Great Plains engaged in bitter warfare with white settlers and the U.S. Army.[1] That conflict is the longest armed struggle in U.S. history, beginning with a tense showdown between the Sioux and Lewis and Clark in 1803 and terminating in the last "battle" of the Indian wars at Wounded Knee, South Dakota, eighty-seven years later. That is a long time to be in armed conflict. It is not possible to understand the current legal and political relationships between Indians and whites in South Dakota without understanding at least the rudiments of that struggle.

South Dakota has had more Indian voting rights cases than almost any other state – eighteen by our count. There are a number of possible reasons. First, there is the extensive history of armed conflict between the races; old animosities die hard, and they are often reflected in the contemporary attitudes of both Indians and whites. Second, there are many Indians in South Dakota, especially in proportion to the white population. According to the most recent census, South Dakota has a population of 761,000; 63,400 of them are American Indians – about 9 percent. There are nine federally recognized Indian reservations in the state, all of them Sioux. And finally, if the Indian plaintiffs' arguments are correct in the litany of voting rights cases in South Dakota – nearly all of

[1] We use "Sioux" because it is the term most commonly used in legal documents. However, the people we call the Sioux refer to themselves as Lakota, Nakota, and Dakota. The *Bone Shirt* case involved Lakota people.

which they won – there is a considerable amount of discrimination in the state.[2]

Rosebud Reservation, in Todd County, and Pine Ridge Reservation, in Shannon and Jackson Counties, are located along the southern border of the state in a landscape of rolling hills and open prairie. Dense grasses cover the swales, and lodgepole pines crowd along hilltops. It is spacious, attractive country that retains much of its wild character. The two reservations were once coterminous, but an enormous chunk of land was carved out of Pine Ridge in 1912 and organized as Bennett County. However, there are still large tracts of Indian trust land in that county. It was here that tensions between whites and Indians reached the breaking point recently when a new county sheriff was appointed with a "get-tough" agenda. Indian people felt he was racist; the sheriff vehemently denied this and said he was only doing his job. Some local Indians formed the LaCreek Civil Rights Committee and contacted the American Civil Liberties Union's (ACLU's) state representative for help. She suggested that they organize a voter registration drive and attempt to change things through the ballot box. The LaCreek Committee began a voter registration drive as part of an effort to drive the sheriff and his supporters from office.[3]

It was in this volatile atmosphere that the ACLU filed *Bone Shirt v. Hazeltine* with the U.S. District Court for South Dakota, in December 2001, alleging both Section 5 and Section 2 violations. The lead plaintiff, Alfred Bone Shirt, was a fiery, outspoken activist with a taste for confrontational politics.[4] But he had learned over the years that the ballot box was perhaps a more effective path to power than high-profile conflicts. The Section 5 claim was based on the state's failure to preclear its 2001 legislative redistricting plan prior to its implementation (*Bone Shirt v. Hazeltine* 2002, 9). The Section 2 claim concerned two legislative districts, 26 and 27. Two plaintiffs, Bone Shirt and Belva Black Lance, lived in District 27, and two additional plaintiffs, Bonnie High Bull and Germaine Moves Camp, lived in District 26. The Section 2 claim charged that the 2001 legislative redistricting packed Indians into District 27; 90 percent of the people in that district were Indian. But right next to it was District 26, which was only 30 percent Indian (Complaint, December 26,

[2] Several of the cases were settled to the satisfaction of the plaintiffs; the rest were court victories except for *Cottier*, which was appealed, overturned, and remanded to district court.

[3] This effort continues. See Harriman (2006).

[4] Bone Shirt is part of an organization called the Dakota-Lakota-Nakota Human Rights Advocacy Coalition. See www.dlncoaltion.org

2001, 2, 7).[5] An adjustment in the boundary lines of four districts in the area would result in two majority-Indian districts. Another possible solution was to divide District 26 into two single-member districts for the state's house of representatives rather than electing two members from the entire district. This remedy had already been implemented in another legislative district (28), in response to the threat of a Voting Rights Act (VRA) lawsuit (see *Emery v. Hunt* 2000; *U.S. v. South Dakota* 2001). Did the legislature's 2001 redistricting plan pack Indians into District 27? Should it have been precleared? Could this case put another Indian in the state house?

This chapter will examine the Section 2 claims in the *Bone Shirt* case. As the appellate court pointed out in the *Blaine County* case, a Section 2 case is long and involved. The *Bone Shirt* case was no exception, with a panoply of expert witnesses – including a prolonged fight over research methodology, a motion for summary judgment, and a lengthy trial with numerous lay witnesses.

The first section of this chapter describes the historical context of Indian voting in South Dakota at some length because it is relevant to so many Indian voting rights cases. This is followed by an examination of the current social, economic, and political climate of Indians in South Dakota. The next section examines the Section 2 claim. The conclusion of this chapter summarizes Judge Karen Schreier's 144-page decision in the Section 2 case and its implications for future VRA claims in Indian Country. Due to space limitations, the Section 5 claim will not be covered, except to note that a three-judge court voted two to one in favor of the plaintiffs and ordered preclearance for District 27 (*Bone Shirt v. Hazeltine* 2002). The Justice Department has since approved the redistricting plan, but preclearance does not preclude a Section 2 claim, certainly not one by private litigants, as in this case.

The Historical Context

General William T. Sherman was the government's principal signatory to the Fort Laramie Treaty of 1868. He was widely known for his antipathy toward Indians, especially the Sioux. In a telegram to President Ulysses S. Grant he opined: "We must act with vindictive earnestness against the Sioux, even to their extermination, men, women, and children" (quoted

[5] The corresponding numbers for voting-age population are 86% and 23%. See Plaintiffs' Proposed Findings of Fact and Conclusions of Law (March 22, 2004, 11).

in Connell 1985, 132). This attitude was not uncommon at the time. The 1877 federal Manypenny Treaty Commission noted: "We are aware that many [white] people think that the only solution of the Indian problem is in their extermination" (Karolevitz 1975, 23). Dakota Territory's first delegate to Congress told the House of Representatives: "The future of that country [the Dakotas] is already fixed; the fate of the Indian is sealed as effectually and materially as was that of the Canaanites before the advancing armies of Israel" (Lamar 1956, 103).

The treaty that Sherman negotiated with the Sioux followed years of bloody warfare and treachery. General William Harney, one of the principal negotiators, admitted this during the negotiations: "We know very well that you have been treated very badly for years past. You have been cheated by everybody, and everybody has told lies to you..." (Lamar 1956, 101). The Fort Laramie Treaty greatly reduced Sioux lands and tribal freedom; "[t]he Sioux could surrender most of what made them Sioux, settle on the Great Sioux Reservation, and yield their independence to white officials" (Utley 1993, 85). Despite these losses, most Sioux decided eventually that the treaty was the best deal they would get. The treaty took most of their traditional homeland but allowed them to keep what became known as the Great Sioux Reservation, which consisted of what is now the western half of South Dakota.

Some local white people disapproved of the new reservation; "[t]he Dakota settlements received the news of the Laramie Treaty with loud protestations" (Schell 1975, 89). During negotiations, the territorial legislature sent a "Memorial to Congress" requesting that Indians be given only worthless land and that all valuable land be awarded to whites (Lamar 1956, 106). After the details of the treaty were made public, the *Yankton Press and Dakotaian* called it an "abominable compact" and asked rhetorically: "What shall be done with these Indian dogs in our manger?" (Connell 1985, 238). The years following the treaty signing consisted of a litany of broken promises, and "violations of the treaty became common" (Greene 1993, xvi). Especially galling to the Sioux was the construction of the "Thieves' Road" into the sacred Black Hills and the subsequent ceding of the Black Hills through deception in 1877 – an act described by the Indian Claims Commission and quoted by the U.S. Supreme Court as follows: "A more ripe and rank case of dishonorable dealing will never, in all probability, be found in our history" (*U.S. v. Sioux Nation of Indians* 1980, 387). Violence was inevitable as whites demanded more Indian land. The *Bismark Tribune* editorialized: "The American people need the country the Indians now occupy.... An Indian war would do no harm, for it must come, sooner or later" (Karolevitz 1975, 99).

Two major clashes occurred in what is now South Dakota. At Slim Buttes in 1876 the U.S. Army cornered a small band of Sioux in a ravine; many women and children were killed or wounded. It was, in the words of one of the soldiers, "enough to touch the heart of the strongest man..." (Greene 1993, 115). Perhaps the most shameful event in all the Indian wars took place at Wounded Knee in 1890. The U.S. Army massacred between 175 and 340 Sioux, including many women and children and unarmed men (Utley 1993, 309). That epic tragedy "poisoned relations between the Sioux and the whites for generations to come" (South Dakota Advisory Committee 2000, 4). Former U.S. Senator James Abourezk stated that the Wounded Knee massacre "irrevocably affected the Lakota and Sioux people. The event's significance and memory have not diminished throughout the hundred and more years since it occurred" (South Dakota Advisory Committee 2000, 4). These "generations to come," these people with undiminished memory, were the plaintiffs in *Bone Shirt*.

When the Dakotas achieved statehood in 1889, it was, in the words of a South Dakota governor, "a very sad time for the Native American" (Mickelson 1990). There was a nearly constant clamor from the white citizens to drastically reduce the land reserved for the Sioux. However, the call for extermination was replaced by a realization that having troops stationed in the area and getting ration contracts with the Bureau of Indian Affairs (BIA), could prove lucrative. According to Howard Lamar's well respected history of the Dakotas: "[T]he Dakotan feared that extermination of the Indians might remove a valuable source of federal income to the local settler. Thus for the first time in the history of the American western movement, the Indian's continued presence was desirable" (1956, 106). This inevitably led to graft and corruption: "The local alliance eventually became so powerful that [Secretary of the Interior] Carl Schurz endeavored to clean up some of the corrupt Indian rings in Dakota.... But he ran into a thousand protests. The entire officialdom of the Territory turned upon him in wrath..." (107).

Thus, the white citizens of the Dakotas wanted profits from Indian contracts, but they also wanted Indian lands. Under great pressure from locals, the U.S. Congress in 1889 forced the Sioux to accept a new agreement that abandoned most of what had been promised in the Laramie Treaty. Historian Frederick Hoxie described this agreement: "There should be no doubt that the Great Sioux Agreement of 1889 was designed to destroy what remained of the Teton Bands' [i.e., western

Lakota] traditional way of life" (Hoxie 1985, 56). This agreement forced the Sioux to cede 11 million acres of land – land that had been promised to them in the Treaty of 1868 as their "permanent home" (Article 15). The Great Sioux Reservation was broken into five much smaller reservations, including Pine Ridge and Rosebud.

But even this enormous loss of land did not put an end to Indian losses. The General Allotment Act of 1887 (Dawes Act) provided for the division of Indian reservation lands into 160-acre parcels; the rest could then be sold as "surplus" land to settlers. Historian Herbert Schell described this process:

> The surplus lands on the Indian reservations supplied the principal stimulus for the intense activity in the trans-Missouri region. Between 1904 and 1913 the government negotiated a series of agreements with the Teton subtribes on the Rosebud, Lower Brule, Pine Ridge, Cheyenne River, and Standing Rock reservations whereby over half the reservation lands, a total of over four million acres, were made available for purchase by white settlers. (1975, 253)

More lands were lost when the reservations were opened; in 1912 the Pine Ridge Reservation lost nearly 1 million acres (land that would become Bennett County). The Rosebud Reservation, which originally included what is now Mellette County, Tripp County, and most of Gregory County, was greatly diminished through a series of statutes passed by Congress.

It should be noted that these land losses occurred after statehood, despite the fact that the South Dakota Constitution provided that the state would "forever disclaim all right and title to . . . all lands lying within said limits owned or held by any Indian or Indian tribes. . . ." (Article XXII). Writing in support of the land takings, the South Dakota state commissioner of immigration wrote that these massive land cessions transformed "a magnificent domain, red-peopled and virgin, from the way of barbarism to the way of enlightened civilization" (quoted in Bilosi 2001, 23).

In sum, the history of the relationship between the Sioux Indians and the territory of Dakota, and later the state of South Dakota, was marked by prolonged warfare, enormous losses of Indian land and freedom, and enmity between the two groups. The Ku Klux Klan became active in the state, and by 1925 "the klan blanketed the entire state with klaverns in virtually every major county" (Rambow 1973). According to political scientist Frank Pommersheim, this history of racial confrontation still has a direct impact on Indian – white interaction: ". . . in states such as South Dakota, tribe–state relations are often caught in a history of actions that are perceived (rightly or wrongly) by many tribes as having as their main objective the undermining of the tribe's very existence" (1995, 153). The unhappy events of the past have resulted in continuing ill will. According to state Senator (now state Representative) Paul Valandra, "There is a mistrust among Indian and non-Indian alike" (*Indian Country Today* 1986, B1).

Historical documents in South Dakota reflect the racial hostility of the times. Indian people were labeled as "revengeful and murderous savage" (Territorial Laws 1866, 551), "implacable enemies" (Territorial Laws 1867a, 120), "hell hounds" (Territorial Laws 1867b, 122), and "uncivilized" (South Dakota Laws 1901, 248). Such language is no longer found in official documents. Indeed, the official policy of the state emphasizes equality under the law without regard to race or heritage, as specified in the 1972 South Dakota Human Relations Act. From 1973 to 1975 the state had a task force on Indian–state relations, which made numerous recommendations, mostly dealing with taxation. In 1990 Governor George Mickelson and the state's nine tribal governments proclaimed a "Year of Reconciliation." This was followed a year later by a "Century of Reconciliation" (South Dakota official state website: www.travelsd.com/onlyinsd/sioux/milestones.asp).

However, statements hostile to Indian people are still made by some officials in the state. A county attorney described Indian culture as "godless, lawless, hopeless, and jobless" (*Lakota Times* 1990, A1). A state attorney general described Indian reservations as a "'divisive system' of government that have outlived their usefulness" (*Sioux Falls Argus Leader* 1989, A1). When the VRA was amended in 1975 to include Indians and other language minorities, then Attorney General William Janklow termed the new law a "facial absurdity" and an "unworkable solution to a non-existent problem" (Report of the Attorney General 1977).[6]

Not surprisingly, the conflicts between Indians and whites in South Dakota have been reflected in the voting laws. The first attempt to define Indians' political status was in the Fort Laramie Treaty, which offered citizenship to any Indian receiving a land patent (see Chapter 1 for the exact language). However, for those individuals who chose to obtain an allotment and citizenship, the treaty did not result in the right to vote in Dakota Territory. The first territorial legislative assembly passed a law limiting the right to vote to "[e]very free white male person" (Territorial

[6] Janklow later became governor of South Dakota and then representative in the U.S. Congress. He resigned after being convicted of manslaughter.

Laws 1862). The state revoked the race provision in 1867 but the franchise was limited to U.S. citizens, which excluded nearly all Indians (Territorial Laws 1867c). When the territory developed a civil code, it stated categorically that Indians "cannot vote or hold office" (Territorial Rev. Civil Code 1866, 4).

When South Dakota became a state, the new constitution limited suffrage to citizens of the United States, again excluding nearly all Indians (South Dakota Constitution 1890, Art. 7, Sec. 1). The fourth session of the state legislature developed criteria for voting and specifically excluded "any unorganized county within the boundaries of any Indian reservation" (S.D. Laws 1895; see the discussion in Chapter 3 of unorganized counties). The state's civil code in 1903 stipulated that Indians "cannot vote or hold office" while "maintaining tribal relations" (S.D. Revised Civil Code 1903). This language was included in the codification of 1939 (S.D. Laws 1939), and was not repealed until 1951 (Act of Feb. 27, 1951).

Until the repeal of that statute, it was assumed that at least some voting rights accrued to Indians who had taken up allotments, by virtue of the language in the Fort Laramie Treaty and similar language in the General Allotment Act, and thus had "severed tribal relations." Political participation for Indians at this time was no idle question. Local politicians were incessantly demanding that more Indian land be taken for settlement. After the opening of the reservations, the tribes soon realized that they did not have a voice in determining the policies that affected them. A year after the Cheyenne River Reservation was opened to settlers in 1908, the local Indian superintendent wrote that "the people of this reservation cannot become reconciled to the idea that they did not have a proper voice in the recent ceding of the lands. . . ." (Hoxie 1985, 65).

When a proposal was made in 1910 to open the Pine Ridge Reservation to non-Indian settlers (and to excise a major part of it in order to create Bennett County), the principal chiefs protested vigorously. One of them stated: "You owe us much by the treaties you make with us but give us only a little part of it." The government ignored their pleas and removed 1,273 square miles from the reservation (Robertson 2002, 110; Wagoner 2002, 39–44). A proposal was immediately made to organize the newly obtained lands as a county, which required a vote of the residents. The referendum to create Bennett County, held in 1912, excluded all voters who were "ration-drawing Indians who have not severed their tribal relations" (Robertson 2002, 112).

Confusion over which Indians were allowed to vote is reflected in various opinions issued by the state's attorneys general during that time. In

1908 the Indian agent at Standing Rock wrote to the state attorney general, asking if voting precincts could be established on the reservation so that the men who had taken allotments could vote. The attorney general's response was a classic "catch-22." He explained that Indians "who had severed tribal relations" had voting rights if an election precinct had been established, but "there is no provision of law in this State for receiving the vote of any person, whether Indian or white, whose residence is upon an Indian Reservation" (Report of the Attorney General 1908, 123).

In the meantime, the issue of Indian voting arose again in Corson County when the county judge inquired whether Indians could vote. Again the attorney general said it depended on whether tribal relations had been severed. He quoted the relevant language in the General Allotment (Dawes) Act and then concluded: "The test then is whether the Indian has severed his tribal relations and adopted the habits of civilized life, and that would be a matter of proof in each separate case" (Report of the Attorney General 1912, 400). Thus, each individual Indian would have to prove that he had become "civilized" in order to vote.

One of the most profound statements regarding Indian voting is found in an attorney general's opinion that dealt with non-Indians living on the Crow Creek Reservation. The attorney general noted that these citizens had the right to vote but that a mere right to vote was insufficient:

> ...there is a distinction between the constitutional right of a citizen to vote and the actual ability of such citizen in a given case to express his will at the polls. His constitutional right may be undisputed, yet he may at the same time be left without the facilities for the exercise of that right by reason of his geographical location, and by reason of the failure of the state legislature to provide for the territory within which he lives the necessary facilities to enable citizens residing therein to exercise the right of suffrage. (Report of the Attorney General 1918, 277)

The attorney general was correct; the "failure of the state legislature to provide" facilities could effectively disenfranchise people who otherwise had a right to vote. An early example comes from the Pine Ridge Reservation. According to a 1917 attorney general's opinion, state law forbade the establishment of election precincts on Indian reservations in unorganized counties; this left the residents of the reservation without an effective method of exercising a right to vote. (Report of the Attorney General 1917, 261).

In 1919 another form of disenfranchisement occurred when Indians tried to vote in a school district election. The attorney general, citing previous attorneys' general opinions, held that Indians "who are not voters and taxpayers in an organized school district are not residents within the meaning of the school laws of this state" (Report of the Attorney General 1919, 169). This statement appears to contain another catch-22: Indians who are not voters are not residents, and thus cannot vote. This opinion also reflects the claim that Indians cannot vote because they do not pay local property taxes.

Indians' political status changed with the passage of the 1924 Indian Citizenship Act, a change immediately reflected in an attorney general's report (Report of the Attorney General 1924, 204). But, as explained in Chapter 1, the act did not automatically bestow suffrage. In 1932 Indians at Cheyenne River tried to vote in a school district election, but the attorney general stipulated that their right to vote was limited by several factors: "Indians are entitled to vote in South Dakota under the same conditions as white people, and if they reside within a voting precinct on the Indian Reservation and not upon the land... under the exclusive jurisdiction of the federal government, they are entitled to vote in school elections" (Report of the Attorney General 1932, 360). These conditions effectively prevented most Indians from voting since few if any precincts had been established on reservations and many Indians still lived on trust lands.

After the prohibition against Indian voting was revoked in 1951, Indians still had to contend with other methods of prohibiting or limiting their suffrage. In 1963 Indian people living in Charles Mix County wanted to sign a petition and vote in a referendum to establish a water district. The attorney general denied their right to vote, even though they lived in the affected jurisdiction; he concluded that they failed to qualify as voters because their names did not appear on the tax rolls and the federal government had full jurisdiction over their affairs (Report of the Attorney General 1963, 115).

Until 1975, voters in the unorganized Shannon and Todd Counties were deprived of the right to vote for county officials; it took a federal court case to solve the problem (*Little Thunder v. South Dakota* 1975). This case had a direct and immediate impact on the right to vote. Testimony before a 1978 Civil Rights Commission hearing explained the importance of the case:

> ...prior to what is known as the *Little Thunder* decision, people in Washabaugh [and Todd and Shannon] County could not vote for county officials that [sic] served them.... That case, the *Little Thunder* case, ruled that that was

a constitutional denial of their right to vote. So consequently, now people in Washabaugh County can and do vote for county officials. I think that fact will increase the interest that people in Washabaugh would have in becoming a registered voter [sic]. (Hogan 1978, 91)

Thus, even as recently as thrity-one years ago, the people of the Pine Ridge and Rosebud Reservations (Shannon and Todd Counties) were still being officially deprived of the right to vote in some elections.

The Contemporary Context

Much of the historical discussion in the preceding section is directly related to the current political context of Indians in South Dakota. This section describes the political, economic, and cultural contexts of the *Bone Shirt* case. During the trial, there was considerable disagreement concerning the causes, severity, and relevance of some of these factors. Thus, it is helpful to examine the results of relevant studies and reports.

Indians' efforts to participate in nontribal elections have been the focus of several advisory commissions to the U.S. Commission on Civil Rights. A 1977 report listed "voting problems of minorities" as one of South Dakota's items of "unfinished business in the area of civil rights" (U.S. Commission on Civil Rights 1977, 179). In 1981 the Commission's South Dakota Advisory Committee issued a lengthy report devoted exclusively to identifying the hurdles and roadblocks Indians faced when trying to participate in elections. In its covering letter to the U.S. Commission on Civil Rights, the Committee stated that "Native Americans encounter problems in the political process which hamper their participation." One of the specific problems noted was "a districting plan which divided the Pine Ridge and Rosebud Reservations so that no district had a majority of Indian voters..." (South Dakota Advisory Committee to the U.S. Commission on Civil Rights 1981, 4).

The Advisory Committee issued another report on South Dakota in 2000. This report focused on perceptions of racism and bias in the state's criminal justice system but also noted problems in the electoral system: "Native Americans do not fully participate in local, state, and federal elections. This absence from the electoral process results in a lack of political representation at all levels of government and helps to ensure the continued neglect and inattention to issues of disparity and inequality" (South Dakota Advisory Committee to the U.S. Commission on Civil Rights

2000, ch. 3, 2). This report lamented that "It is both remarkable and disconcerting that many of the concerns brought before the Commission in the 1970s were the same ones heard more than 20 years later in Rapid City" (ch. 1, 2).

Indian voting difficulties in South Dakota have also been the subject of numerous court cases, which were summarized in Chapter 3. And a recent study of the Rosebud Reservation noted that both Indians and non-Indians "agree that there is deep-seated racial tension" (Bilosi 2001, 4). Two anthropological studies of the region concluded that negative stereotypes of Indians, especially full-bloods, are still common (Daniels 1970; Wagoner 2002, 58–9). Accusations of racism can be heard from non-Indians as well.[7]

Another major issue concerns allegations that "Indian voting fraud" has occurred. The 2002 voter registration drive provoked a barrage of such claims. Accusations by some members of the Republican Party that Indian voter registration workers had bribed people and forged voter registration cards received widespread media coverage. A story in a national magazine, *The National Review*, claimed that "the Democrats Stole a Senate Seat," referring to Senator Tim Johnson's narrow victory in 2002 – a victory secured by late returns from Indian reservations (York 2002, 33–6). State Attorney General Mark Barnett, a Republican, investigated fifty such charges and proclaimed *The National Review* article to be "shoddy, irresponsible, sensationalistic garbage" (Woster and Ross 2002). He also stated that "There was no widespread fraud and the election results are valid. No one stole the election" (Associated Press 2002, 1).

The reports by the U.S. Commission on Civil Rights, the numerous court cases, and false accusations of Indian voting fraud are all part of the larger sociopolitical context in which the controversy over voting rights has taken place. Another element in that context is the contrasting economic well-being of the contending parties, which has an impact on political participation. The Sioux people of South Dakota have endured dire poverty for a long time. In 1869 the Sioux, having been confined to the Yankton and Lower Brule Reservations, soon found themselves in desperate straits. The territorial government asked the secretary of the interior to help feed these Indians, who had been "reduced to a state of starvation"

[7] See Darrel Smith, "Who Are the Radical Racists?", an editorial published on the website of the Citizens for Equal Rights Alliance. Mr. Smith, a resident of South Dakota, quotes an Indian newspaper as calling some of his friends "loudmouthed racist partisans." He then opines, "it is the supporters of Federal Indian policy who are racist by definition" (www.citizensalliance.org/links/pages/news, accessed November 12, 2002).

(Territorial Laws 1869, 352). In 1889, following huge land cessions and a dramatic cut in government rations, all the Sioux on reservations were reduced to a state of abject poverty: "The Sioux were brought to the verge of starvation and suffered an epidemic of diseases attributable in part at least to the food shortage. Many children died, and some adults" (Schell 1975, 325).

One hundred years later the poverty remained. According to 1990 census data, four of the ten poorest counties in the United States were on Indian reservations in South Dakota. A 1992 special report, published in the *New York Times*, described the legacy of poverty on the Pine Ridge Reservation: "The conditions here also show influences that drag people down anywhere: bad nutrition, bad personal habits, high unemployment, racial discrimination, the two-decade-long erosion of American wages and Federal welfare programs that foster dependence" (Kilborn 1992, 1).

It is instructive to compare Todd County (85.6 percent Indian) and Shannon County (94.2 percent Indian) with South Dakota as a whole. The median household income for the state as a whole was $35,282.[8] In comparison, household income in Shannon County was $20,916, and in Todd County it was $20,035. The per capita income for the state was $17,562; for Shannon County it was $6,286, and for Todd County it was $7,714. The percentage of people in all of South Dakota living under the poverty line was 13.2 percent; for Shannon County it was 52.3 percent, and for Todd County it was 48.3 percent (U.S. Census 2002).

These data can also be analyzed by comparing American Indian and non-Indians in Districts 26 and 27. The unemployment rate among Indians in those districts was 31 percent; for whites it was 2.3 percent. In regard to household income, 30.2 percent of Indians earned less than $10,000; the same figure for non-Indians living in the same districts was 14.2 percent (U.S. Census 2000).

It was in this highly conflictual milieu that the state of South Dakota and the ACLU, on behalf of four Indian plaintiffs, went to court over the boundary lines of Districts 26 and 27.

The Case

The involvement of the ACLU's Voting Rights Project in the conflict over Districts 26 and 27 began before this case was filed. The Voting Rights

[8] Keep in mind that this figure includes data from all the Indian reservations in the state; if only non-Indian income had been included, the figure would be considerably higher.

Project and their local attorney played a role in the legislative hearings on the 2000 reapportionment. At that point, disagreements began to emerge as to how to draw the boundary lines of Districts 26 and 27, given the changes in population that had occurred since the last redistricting following the 1990 census. The Voting Rights Project argued that significant population changes since the last census made District 27 retrogressive and constituted a change under Section 5. The legislature, however, disagreed, and refused to make any changes. The Voting Rights Project then decided to challenge District 27 in the redistricting plan when it came up for Section 5 review before the Justice Department. But the state declared that, because no actual boundary changes had occurred, they would not submit the plan for Section 5 review. At that point, the ACLU filed both Section 5 and Section 2 complaints. The Section 5 case, cited at the beginning of this chapter, was decided fairly quickly. The Section 2 case, in contrast, required the whole panoply of *Gingles* tests and Senate factors and a full trial.

Both sides in the case hired multiple expert witnesses. The defendants hired a historian, Michael Lawson, to write a descriptive narrative of the political history of the Oglala and Rosebud tribes (Lawson and Muhn 2003). He and coauthor James Muhn argued that these two tribes have historically lacked political cohesion because of a "long tradition of internal factionalism and divisiveness" (2). They concluded that tribal members have "much less to gain through political participation in State and local elections" compared to their relationship to the federal government (64). For the plaintiffs, political science professor Daniel McCool utilized qualitative analysis to analyze historical, cultural, social, and economic factors and how they have affected the ability of Indians in Districts 26 and 27 to elect candidates of their choice (McCool 2003a). He concluded that "The combination of past and present discrimination, resistance to Indian voter registration, a hostile political and social environment, limited reading comprehension . . . and extreme poverty among Indians have prevented, reduced, or hindered Indian political participation, and caused a marked political polarization between Indians and Anglos" (55).

The statistical expert for the defendants was economics professor Jeffrey Zax, who found Indian voter cohesion in all of the exogenous elections he examined. However, he took a unique approach to the question of polarization and endogenous versus exogenous elections; he omitted all elections that encompassed only part of Districts 26 and 27, such as local county races, because such races "cannot reveal whether these same races would have been polarized, had they been extended to the rest of the electorates of the State Senate Districts in which they were contained" (Zax 2003, 14). Professor Zax also excluded all endogenous elections – races for house Districts 26 and 27 – because "These are multi-member districts, with first-past-the-post elections. Ecological inference cannot be applied to this electoral structure" (15). The only races included in Zax's analysis of polarization were statewide races and ballot issues (15). In these races he found a moderate level of cohesion among Indians (twenty-four out of forty-seven races) and whites (thrity-two out of forty-seven races) but found little evidence of polarization, which occurred in only six of the fifty races in District 27 and in fourteen of forty-seven in District 26. He concluded that, in District 27, "dilution does not occur," and in District 26, "the instances of polarization... are not sufficient to constitute a pattern in which '(t)he white majority votes... to usually defeat the minority's candidate'" (49). Zax relied upon a statistical method known as "ecological inference" or the "King method" (developed by political scientist Gary King) and argued, citing his own publication, that the ecological regression methodology utilized by most statistical experts had been proven unreliable (7–15).[9]

The statistical expert for the plaintiffs was psychologist Steven Cole. Dr. Cole focused primarily on the races that were excluded from Zax's analysis. Using the standard procedures of ecological regression analysis and homogeneous precinct analysis, Cole analyzed the multimember endogenous House districts. Zax had argued that ecological inference could not analyze such elections, but Cole offered a different interpretation: "For multi-member elections, there are no simple numerical thresholds to define racial polarization or cohesion. However, significant racial polarization is exhibited whenever the set of candidates that would be chosen by voters of one race differs from the set of candidates that would be chosen by voters of the other race" (Cole 2003, 7). Thus there were fundamental methodological differences between Zax and Cole that determined which elections were included in their sample. And Cole, unlike Zax, focused on Indian versus white elections because they "are most probative of racial bloc voting because they present voters with a racial choice" (11, 18). Unlike Zax, Cole also emphasized endogenous elections because "analysts generally first examine elections for the office(s) under challenge, in this case, state legislative offices" (11).

[9] Ecological regression has indeed been the subject of significant criticism. However, it is still the "principal technique" used to assess racial polarization (Kousser 2001).

Cole analyzed a series of elections, most of which were not in Zax's sample, and found that most, but not all, of them were racially polarized and that the Indians voted cohesively. For Indian versus white elections in state senate contests, he found that "for these five Indian/non-Indian contests, average Indian cohesion was 83% and average non-Indian crossover support for the Indian preferred candidates was 22%. In all five contests, no one candidate was preferred by both Indians and non-Indian voters" (18).

Cole's analysis provided a unique opportunity to compare election results in two racially distinct districts: District 27, with an Indian majority, and District 26, with an Indian minority. In District 26 he found that the one white versus Indian contest was polarized, that the Indian-preferred candidate lost, and that, of the legislative elections involving only non-Indian candidates, "over 80% of the contests were racially polarized" (24). In District 27 he found that most of the Indian versus non-Indian general elections, and Indian-only general elections, were polarized, but the all-Indian primary elections were not (25).

The plaintiffs utilized another expert, demographer William Cooper, to generate five possible redistricting plans that would satisfy the VRA (Cooper 2004).

As in the *Blaine County* case, the experts used different approaches and interpretations to arrive at different conclusions. As a result, there were fundamental disagreements among the various experts. For example, there were significant differences between Zax's and Cole's samples, and they used different quantitative methodologies. In another expert–expert exchange, Dr. McCool wrote a rebuttal report to the Lawson–Muhn report, arguing that their report utilized "inadequate and inappropriate methodology and data, omit[ted] critically important elements of the historical record, misrepresent[ed] tribal relationships, and reache[d] erroneous or unsubstantiated conclusions" (McCool 2003b). Dr. Lawson did not submit a rebuttal to Dr. McCool's report. However, the state took issue with Dr. McCool's use of qualitative methodology and tried to have his report disqualified – a move rejected by the judge after much conflict between the parties concerning the legitimacy of qualitative analysis (*Bone Shirt v. Hazeltine* 2004a).[10]

[10] This conflict produced at least eight entries in the case docket with titles such as "Brief in Support of Motion to Strike Report and Testimony of Dr. Daniel McCool"; "Plaintiffs' Brief in Opposition to the Defendants' Motion to Strike the Report and Testimony of Dr. Daniel McCool"; "Reply Brief in Support of the Motion to Strike Report and

Following the submission of the experts' reports, the defendants filed a motion for summary judgment, arguing that the plaintiffs "cannot demonstrate that the legislatively adopted redistricting violates even one of the three *Gingles* prerequisites" (Defendants' Brief in Support of Motion for Summary Judgment, July 18, 2003, 12). The plaintiffs filed a brief in opposition to the motion for summary judgment and moved for a partial summary judgment in their favor (Plaintiffs' Brief in Opposition to the Defendants' Motion for Summary Judgment, August 11, 2003). The judge denied the motions of both parties, noting that the "varying interpretations and statistics by plaintiffs' and defendants' experts create a material issue of fact as to whether the majority votes as a bloc... the court will weigh the merits of the experts' methods and their outcomes during trial" (*Bone Shirt v. Hazeltine* 2004b, 20–1). Thus, after much wrangling and disagreement over the experts' methodology and the extent to which the *Gingles* criteria were met, both sides prepared to go to trial.

Prior to the trial, each side prepared "proposed findings of fact and conclusions of law." These briefs essentially mimic a judge's opinion in that they are written as if the court had produced them. Of course, each side writes as though the judge saw the case entirely from its perspective.

The plaintiffs' proposed findings ran to 188 pages. In considerable detail, the plaintiffs' brief went through the *Gingles* factors, the Senate factors, and relevant case law. In regard to the first *Gingles* factor, numerosity and compactness, the brief explained the five proposed solutions that were presented in William Cooper's report and noted, "There are many ways to draw majority-Indian districts in South Dakota because Native Americans on and around the state's Indian reservations are numerous and geographically compact" (Plaintiffs' Proposed Findings of Fact and Conclusions of Law, March 22, 2004, 22). The brief then took issue with several claims made by the defendants regarding supermajorities, complete remedies, and the Fourteenth Amendment (24–36). The plaintiffs also pointed out that their proposed districts did not have the bizarre, irregular boundaries that invoked the disapproval of the Supreme Court in *Shaw v. Reno* (1993).

Testimony of Dr. Daniel McCool; Plaintiffs' Motion to Strike, or, in the Alternative Leave to File a Surreply Brief"; "Defendants' Response to Plaintiffs Brief in Support of Their Motion to Strike, or, in the Alternative, For Leave to File a Surreply Brief'(McCool)"; "Plaintiffs' Reply to the Defendants' Response to the Plaintiffs' Motion to Strike, or, in the Alternative, For Leave to File a Surreply Brief"; "Order Denying Defendants' Motion to Strike McCool and Plaintiffs' Motion to Strike"; and "Order Denying Defendants' Motion in Limine Regarding Dr. McCool."

The plaintiffs' proposed finding then tackled the second *Gingles* test concerning the political cohesiveness of American Indian voters. This required an explanation of why the methodology of the plaintiffs' experts was superior to that of the defendants' experts. Much of the discussion focused on which elections are most probative, as determined by previous court decisions; the plaintiffs argued that the elections included in Professor Cole's analysis were the most probative (most of which were excluded by Profesor Zax) and that the least probative elections – ballot issues – were included in Zax's sample (37–40). Nevertheless, both experts found that "Native Americans were usually politically cohesive in the elections they analyzed" (Plaintiffs' Proposed Findings of Fact and Conclusions of Law, March 22, 2004, 43).

The third *Gingles* factor, that the Indian-preferred candidate is usually defeated, also required an extensive discussion of the experts' methodology, with the plaintiffs arguing that "Notwithstanding their several differences in methodology, the results of both statistical experts' analysis demonstrate that white majorities voted sufficiently as a bloc to defeat the Indian-preferred candidates in the overwhelming majority of the elections that they analyzed" (79). This is followed by a detailed discussion of each of the Senate factors, including a lengthy description of discrimination against Indians (90–136). The plaintiffs concluded with a section titled "Blaming the Victim Is No Defense," which takes issue with the defendants' claim that Indian voter apathy is their own fault; rather, it is due to "outright discrimination and informal barriers" that have prevented Indians from participating (184).

The defendants' proposed findings began with a brief history of how District 27 was created, pointing out that it was created in response to input from the South Dakota Task Force on Indian/State Relations, which existed from 1973 to 1975 (Defendants' Proposed Findings of Fact and Conclusions of Law, March 29, 2004, 3–5). The defendants' brief noted that, in discussions regarding possible changes to Districts 27 in 2001, "Legislators who were tribal members from the area, and the people who lived in Districts 26 and 27, supported the continuation of the 1990 configuration" (6). Perhaps the defendants' strongest point was testimony from Representative Paul Valandra, the tribal member who represented District 27, who wanted no changes to District 27 (8).

Like the plaintiffs' brief, the defendants' proposed findings included an extensive discussion of statistical methodology. The brief denounced the methodology used by Professor Cole – ecological regression – as "gibberish," even though it is widely accepted by the courts (12). The defendants also took issue with Professor Cole's use of homogeneous precinct analysis and said it was "of little use" (28).

The defendants' brief then turned to the first *Gingles* factor, numerosity and compactness, and argued that, because of low turnout, the state was justified in placing a "supermajority" of Indian voters in a single district (29–40). In contrast, the legislative districts suggested by the ACLU "contain bizarre or uncouth shapes" (38). As a result, the brief argued, "the plaintiffs necessarily fail to prove the existence of the first *Gingles* factor" (40).

The defendants' proposed findings combined the second and third *Gingles* factors into one section, which focused on different cutoff points regarding cohesiveness and polarization:

> Plaintiffs insist that polarization is shown "when a majority of the voters of one race would elect different candidates than would the majority of voters of the other race." Cole, p. 6. This standard of polarization must be rejected. It makes trivial the definition of cohesiveness, essentially defining it as 50% plus one, and it makes trivial the definition of white bloc voting, again making it essentially 50% plus one. (45)

The defendants argued that the split must be at least 60/40 to constitute cohesion and polarization (46) and concluded: "Plaintiffs have thus failed to show dilution of the minority's right to vote even using their own statistics" (48).

Next, the defendants' proposed findings turned to their explanation of why Indians do not participate in state and local politics on an equal basis with whites and argued that it is due to Indians' preference for tribal over state government: "The special relationship of the Indian tribes and the United States is a significant reason that tribal members declined to participate in State political matters" (50). This special relationship creates advantages for Indians: "Among the opportunities available to tribal members who [sic] are not ordinarily available to state legislators or local government leaders is the opportunity to testify before Congress" (53). The gap between whites and Indians in socioeconomic well-being is explained, according to the defendants, by "the fact that tribal members tend to be less materialistic than non-members" and by "placing land in trust [has a] significant adverse effect on productivity" (60). In addition, "the failure of tribes to live up to their contracts hurts the economic status of the tribes" (62).

The defendants then argued that, rather than having a history of discrimination, the state of South Dakota had provided numerous services and benefits to Indians, that voting in the state is an unusually open and fair process (63–84), and that Native Americans "have a long and consistent history of being elected and appointed to public office in Districts 26 and 27" (84).

The competing motions for summary judgment and the proposed findings of fact filed by each side clearly demonstrated the complexity of a Section 2 claim. These documents also reveal vastly different interpretations of everything from statistical methodology to historical fact to explanations of Indian poverty. At the trial, which lasted for nine days, each side presented a large number of lay witnesses in addition to their experts.

The Decision

On September 15, 2004, Judge Karen Schreier issued a 144-page opinion (*Bone Shirt v. Hazeltine* 2004c). It is a comprehensive, detailed explanation of each of the many factors that must be considered in a Section 2 case. With meticulous care, Judge Schreier summarized the history and background of the case, then evaluated the claims of both parties in regard to each *Gingles* test and each Senate criterion. In doing so, she evaluated competing methodologies, passed judgment on the validity of the reports filed by each side's experts, and determined the credibility of lay witnesses.

Judge Schreier noted that Representative Valandra and Senator Richard "Dick" Hagen, the American Indian legislators from District 27, had spoken out against changing the district boundary lines, but "the court gives little weight to this evidence because as incumbents, they had a vested interest in resisting change to their district's boundaries" (985). In contrast, the court found Representative James Bradford to be "highly credible" (985). Bradford also represented District 27, is of Indian heritage, and had requested that the legislature change the district's boundaries to create an additional Indian majority district – a proposal that was rejected by a decisive vote in the legislature.

Judge Schreier dismissed the defendants' claim that a supermajority of 65 percent Indian was required in any proposed remedy (990), but then noted that most of the new districts proposed by plaintiffs actually met that standard (991). She also dismissed the defendants' claims that the proposed remedies were impermissibly race-based and failed to account for communities of interest, noting that drawing racial distinctions is permissible when it serves a "compelling state interest" and that the proposed districts "are no more irregular than the current districting plan" (992). Thus, she found that the plaintiffs met the first *Gingles* test (995).

In evaluating the second Gingles test, the judge delved into the sticky controversy over methodology. She summarized the three most popular statistical methods used in Section 2 cases, then indicated that the most probative elections are interracial, endogenous, and recent (996). First, she examined Dr. Cole's analysis in considerable detail and summarized his findings. She disputed the defendants' characterization of his definition of cohesion as 50 percent plus one, noting that that was simply a starting point and indicated only weak cohesion (997). Next, the judge examined Dr. Zax's report. Given the level of disagreement that preceded the trial, one would think that the two reports had nothing in common, but the judge found that both had consistent definitions of cohesion (999). She noted that Zax found high levels of Indian cohesion in nearly every kind of race except ballot issues, but that "the court does not give these results any weight, however. Defendants have not explained why or how Indian voting behavior with regard to ballot issues would be probative of vote dilution" (1000).

Judge Schreier then took a close look at the competing methodologies offered by Cole and Zax. She pointed out that ecological regression was widely accepted by the courts, and even Zax had relied upon it in previous testimony (1001). While acknowledging some problems with ecological regression, she noted that it was still relatively reliable (1002). She also approved of homogeneous precinct analysis but admitted that it had some limitations too (1003). In regard to Zax's method of choice, ecological inference, she also recognized its reliability, but noted that Zax did not give more weight to endogenous and interracial contests, which are more probative (1003). The judge then concluded that all three methods are acceptable and that they produce very similar results. In this case, both experts found high levels of Indian cohesion (1004). She also examined nonstatistical evidence of cohesion, relying upon the reports of McCool, Lawson, and lay witnesses, and found considerable evidence of Indian cohesion (20–3). Thus, the second *Gingles* factor was satisfied (1010).

In discussing the third *Gingles* factor, the judge quoted the *Buckanaga* court: "The presence of racially polarized voting 'will ordinarily be the keystone of a vote dilution case'" (1010). In other words, racial polarization had to be demonstrated decisively for a successful Section 2 claim. The judge pointed out that the most important races for ascertaining polarization were those in white-majority districts (1011). This is critical because the VRA is concerned with the inability of minorities to elect candidates of their choice; in a majority-minority district, such as District 27, this is not a problem. Thus, the most probative races are those where racial minorities are also numerical minorities; in such districts, do whites and Indians consistently vote for different candidates?

To answer that question, the judge adroitly compiled a spreadsheet that included the results of both Cole's and Zax's analyses, with elections arranged according to their probativity. She excluded elections that rank low in probativity such as ballot issues, Bennett County elections, and elections more than twelve years old – all of which were included in Zax's sample. This probative ranking of elections was exactly what was missing from Zax's analysis, and the court rejected his "skewed" conclusions (1016). Instead, "considering all this evidence in the aggregate," the court concluded that the white majority in District 26 "votes sufficiently as a bloc to enable it . . . usually to defeat the [Indian] preferred candidate" (1017).

The judge then embarked on a point-by-point assessment of the Senate factors. Perhaps the most important of these is the history of discrimination; the judge wrote about this factor for sixteen pages, and concluded:

> Based on the wealth of evidence and testimony in this case, the court concludes that there is a long and extensive history of discrimination against Indians in South Dakota that touches upon the right to register and to vote, and affects their ability to participate in the political process on an equal basis with other citizens. Indeed, Indians faced voting discrimination in both the Dakota Territory and the state of South Dakota, ranging from outright vote denial to more subtle restrictions on the right to vote. The effects of this history are ongoing (1034).

The judge then returned to the question of polarization, the second factor, and found that "substantial evidence, both statistical and lay, demonstrates that voting in South Dakota is racially polarized among whites and Indians in Districts 26 and 27" (1036). In regard to the third factor – the use of discriminatory voting procedures – the judge noted that South Dakota had taken measures to improve access and participation, but that this was outweighed by the multimember system in the state house (1037). The fourth factor – a slating process – was of minor consequence.

The fifth factor provoked considerable discussion. The judge presented a comprehensive picture of socioeconomic disparities between whites and Indians, finding that Indians bear the effects of discrimination in education, employment, and health and that this hinders their ability to participate in politics (1041). For all of the remaining factors, the judge unequivocally found in favor of the plaintiffs (1041–52), and concluded that "Indians in Districts 26 and 27 have been denied an equal opportunity to access the political process. The current legislative Plan impermissibly dilutes the Indian vote and violates Section 2 of the Voting Rights Act" (1052).

The state of South Dakota appealed the *Bone Shirt* case to the Eighth Circuit Court of Appeals, but lost. The appellate court affirmed the lower court's decision to impose the plaintiffs' remedial plan (*Bone Shirt v. Hazeltine* 2006).

Conclusion

Redistricting is a responsibility of the states, and thus it is state government that must correct deficiencies in districts that have been found to be in violation of the VRA. The state of South Dakota was ordered to correct the problems with Districts 26 and 27. However, the state legislature chose not to act on the court's decision, so in August 2005, the district court issued a remedial order based on recommendations made by the plaintiffs (*Bone Shirt v. Hazeltine* 2005).

The *Bone Shirt* case is only one of numerous VRA cases that have been filed in South Dakota (see McDonald, Pease, and Guest 2006; South Dakota Equal Justice Commission 2006). It reflects the continuing animosity between whites and Indians in that state, but it also creates a forum for both sides to engage in a dialogue and possibly create an electoral system that meets everyone's needs. As more Indians get elected to the legislature, they may help sensitize state officials to Indian issues and thus avoid future litigation.

The *Bone Shirt* case also demonstrates the complexity of a Section 2 claim; the briefs and decisions filed in the case filled hundreds of pages and had to address a litany of issues using complex and controversial methodologies. Also, it is important to remember that this was no cut-and-dried example of whites overtly and purposefully standing in the way of Indian voters while screaming racist epithets. There was no Lester Maddox handing out axe handles; there was no Governor George Wallace standing in the doorway. The issues in this case were much more nuanced, much more susceptible to interpretation; today very few people openly espouse electoral racism. However, the resulting impact may be much the same; a vote not cast, for reasons that are either subtle or overt, has the same effect on the outcome of an election. In the same manner, a vote that does not count because of packing, cracking, or some other form of voting abridgment is equally repugnant to the concept of an open and fair democratic process. The *Bone Shirt* case alerted both Indian and non-Indian people in South Dakota that electoral fairness matters and that advocates for voting rights are willing to go to great lengths to support that goal.

7

An Equal Opportunity

The Impact of the Voting Rights Act

The Voting Rights Act (VRA) of 1965 and its subsequent amendments unquestionably changed the nature of the American political system. Within ten years of its passage, more blacks were registering, voting, running for elected office, and winning, due directly or indirectly to the VRA, (U.S. Commission on Civil Rights 1975, 39). The significant gains in black participation and the success of black candidates have been thoroughly studied; however, little research exists regarding the effects of the VRA on American Indians. Has the VRA resulted in increased registration and turnout among Indians? Has the act affected the success rate of Indian candidates? Once Indians are elected, are they able to become influential players in the political process and affect policies?

This chapter attempts to answer these questions. The first section explores the impact of the language provisions on registration and turnout among American Indians. The second section examines the success of Indian candidates after at-large electoral systems are dismantled. The third section focuses on the impact Indian elected officials have on public policy in those jurisdictions that have abandoned atlarge elections as a result of litigation.

The Impact on Registration and Turnout

The VRA of 1965 directly influenced the number of registered blacks in the seven southern states originally targeted by the act.[1] Within seven years,

[1] The seven states originally targeted by the 1965 VRA are Alabama, Georgia, Louisiana, Mississippi, South Carolina, Virginia, and parts of North Carolina.

more than 1 million blacks registered to vote, more than doubling the number of registered black voters prior to 1965 (U.S. Commission on Civil Rights 1975, 40). The abolition of poll taxes and literacy tests combined with the use of federal examiners is credited with these significant gains (Alt 1994).

In 1975 Congress recognized that elections held only in English constituted barriers to registration and voting just as great for non-English speakers or those with limited proficiency as literacy tests had been for African Americans. Implementation of the bilingual provisions of the 1975 amendments, often forced by litigation, has increased registration and turnout among language minorities. Hispanic and Asian-American participation rates are significantly higher in areas with language assistance compared to those without such assistance. The effects of bilingual assistance remain after controlling for various demographic factors including education, poverty, nativity, residential mobility, and English proficiency (Jones-Correa and Ramakrisham 2004).

Language assistance provided to American Indian voters has had similar positive effects on registration and turnout. We examined registration and turnout in two jurisdictions, San Juan County, Utah, and the state of New Mexico, which implemented bilingual voter programs following litigation. San Juan County implemented a bilingual program in 1984 following a Section 203 case filed by the Department of Justice. We examined twenty years of registration and voting data provided by the San Juan county clerk. In addition, interviews with elected officials and the bilingual program coordinator in San Juan County were conducted to determine the impact of the bilingual program on registration and turnout. Participation rates among Navajos in San Juan County increased substantially following the settlement of the Section 203 case in 1984 (*U.S. v. San Juan County, Utah* 1983b*). Registration in five precincts heavily populated by Navajos rose from 1,719 in 1984 to 3,358 in 2004, an increase of 95 percent. Turnout in those five precincts during the twenty-year period jumped from 1,000 voters to 1,480, an increase of 48 percent.[2] Turnout in 1984 within the selected precincts was 58 percent among registered voters. In 2004, turnout among registered voters in the same precincts declined to

[2] The five precincts selected for analysis are located on the Utah portion of the Navajo Reservation. They are Precincts 2, 3, 13, 14, and 16. All except Precinct, 2 are located wholly on the reservation. Only a small portion of Precinct 2 is off the reservation. Precincts 1, 12, and 17 are only partially on the reservation and were excluded. The total Indian population of San Juan County grew from 5,622 in 1980 to 8,157 in 2000, an increase of 45 percent.

44 percent. The county clerk believes that the decline is actually due to duplicate registrations, not to a decline in voter turnout. According to the county clerk, approximately 800 names on the voter registration lists are duplicates. Most of these persons were registered on the reservation in 1990, during a large registration drive, causing the voter turnout percentage to decline. Again, the county clerk believes that the actual number of Indians who vote has not declined, but rather has increased (N. Johnson 2005b). The increase in registration and turnout among Indians is partially attributed to the implementation of the Navajo Language Election Information Program (N. Johnson 2004a; Stevens 2004; Tapaha 2004). Other factors including voter registration drives, holding tribal elections on the same day as county elections, and population growth may have also contributed to the increased participation among Navajos in San Juan County.

The experience of New Mexico after Section 203 litigation has been much like that of San Juan County. The state implemented a statewide Native American Election Information Program (NAEIP) in 1988 following a Section 203 suit filed by the Department of Justice (*U.S. v. State of New Mexico* 1988*). The NAEIP is the "only one of its kind in the nation" (James 2004). The program, located in the Secretary of State's Office, is staffed by a director and two Native American coordinators (James 2005). It is coordinated with eleven New Mexico counties and twenty-two tribes.[3] County and state election coordinators educate the Native American population on upcoming election issues, produce a candidate guide, interpret and translate election documents, and conduct voter registration drives (James 2004). A former coordinator for the NAEIP claims that there has been a "steady increase over the past years" in the number of Native Americans who registered to vote because of the NAEIP, but the data necessary to measure the increase have not been compiled (James 2004).[4] The Secretary of State's Office estimated the total number of American Indian registered voters in select precincts at 57,228

[3] The eleven counties are Bernalillo, Cibola, McKinley, Otero, Rio Arriba, Sandoval, San Juan, Santa Fe, Socorro, Taos, and Valencia. The twenty-two tribes are Jicarilla Apache Nation, Mescalero Apache Nation, Pueblo of Acoma, Pueblo of Isleta, Pueblo of Laguna, Pueblo of Picuris, Pueblo of Sandia, Pueblo of San Ildefonso, Pueblo of Santa Ana, Pueblo of Santo Domingo, Pueblo of Tesuque, Pueblo of Zuni, Pueblo of Cochiti, Pueblo of Jemez, Pueblo of Nambe, Pueblo of Pojoaque, Pueblo of San Felipe, Pueblo of San Juan, Pueblo of Santa Clara, Pueblo of Taos, Pueblo of Zia, and the Navajo Nation.

[4] The New Mexico Secretary of State's Office provided data only on the 2004 election. Data on the number of Indians registered and voting in past elections were not available.

in 2004. Turnout in those precincts was 36,420 in the November 2004 election.[5]

The Impact on Indian Candidates

Previous chapters provide an overview of various structures, including at-large systems, that hindered the ability of Indians to elect candidates of their choice. Research shows that the increase in the number of African American and Hispanic elected officials is due not just to ballot access, but also to the elimination of at-large and gerrymandered districts. At-large systems have been found to diminish the success of minority candidates (see Karnig 1976; Robinson and Dye 1978; Taebel 1978; Engstrom and McDonald 1981; Davidson and Korbel 1984; Grofman and Davidson 1994). Only a handful of studies have failed to show the detrimental effects of at-large elections on minority candidates (see Cole 1974, 1976; MacManus 1978; Welch and Karnig 1978). A 1994 study of eight southern states found that at-large elections reduce the success of African American candidates in municipalities and state legislatures. Dramatic gains in the number of African Americans elected to office occurred following the dismantling of at-large systems in cities (Grofman and Davidson 1994, 319).

Our research supports the finding that minority candidates are rarely successful when running in an at-large system. Our study examined nineteen jurisdictions in Indian Country where an at-large system had been used. In those jurisdictions, only six American Indians had ever been elected in an at-large system. We examined whether replacing an at-large system in these nineteen jurisdictions with a single-member system, a mixed system, or a cumulative voting system resulted in the election of Indian candidates. Our findings indicate that when at-large structures are replaced with single-member districts, Indian candidates are very successful. Indian candidates, however, are less successful in cumulative voting systems and mixed electoral systems in our study.

Single-Member Districts

The success of minority candidates has been largely attributed to the implementation of single-member districts. Handley and Grofman found

[5] Data for registration figures were provided by the NAEIP. The figure is for seventy-five precincts identified by the New Mexico Secretary of State's Office as having an Indian population of 80 percent or more.

that instituting single-member state legislative districts contributed to the increase in black legislators in the South (Handley and Grofman 1994, 341). Similar gains in the number of Hispanic elected officials occurred in Texas following the replacement of at-large systems with single-member or mixed systems (Grofman and Davidson 1994, 384). Engstrom and McDonald determined that at-large electoral structures underrepresent blacks more than district electoral structures. They also found that once a black population reaches about 15 percent of the total population, the type of electoral structure used to elect city council members has a greater influence than socioeconomic factors (Engstrom and McDonald 1981). Other studies support the finding that establishing single-member districts with a Latino population above 40 percent frequently results in the election of Latinos (Pachon and DeSipio 1992, 216).

Our findings indicate that American Indians are more successful in single-member systems than in at-large systems. We examined fifteen cases where the at-large system was replaced with single-member districts. In only one of the fifteen had an Indian won under the at-large system. In all but two instances, once the single-member district system was implemented, Indian candidates were successful.

The first at-large voting rights case in Indian Country challenged Thurston County, Nebraska's, system for electing county supervisors (*U.S. v. Thurston County, Nebraska*, 1978*). Under the at-large system, no Indian had ever been elected to the seven-member board of supervisors. Thurston County agreed to replace its at-large system for electing the board with a single-member system in 1979. Two of the seven districts, District 4 and District 6, were majority Indian. The first election under the district system in 1980 resulted in the election of Ed McCauley, a Native American, from District 6. McCauley was reelected in 1984 (Moore 2005). In 1993, Thurston County was again involved in voting rights litigation. The court ruled that at-large methods for electing school board members or members of the Wathill Village Board of Supervisors did not violate Section 2 of the VRA; however, the court found that the plaintiffs were entitled to a districting plan that provided three Native American majority districts for the Thurston County board of supervisors (*Stabler v. Thurston County* 1997). Included in the court's ruling was the fact that District 6 has consistently elected an Indian since 1980. As of 2005, two of the seven board members are Native American. Paul Snowball, a member of the Winnebago tribe (Snowball 2005), and Darren Wolf, a member of the Omaha tribe, were elected in 2004 (Wolf 2005).

Similar changes in electoral structures were enacted in counties throughout the West. In San Juan County, New Mexico, no American Indian has ever been elected to the county commission under the at-large system. The county agreed to implement a single-member system following a lawsuit filed by the Department of Justice (*U.S. v. San Juan County, New Mexico* 1979a*). As of 2005, two of the five commissioners, Wallace Charley and Ervin Chavez, are Native American (Charley 2005; Chavez 2005). San Juan County, Utah, has a similar story. There several American Indians ran unsuccessfully for the commission under the at-large system in the 1970s. In 1984, the county agreed to replace that system with a single-member system (*U.S. v. San Juan County, Utah* 1983a*, Agreed Settlement and Order, April 4, 1984). The first election under the single-member system in 1986 resulted in the election of Mark Maryboy, a Navajo. Maryboy held the position until 2002, when he chose not to seek reelection. Manuel Morgan, a Navajo, won the seat in 2002. Cibola County, New Mexico, relied on an at-large system for electing its county commissioners, under which no American Indian was elected. In 1985, the National Indian Youth Council (NIYC) sued the county for violating Section 2 of the Voting Rights Act. The case was settled in 1987, and the county agreed to replace its at-large system with a single-member system (*Felipe and Ascencio v. Cibola County Commission* 1985*). As of 2005, two of the five commissioners, Freddie Scott and Bennie Cohoe, are Native American.

Four counties in Montana replaced their at-large systems for electing commissioners with single-member systems following lawsuits. No Indian had ever been elected to the commissions in Big Horn County, Roosevelt County, Rosebud County, or Blaine County under the at-large system. Big Horn County dismantled its at-large system in 1986 following a court order (*Windy Boy v. Big Horn County* 1986). John Doyle, Jr., was the first Native American elected to the three-person commission under the single-member system in 1987 (Doyle 2005). He believes his election was the direct result of the case (Doyle 2005). In addition to Doyle, John Pretty-on-Top, also a Native American, holds a seat on the Big Horn Commission (Pretty-on-Top 2005).

Neighboring Roosevelt County replaced its at-large system with three single-member districts in 2000 following a consent agreement with the Department of Justice (*U.S. v. Roosevelt County* 2000*). One of the three districts is majority-Indian; the other two are majority-white. Gary McDonald, a Native American, was appointed to the board in 1999 and was elected in 2000 (McDonald 2005).

Rosebud County dismantled its at-large system in 2000 following a court order (*Alden v. Board of Commissioners of Rosebud County* 1999*, Order, May 9, 2000). The county currently elects its three commissioners by districts, one of which is majority-Indian. However, there has yet to be an American Indian candidate since the change; no American Indian currently sits on the commission (Custer 2005). Blaine County instituted a single-member system in 2002, as required by the court (*U.S. v. Blaine County*, Findings of Fact and Conclusions of Law and Order, March 21, 2002). Of the three districts, one is majority-Indian. The first election under the new system in 2002 resulted in the election of Dolores Plumage, the first American Indian ever elected to the Blaine County Commission.

School districts have also been sued under Section 2 of the VRA and forced to implement single-member districts. School board members in Holbrook Unified School District No. 3 in Navajo County, Arizona, were elected at-large until 1989, when the district implemented a single-member system (*Clark v. Holbrook Unified School District* 1989). No Native American had ever been elected under the at-large system. Currently, two of the five board members, Alfred Clark and Linda Yazzi, are Native American. In the mid-1980s, the NIYC filed lawsuits against four New Mexico school districts. The suits claimed that the at-large method for electing school board members violated Section 2 of the VRA. The Grant-Cibola County School District implemented a single-member district following a lawsuit (*Estevan v. Grants-Cibola County School District*, 1984*). Currently, two of the five board members, Lloyd Felipe and Rita Suazo, are Native American (Felipe 2005). In 1986, the McKinley Consolidated School District in New Mexico agreed to implement a single-member plan for electing school board members (*Largo v. McKinley Consolidated School District* 1984*). Currently, three board members, Mavis V. Price, Johnny R. Thompson, and Adreanne Sloan, are Native American. The Cuba Independent School District agreed to replace its at-large system for electing school board members with a single-member system in 1987 (*Tso v. Cuba Independent School District* 1985*). The five-member school board currently has three Native American members: Marlene Waukazoo, Theresa Castillo, and Wally Toledo. The Bernalillo School School District agreed in 1988 to replace its at-large system for electing board members with a single-member system (*Bowannie v. Bernalillo School District* 1988*). As of 2005, two of the five school board members are Native American: Lorenzo Tafoya and Ray Trujillo.

The San Juan College Board in Farmington, New Mexico, used an at-large system to elect its members until 1987, when ordered by a court to adopt a single-member system (*Kirk v. San Juan College Board* 1986*). Under the at-large system, only one Indian had ever been elected to the five-member board. The seven-member board is now elected under a single-member system. Currently, two board members, Evelyn Benny and Eva Stokely, are Native American.

The city of Gallup, New Mexico, also relied upon an at-large system for electing members of the city council until it was sued in 1986 under the VRA (*Casuse v. City of Gallup* 1987). Under the at-large system, no Native American had ever been elected to the four-member city council. The single-member system was enacted in 1987; however, no American Indian has yet been elected to the city council (Rosebrough 2005).

Cumulative Voting Systems

Single-member systems are only one method of resolving vote dilution problems; cumulative voting systems are another (McDonald 1989, 1284). A cumulative voting system can be an effective alternative to at-large systems, especially when minority voters are too geographically dispersed to constitute a majority in a single-member district (Engstrom and Barrilleaux 1991, 392). African American candidates have been extremely successful under cumulative voting systems. Futhermore, there is no evidence that cumulative systems have an adverse effect on local politics or undermine American democratic traditions (McDonald 1989, 1284).

Hispanic success under cumulative systems has been mixed. A study of fifteen cumulative systems with large Hispanic populations in Texas indicates the limited success of Hispanic candidates. In the Texas jurisdictions studied in 1995, "Hispanics were elected in just over half of the elections in which they ran" (Brischetto and Engstrom 1997, 976). "Such mixed results raise doubts about the viability of cumulative voting as a remedy for minority vote dilution" (976). Research indicates that four factors must be present for Hispanic candidates to win in cumulative systems (Brischetto and Engstrom 1997; Brockinton and Donovan 1998). First, there must be a sufficient number of Hispanic voters. Second, voter cohesion is necessary. Third, voter mobilization efforts, including registration drives, education, and get-out-the-vote efforts, are needed to get voters to the polls. Finally, minority candidates must be recruited. In five of the elections studied by Brischetto and Engstrom (1997), there were no Hispanic candidates (988–9).

In two instances, cumulative voting systems have replaced at-large structures following a voting rights case in Indian Country. The Sisseton School District in South Dakota implemented a cumulative voting system as required by a consent decree (*Buckanaga v. Sisseton School District* 1986, Consent Decree, 1988). The success of Native American candidates in the at-large system had been limited. No Indian served on the school board until 1967, when Francis Crawford was appointed to serve an unexpired term. Crawford won the seat in a 1968 election; she ran unopposed. Two other Indians won under the at-large system: Hildreth Venegas in 1973 and Daryl Russell in 1982 (*Indian Country Today*, October 24, 1984, 2). The first election using cumulative voting was held in June 1989 and resulted in the election of David Selvage, a Native American (Karst 2005). Celine Buckanaga, a plaintiff in the case, attributes Selvage's success to canvassing efforts, informing voters about the new system, and getting the voters to the polls on election day: "... we just worked every day canvassing the people, encouraging them to vote. On that day of voting we gave them rides and we told them they could cast all three of their votes on this one Indian person" (Buckanaga 2005). Selvage chose not to seek reelection in 1993, when his term expired. Although an Indian woman ran for the school board in 2001, no other Indian has been elected under the cumulative system (anonymous interview). Buckanaga believes that two or three of the seven seats could be won by Native Americans, but it would require more canvassing to encourage people to run and to vote (Buckanaga 2005).

In 2003 the Wagner School District in South Dakota agreed to implement a cumulative voting system to elect its seven school board members (*Weddell v. Wagner Community School District* 2002*). Only one Native American had been elected to the school board under the at-large system (Kent 2002). Under the cumulative system, one Indian candidate was elected in 2003 and another in 2004 (Smith 2005). Two Native Americans, John Sully and Raymond Cournoyer, currently sit on the seven-person school board.

Mixed Systems

Single-member and cumulative voting systems are the most common solutions for vote dilution problems. Mixed electoral systems are the third solution. These systems are a combination of at-large and single-member districts. Some members are elected from districts; others are elected at-large (Davidson and Grofman 1994, 7). Mixed electoral systems often result in the election of minority candidates; however,

TABLE 7.1. *Ronan School District Population*

District	Population	White Voting-Age Population	Indian Voting-Age Population	Percent of Voting-Age Population That Is Indian
1	1,852	1,174	707	60%
2	4,494	3,072	553	18%
Total	6,346	4,246	1,260	30%

Source: Matt v. Ronan School District (1999*).

minority candidates are usually elected from single-member districts. Grofman and Davidson's study of eight states found that black officeholding in mixed systems was "largely or almost entirely the result of black success in the district component of the plan" (1994, 319). Mixed systems have been required by the courts in only one Native American case. In 1990, Montezuma-Cortez School District in Colorado agreed to replace the at-large system for electing school board members with a mixed system (*Cuthair v. Montezuma-Cortez, Colorado School District*, 1998). The mixed system resulted in one single-member district. The majority of the voting-age population in the single-member district is Native American. However, there is still a significant non–Native American population there (Thompson 2005). The six remaining board members are elected at-large. A Native American has yet to be elected to the school board.

Multimember Plans

A fourth solution to at-large electoral structures is a multimember plan. The Ronan School District in Montana abolished its at-large system for electing school board members following a court order in 2000 (*Matt v. Ronan School District*, 1999*, Order, January 13, 2000). Prior to 2000, the five school trustees were elected at-large, and although Native Americans ran seventeen times since the early 1970s, only one was successful. The U.S. District Court for Montana ordered the district to establish two multimember districts for the seven trustees. District 1, which is majority Indian, elects two trustees. District 2, which is majority white, elects five trustees (see Table 7.1).

The first election using the multimember plan resulted in the election of two Native Americans, Patty Stevens and Ron Koutere, both from District 1. In 2002, Jason Adams, also an American Indian, was elected to

Ron Koutere's seat (Adams 2004; Stevens 2005a). Ms. Stevens attributes her success directly to the voting rights case (Stevens 2005a). "I am an elected member of the Ronan Board of Trustees as a direct result of this case. I know there wouldn't be two Indians on the Board without this case" (Stevens 2005b). Mr. Adams also attributes his success to the case: "I think it gave me a fair opportunity to participate in the process" (Adams 2004).

Impact on Policy

The previous two sections have discussed the effect of the VRA on minority enfranchisement and the success of Indian candidates once at-large voting systems are dismantled. This section explores the impact of Indian-elected officials on policy outcomes. Research indicates that minority officeholding is associated with substantial shifts in "responsiveness to minority interests and the inclusion of minorities in decisionmaking" (McDonald 1989, 1277). We examine whether elected officials perceive a shift in responsiveness in jurisdictions that elected Indian candidates after at-large electoral structures were dismantled.

The experiences of African Americans demonstrate that those lacking the capacity to influence government received few public benefits (Morris 1984, 271). "Their streets were the last paved or went unpaved; they were the farthest from the parks and recreational facilities; their neighborhoods were less frequently or properly patrolled by the police; and in virtually all areas of benefit distribution, they were generally served last and least" (271). In contrast, representation in the political arena leads to a variety of benefits.

Numerous studies have found that African Americans elected to office increase the benefits to the African American community (see Keech 1968; Cole 1976; Campbell and Faegin 1975; Dye and Renick 1981; Eisinger 1982; Browing, Marshall, and Tabb 1984). Campbell and Faegin found that black elected officials have provided constituents with benefits in employment, housing, health care, education, consumer protection, police relations, and psychological recognition (156). Browning, Marshall, and Tabb reached similar conclusions. They determined that black and Hispanic city council members are associated with changes in four policy areas: police civilian review boards, minority appointments to boards and commissions, city contracts with minority firms, and minority employment. Other studies, noted subsequently, have confirmed these findings.

African American elected officials are associated with increases in minorities in government jobs (see Dye and Renick 1981; Eisinger 1982; Browning, Marshall, and Tabb 1984; Mladenka 1989). Eisinger found that black employment in city government is a function of the size of the black population and the presence of a black mayor. His study of forty-three cities with black populations above 10 percent found that the presence of a black mayor is the best predictor of black employment. It appears that black city council members have little influence on personnel policies and thus are unrelated to the level of black employment (388). Other studies found that Hispanic representation on city councils increases the number of Hispanics in government jobs (Dye and Renick 1981; Browning, Marshall, and Tabb 1984; Mladenka 1989). Dye and Renick found that Hispanic city council members are associated with greater Hispanic employment in administrative, professional, and protective jobs. They regard Hispanic city council members as the single most important determinant of those types of jobs. For less prestigious office jobs and service work, such as truck drivers, custodians, groundskeepers, and clerks, Hispanic representation on the city council is not essential (Dye and Renick 1981, 483–4). Other studies have found that Hispanic school board members have a positive effect on the number of Hispanic teachers (Fraga, Meier, and England 1997, 295).

Minority elected officials also increase minority access to the political process. A twenty-year-old study of ten cities in California found that the presence of African American and Hispanic city council members increased minority access to city councils and changed the decision-making process (Browning, Marshall, and Tabb 1984). The authors were "told repeatedly that minority council members were important in linking minorities to city hall, providing role models, and in sensitizing white colleagues to minority concerns" (141). Smith, Kedrowski, and Ellis (2004) examined the effect of electoral structures on school boards and school desegregation efforts. In addition to finding that single-member districts increase the number of African American board members, they found that African Americans' presence on school boards facilitates desegregation. In the Rock Hill School District of South Carolina, the all-white school board replaced its at-large system with a mixed system after receiving a notice letter from Department of Justice indicating their intent to file a Section 2 VRA case. The seven members of the school board are now elected under a mixed system; two are elected at-large, and five are elected by single-member districts. The November 2000 election resulted in the election of two African Americans, who made desegregation a high priority. Other studies have confirmed that the election of minorities to public office makes a difference in public policies. Cole's study of sixteen New Jersey cities found that minorities elected to city office influence the formation and implementation of public policies in areas such as jobs, housing, food, health care, day care, education, and job training (Cole 1976, 221–3).

The election of minorities to public office can have a substantial impact beyond public policy. Research confirms that minority elected officials also sensitize white colleagues, act as role models for minorities, reverse images of white superiority, and provide a sense of legitimacy for blacks who hold office (Cole 1976, 221–3). Eisenger also found that minority city council members provide role models and sensitize white colleagues to minority concerns (1982, 141). McDonald concluded that increased minority officeholding has provided "minority role models, conferred racial dignity, and helped dispel the myth that minorities were incapable of political leadership. It also required whites to deal with minorities more nearly as equals, a change in political relationships whose implications have been profound" (1992, 80).

Although most studies indicate that the election of minorities to public office positively affects policies concerning the minority community, others have found that majority-minority districts must be carefully designed or they can undermine substantive representation of minority interests. Epstein and O'Halloran examined the impact of alternative districting plans on substantive representation of minority interests in South Carolina, focusing specifically on "whether the effect of electing a minority candidate to office gains more than it loses in terms of support for minority-sponsored legislation" (1999b, 386). Their analysis revealed that (1) minorities may win office outside majority-minority districts; (2) majority-minority districts may overconcentrate minority voters, to the detriment of their impact on policy; and (3) a "race-neutral approach to districting will probably result in a minimization of minority influence on public policy, as minorities do still face significant difficulties in gaining office. Consequently, the argument favoring some degree of concentrated minority districts remains strong" (394).

To assess the impact of Indian officeholders on policy, we conducted fifty semistructured interviews with Indian and non-Indian elected officials in jurisdictions that had dismantled their at-large systems as a result of VRA litigation. The interviews were conducted by telephone with current officeholders in fourteen jurisdictions.[6] We consider these individuals "elites" – influential, prominent, and/or well informed about an organization or a community. Elites are more likely than others to be familiar with the legal and financial structures of the political body, and are able to report on the organization's policies, history, and future plans (Marshall and Rossman 1999, 113). Semistructured interviews allow a researcher to gain detail, depth, and an insider's perspective on a research question (Leech 2002, 665). We relied upon open-ended questions, which are potentially the most valuable because they provide flexibility, allow follow-up questions, and do not force respondents to make categorical answers predetermined by the researcher.

In 2005, seventy-two people served as elected officials in the fourteen jurisdictions in this study (see Table 7.2); twenty were Indian and fifty-two were non-Indian. We conducted interviews with fifteen of the twenty Indians officials and thirty-five of the fifty-two non-Indian officials.[7] Several officials requested anonymity; therefore, we will not identify any individuals because, in doing so, we may reveal the identities of others. The interviews were conducted between December 2004 and April 2005. We asked each Indian elected official this question: "As an American Indian officeholder, what impact do you think you have had on laws and regulations, the delivery of services, Indian people's access to local government, and Indian people's perceptions about local government?" We a similar question of non-Indian officials: "What impact has the election of an American Indian had on laws and regulations, the delivery of service, Indian people's access to local government, and Indian people's perception about local government?"

Impact on Laws and Regulations

Seven of the fifteen Native American elected officials believed that they had made an impact on laws and regulations in their jurisdictions. In one jurisdiction, two Native Americans hold office. One believes that together they have been able to shift money to areas that were once ignored. This commissioner believes that having two Native Americans on the commission

[6] The authors identified nineteen jurisdictions that had used at-large elections, were sued under the VRA, and subsequently dismantled the at-large system. We attempted to conduct interviews with elected officials in all jurisdictions; however, we were only able to interview elected officials from fourteen jurisdictions.

[7] We attempted to contact all elected officials in the jurisdictions; however, not all agreed to participate in our study, and some we were unable to contact.

TABLE 7.2. *Number of Elected Officials in Selected Jurisdictions in 2005*

Jurisdiction	Total Number of Elected Officials	Native American Elected Officials	Non–Native American Elected Officials
Thurston County Commission, Nebraska	7	2	5
San Juan County Commission, New Mexico	5	2	3
Big Horn County Commission, Montana	3	2	1
Grants-Cibola School District, New Mexico	5	2	3
Sisseton School District, South Dakota	9	0	9
San Juan College Board, New Mexico	7	2	5
Gallup City, New Mexico	5	0	5
Holbrook Unified School District, Arizona	5	2	3
Roosevelt County Commission, Montana	3	1	2
Ronan School District, Montana	7	2	5
Rosebud County Commission, Montana	3	0	3
Wagner School District, South Dakota	7	2	5
McKinley School District, New Mexico	5	3	2
Cibola County Commission, New Mexico	5	2	3
Total	72	20	52

has made the biggest impact: "Before, [commissioner A] was by himself and he always got outvoted."

However, five other elected officials believed that they had no impact on laws and regulations. One commissioner replied that he "hasn't had any, because we're only one vote." Another commissioner said, "I don't believe so." He stated later in the interview that "I'm only one vote here, we get overrun on anything." School board members expressed similar disappointment. "I don't know that I've had any impact. I haven't, because it seems like the decisions and those things that myself and the other Native American person that's on the board, if we have any option or opportunity to express our view, we're in the minority. And so the issues that we feel are significant are just voted down." He noted two instances in which that happened. One dealt with the volatile school mascot issue in the district. Three of the Native American elected officials provided unclear replies to this question or simply did not answer.

Although Native American elected officials had mixed opinions about whether they were able to impact laws and regulations in their jurisdiction, several noted that they believed they were able to have input, advocate for Native American issues, and make others more aware of problems facing the Native American community. One school board member mentions that "Indian issues, if you will, are considered now, and I don't believe they were given fair consideration in the past." Another school board member stated that others on the school board are more aware of the problems facing Native American students. He also noted that because two of the board members are Native American, they are "able to have more relevant or pertinent Native American issues brought to the forefront and dealt with by the district."

In our interview, we did not directly ask about the elected officials' impact on employment; however, several mentioned that they believe they have increased the number of Native Americans working in government jobs and elected offices. One county commissioner noted that the elected officials in the county are mostly Native American. When we asked if this was the result of the voting rights lawsuit, he answered, "Yes. If you look at the length of time that the county has been in existence before versus since the case, it's obvious that is the reason." One school board member stated that more Native Americans are working in administrative positions and as teachers, and not just as janitors.

The responses from white elected officials in these fourteen jurisdictions were mixed when we asked, "What impact has the election of a Native American had on laws and regulations?" Fifteen white officials we interviewed stated that American Indian elected officials have had little or no impact on laws and regulations in their communities. However, many of them noted that having an American Indian on their commission or school board has provided American Indians in their community with a voice. This was reported by two white commissioners from the same county. Both of them also noted that the two Native American commissioners have been very effective on behalf of their constituents. Six white school board members noted that Native American board members may not have a major impact, but they have brought Native people's issues to the table, educating them about the needs of tribal members and providing more diverse views. One board member commented, "I don't know that it's had a major impact, but I think it's important to have them there for sure." A colleague responded that "It's definitely brought the [Indian] people's thoughts to the table on issues coming about, issues on the tribe and reservation land. The representatives come back and tell us about their needs." Another stated that "Having Native Americans on the board has been, I think, a positive." Board members from other school districts reiterated these comments. "It was my understanding that before this happened that Native Americans had attempted to run before but until that point none had been elected. From that point of view I think it was very good, because since that time we now have representation from some of our students' areas that we serve. So, in that sense, I think it's excellent that we have fair representation." A board member from another district also believes that having Native American school board members has "brought a wider view to the board," and his colleague stated that "I think the tribe is being well represented by the two members that are on the board. They bring the issues to the table."

One commissioner expressed concern over the costs of the VRA lawsuits that resulted in a single-member district system. He stated that the expense of the case had decreased the ability of the county to provide services. A related economic problem facing counties, according to two commissioners, is their inability to tax federal and reservation land. According to one commissioner, this places a large burden on the remaining citizens, the "taxpayers," to cover the costs of such things as schools and law enforcement. Further, he stated, Indians have "as much right to run for office" as anyone else, but it's wrong that "they don't pay for taxes."

Impact on Services

Most Native American elected officials we interviewed believed that they had an impact on the delivery of services in their jurisdiction. Of the seven county commissioners we interviewed, five responded that they had an impact on services, and two provided unclear responses or did not answer the question. Several commissioners described the differences in services and infrastructure under the at-large system compared to the single-member system. "Back when there was [sic] only three commissioners [under the at-large system], in the [Indian] community . . . there was no infrastructure in place – like basic health and safety issues that the rest of the county was enjoying. Fire stations, road maintenance, trash disposal, those sorts of things. Very little was done. When they went to the five commission districts, it improved about 100 percent because we now have fire districts throughout the county divided up evenly. We have trash pickup systems throughout the county. We also have roads that are being paved even in these Native American districts. So, the impact has been very positive overall and it continues to be so."

Commissioners in other communities believe that they have been able to improve the infrastructure in their counties by shifting funds to address the needs on the reservation that had been ignored under the at-large system. "A lot of the road projects were ignored on the reservation side of the county." "A lot of the services weren't going into the reservation. Now roads, sheriff, fire, just about every service that at one time was denied at the reservation is there. After we got in, we were able to do this." Another county commissioner initially stated that he had had no effect on services in his community; however, later in the interview, he said that Native Americans do seem to get a little better service when applying for license plates or other services at the county courthouse. On follow-up, he said that persons working in the county offices are "more polite. They're willing to help you when you step up to the counter. They don't pass you over and go to the white person, until you're the last person standing. It used to be that way."

The impact of Native Americans on school boards differs from that of county commissioners simply because of the jurisdictional differences. All five school board members we interviewed believed that they had an impact on services in their school districts. Three mentioned an impact on the curriculum, particularly the incorporation of Native American languages, history, and culture. One stated that by being on the school board, he is able to provide input on curriculum issues. When curriculum policies come before the board for consideration, "we have the opportunity to look through and consider and make sure that the other board members and administrators within the schools have considered the Indian perspective on different curriculums that are being proposed." Two Native American school board members noted that since they have joined the school board, classes on Native American language and culture have been added to the curriculum in their districts. One stated that when he joined the board, the district offered no classes in native history, culture and tradition; now it does. "That's a big impact for our Native people here in our area." One school board member stated that she pushed for a policy to send all new teachers to the reservation to see "firsthand . . . where their students were coming from."

We also asked white elected officials what impact the election of an Indian has had on the delivery of services. Three of them, one commissioner and two school board members, responded that American Indians have definitely impacted services. One school board member noted that requests from Native American board members resulted in the establishment of a Native American education office. Another school board member stated: "I think that yes, I think absolutely it has had a very positive impact." She pointed out a new school on the reservation that was built by the district. "It has a definite impact because we have little ones that don't need to ride the bus for long periods of time anymore. So, that was a positive impact. And because we have two Native American board members, it helped to move that process along." Other officials disagreed. Five county commissioners believed that the Native American commissioners in their jurisdictions had little or no impact on services. One replied that the voting rights lawsuit that resulted in the establishment of single-member districts had cost the county $200,000, and "that has decreased the ability of the county to provide services." Seven school board members stated that the impact of Indian members has been little or none. One believes that the single-member district system that resulted in the election of a Native American has divided the community. Five individuals did not respond to the question.

Access to Government

We asked each interviewee if having an American Indian elected official has impacted Indian people's access to government and their perception of government. Of the fifteen Native American elected officials interviewed, eleven said yes, one said no, and three did not address the question. One commissioner responded that he has had no impact on Native Americans' access to government. On follow-up, he replied, "Not really. It gives them a little therapy now and again, and then they're back to their old racist ways." Most others believed that as an American Indian elected officials, they have had a positive impact on Native American people's access to government. One commissioner stated, "Having a Native American on the county commission opened the door and created a better working relationship between the reservation community and the off-reservation community." A commissioner from the same county agreed, saying, "It has opened up a lot of access to the county government." In other counties, commissioners generally agreed that "just by being here," they make a difference. One commissioner stated, "I'm all over, I'm talking to everyone constantly. And when there's an issue/concern that deals with county government, I invite them to come in and visit with the board or whoever they need to visit with. And if they want me to be present, I'll be there."

His colleague agreed, noting that Indian people are starting to meet with commissioners. In another county, the Indian commissioner believed that his presence improves access to government. He points out that he meets with tribal members and the council to keep them informed about issues in county government, and "That really does help."

School board members also agreed that their presence has increased access to government for Native people. One stated, "Access to the board has been a lot easier." Another noted the difference in access before she was elected. "Before, you couldn't just come to a meeting and just comment on anything. So, I tried to shift it to make it more of a friendly place for people in the community to be a part of." She believes her efforts have paid off. "The school board became more of a community-friendly place that you could go to, and I even had people say, 'Wow, it's really different coming to the board'." Her colleague responded, "On the school board, definitely, I think there's a lot more – the Indian people feel like they have a voice now and somebody they can feel comfortable talking to." Members of another school board agreed that "Yes, there has been an impact." One mentioned that "I feel that I have provided a lot."

Perception of Government

The Native American elected officials were asked if their presence had an impact on Indian people's perceptions of local government. Ten of the fifteen believed that Native Americans' perception of government had changed because of their presence, one believed that the results have been mixed, one said no, and three did not address the question.

One Indian commissioner said that a member of the county government travels to the reservation for meetings, talking with tribal staff to improve coordination and communication between leaders on and off the reservation. His colleague believed that Native Americans are participating more in county government. "I think they're now starting to take a more action role." "It's a real positive sign.... If you apply the same picture back in '78, you never saw that, but in the year 2004, 2005, you do." Another Indian county commissioner said that his presence has made a difference because "the tribe is seeing what we have done, shifting monies to where it's needed, not just to one area, one group, kind of an overall shift." Another responded positively as well, noting that the change in perception is due in part to the county's efforts to make sure that voting regulations are posted in both the tribal and county newspapers so that people are well informed. He believes that the redistricting processes a few years earlier may have spurred interest in county government, but this interest has been maintained by efforts of the city, county, and tribal governments. A commissioner from another county believes that his presence has made a difference as well.

Conclusion

The changes due to the VRA have been profound for American Indians. The implementation of bilingual election programs has directly increased voter registration and turnout among American Indians in the two communities in our study. The role of Section 2 has been equally important in altering the political landscape in Indian Country. In the nineteen jurisdictions in our study, only six American Indians had ever been elected under the at-large system. Replacement of this system with single-member districts resulted in remarkable gains in Indian officeholding. In the fifteen single-member systems in our study, there are currently twenty-five Native American elected officials. In only two of the fifteen districts has an Indian not yet been elected. The mixed results of Indian success in cumulative and mixed election systems are noteworthy. In the Sisseton and Wagner School Districts, cumulative voting systems replaced the at-large system. Under the at-large system, three Indians had been elected in the Sisseton District. Although one Indian was elected under the cumulative system, no Indian currently sits on the school board in Sisseton. In Wagner, one Indian had been elected under the at-large system. Currently, two of the seven board members are Indian. No Indian has ever been elected to the Montezuma Cortez School board under either the at-large system or the current mixed system. The multimember plan used in the Ronan school district has resulted in the election of three Indians. Currently, two sit on the board.

The election of Indian candidates has led to positive impacts on services, Indians' access to government, and Indians' perception of government. Our examination of fourteen jurisdictions and interviews with fifty elected officials demonstrate that while Indian elected officials are divided as to their own impact on laws and regulations, they overwhelmingly believe that they have had an impact on services in their community, access to government, and improved perception of government among Indians. This demonstrates the success of the VRA in changing both descriptive and substantive representation in Indian Country.

8

From Extermination to Electorate

Indians in American Politics

In the 1860s, Senator James Doolittle of Wisconsin played a prominent role in the debate over the Fourteenth Amendment and became a proponent of President Grant's "peace policy" toward Indians. On a fact-finding trip to Denver in 1866, Senator Doolittle addressed a crowd, asking rhetorically what should be done with the Indians. The crowd began screaming out a chant, "Exterminate them, exterminate them" (quoted in Goodrich 1997, 58). One hundred forty years later, in 2004, Indians comprised a critical voting bloc that was wooed by all sides: "From the Dakotas and Oklahoma to Arizona, California and Washington state, the Navajo, Cherokee, Yakima and other Native American tribes are being aggressively courted by both parties this year like never before" (Glionna 2004). Things have changed.

The political evolution of American Indians from the focus of ethnic cleansing to swing-vote electorate can be attributed to many factors, but without doubt the Voting Rights Act (VRA) has added meaning and substance to their right to vote. After over seventy lawsuits, Indians now have many legal victories. Chapter 7 demonstrated that many of these victories have led to tangible gains in terms of candidates elected and policies influenced. Where they have not, it is sometimes because Indians have not run for election or Indian voters have not turned out in sufficient numbers. Thus, efforts to mobilize Indian voters and candidates are crucial to fulfilling the potential created by legal victories.

This final chapter examines the role of Indians in recent elections, including voter mobilization efforts by Indian organizations and tribes, and the efforts of both political parties to attract Indian votes. We also point out continuing procedural problems and resistance, and describe how American Indians have expanded their political repertoire beyond voting to include lobbying, contributing to campaigns, and running for office. Finally, we assess the importance of the VRA for the future of American Indians and their role in our representative democracy.

The 2004 Native Vote Campaign

Efforts to mobilize Indian voters have been greatest in a few western swing states, where such voters can make the difference between defeat or victory in certain races. The year 2004 was not the first time that Indian voting power had been noticed, but it became prominent in that election season. In 2000, Indian voters had helped Maria Cantwell defeat Senator Slade Gorton, who was widely perceived as anti-Indian, and the Indian vote helped Al Gore carry New Mexico. Two years later, Indian voters again displayed their potential power. In South Dakota they provided the winning margin for Senator Tim Johnson in his very close reelection bid, and they were credited with helping to elect Governor Brad Henry in Oklahoma (Baker 2004). Janet Napolitano, the governor of Arizona, acknowledged at the 2004 Democratic National Convention that "Without the Native Americans, I wouldn't be standing here today" (Kraker 2004a).

Suddenly, everyone was interested in the Indian vote: "In the last few years, political races from Congress to county sheriff have begun to hinge on the Indian vote..." (Kershaw 2004). O. J. Semans, field director of an Indian get-out-the-vote organization called Four Directions, noted the stark change: "It's like somebody figured out we're here" (Kershaw 2004). In South Dakota, congressional candidate Stephanie Herseth told an American Indian audience:

> The Native vote in 2002 spoke loud and clear about the influence that you can have in our elections in every level of government. And to see the reaction nationally to the strength and to the influence of the Native vote in South Dakota and in other districts throughout [the state] is something which is clear. (Melmer 2004a).

At the beginning of the 2004 campaign, the National Congress of American Indians (NCAI), the same group that supported the *Harrison* case in 1948, took a leadership role in organizing Indian voters. They produced a publication, "Knowing Your Rights," that explained the VRA and its amendments and ended with a section titled "Who Can File a Complaint and How Can They Do It?" (National Congress of American

Indians 2004a). They also initiated a nationwide registration drive called "Native Vote 2004" and made a very ambitious commitment to deliver 1 million Indian votes in November. Their campaign was replete with bumper stickers and lapel buttons ("I'm Indian and I Vote" and "Native Vote"), a dedicated website (www.nativevote.org), and rallies. In a speech at Fort Belknap, NCAI president Tex Hall said, "To prosper, Montana Indian tribes must set priorities, mobilize voters and join with other tribes to push their shared agenda onto Washington's political stage..." (Miller 2004).

The NCAI also recognized that one of the impediments to increased Indian turnout was that many tribes held their tribal elections on a different date from the national elections. They sent out a survey to member tribes, noting that a "record number of Tribes are making proactive decisions to change their Tribal elections to coincide with the National elections," and offered assistance to make the change (National Congress of American Indians 2004b).

The NCAI's Native Vote 2004 campaign was mirrored by similar campaigns at the state and tribal levels. The Seneca Nation registered a record number of its members (Kettle 2004). In Oklahoma a unique "Rock the Native Vote" concert was organized, featuring Native American performers and a goal of registering 3,000 native voters and "rais[ing] the awareness of the importance of being active in the political arena" (Kernell 2004). The concert was part of a larger effort organized by the Oklahoma Indian Bar Association to increase voter turnout among the state's 252,000 Indians and field complaints from Indian voters on election day (Andrews Davis 2004).

On the Navajo Reservation, the venerable code talkers (World War II veterans who had used their native language as a code against the Japanese) traveled throughout the reservation, urging people to register and vote, and the Navajo Nation cosponsored a voter education forum with the Global Exchange (Lee 2004). In New Mexico, Indian voters were assisted by the state's Native American Election Information Program, which had been set up in direct response to the many VRA cases in that state in the 1980s (Lehman and Macy 2004, 29).

In and around Minnesota, an organization called National Voice led an effort to educate Native voters. According to one of the organizers, "There is more get-out-the-vote work going on in Indian Country than we've ever seen before" (Schmidt 2004). Indian voters in that state were also encouraged to vote by a "Native Vote–MN Style" campaign (Lehman and Macy 2004, 23).

In South Dakota multiple efforts were made. Three tribal organizations were set up to register voters. The United Sioux Tribes initiated a Native Vote Project. The Four Directions organization played multiple roles, as did the Northern Plains Tribal Voter Education Project (Lehman and Macy 2004, 36; Melmer 2004).

Even in remote Alaska and Hawaii, voter registration drives were organized for native peoples (Danner 2004; KTUU 2004). And the Gila River Indian Community initiated a "Kids Voting Program" to teach young people the importance of voting (Mendoza 2004). It was two Indians from Gila River who were told in 1928 that they were not entitled to vote (see the previous discussion of *Porter v. Hall*).

In the Pacific Northwest, a voter registration drive coordinated by the Native Action Network used the acronym VICTORY, which stood for "Voters in Indian Country Taking on Regional Elections" (Native Action Network 2004). That effort was enhanced by another organization, founded in 1999, called the First American Education Project (Lehman 2003). In the Southwest, the Moving America Forward Foundation worked to increase voting among Hispanics and Native Americans (Arizona Native Voter 2004). In Arizona, a special celebration was held to honor the fifty-sixth anniversary of the *Harrison v. Laveen* case, and July was declared to be "Arizona Indian Right to Vote Month" (Lehman and Macy 2004, 13).

Efforts were also made to organize urban native voters. The National Indian Youth Council (NIYC) and the Sage Council created a Native American Voters Alliance in Albuquerque, New Mexico (Sage Council 2004). In Phoenix, Arizona, the Native American Community Organizing Project set out to register 3,000 urban Indians for the 2004 election (National Office News 2004). In Montana, the Native Development Corporation led the effort to register urban Indians in Billings (Lehman and Macy 2004, 28). Urban native voters in Seattle were the target of a new group called Native Action Network (Lehman and Macy 2004, 45).

All of these activities led the executive director of NCAI to proclaim that "Native America's voice on the national stage was historically strong in 2004 when a record number of American Indians and Alaska Natives exercised their right to vote..." (Johnson 2005a).

Partisan Appeals

The growing power of the native vote was noted by the major parties. There was a perception that although many Indians were Democrats, party loyalty was weak, primarily because neither party had been very responsive to their interests (Ritt 1979, 52–3; Davis 1983; McCool 1985, 128–9; Kraker 2004b). An article in *Newsweek* noted that "this year both parties are trying to court that often-ignored group" (2004, 12). Republican Congressman Rick Renzi, while campaigning on the Navajo Reservation, said, "This is fertile ground out here. Amazing fertile ground for both sides" (Schmidt 2004). About eighty American Indians attended the Democratic National Convention, and thirty-five went to the Republican National Convention (Kershaw 2004). Both parties made political pitches to Indians who were in Washington in September 2004 to attend the opening of the Smithsonian's National Museum of the American Indian.

The Democratic Party realized quite early in the campaign that the Indian vote was crucial to their success. The party published a Democratic Policy Committee Special Report titled "The American Indian Vote: Celebrating 80 Years of U.S. Citizenship."[1] This report describes five "Continuing Obstacles to Indian Voting," including vote dilution, voter suppression tactics, restrictive identification requirements, linguistic barriers, and distant poll locations (Democratic Policy Committee 2004). These are, of course, the kinds of issues that have been litigated repeatedly in VRA cases.

The Democratic campaign formed a "Native Americans for Kerry–Edwards" organization to "help energize, organize and mobilize the Native American community." In August, John Kerry visited Arizona and New Mexico, met with tribal leaders, and spoke at the Gallup Inter-Tribal Ceremonial (*Ute Bulletin* August 11, 2004). Much of the Democrats' effort focused on the sprawling 17-million-acre Navajo Reservation. Of the 95,000 Navajos registered to vote, about 72,000 are Democrats (Shaffer 2004). Navajo Nation President Joe Shirley, as well as the tribal council, endorsed Kerry (Hoffman 2004).

Late in the campaign, the Democrats' appeal to Native voters intensified. House Democratic leader Nancy Pelosi and other leading Democratic legislators issued a party agenda titled "Restoring the Trust" that pledged to increase spending for Indian programs (Adams 2004a). Pelosi said that the Democrats would "pledge to work together with Native Americans to improve education, create jobs, and provide good health care for our nation's first citizens" (Fogarty 2004). A month before the election, an article in *Indian Country Today* began with this sentence: "John Kerry's

[1] This title is somewhat misleading. As pointed out in Chapter 1, many Indians were already citizens when the Indian Citizenship Act became law in 1924.

secret weapon in the presidential campaign is the Indian vote" (Adams 2004).

The Republicans also made a concerted effort to gain the Indian vote. In years past the Indian vote was assumed by many to belong to the Democrats, but that support has eroded due to several developments. In the 1980s, Navajo chairman Peter McDonald endorsed Ronald Reagan. Senator Ben Nighthorse Campbell, the only American Indian in the Senate until his retirement in 2004, switched parties and became a Republican in 1995. When the Republicans took over the Senate in 1994, the chairmanship of the Indian Affairs Committee switched to Republican John McCain. McCain is generally given high marks for his advocacy on behalf of Indians.

Thus, despite races in 2000 and 2002 where Indians played a crucial role in Democratic Party campaigns; the Republican Party worked hard during the 2004 campaign to woo these voters. That effort began with the writing of the party's platform. An early version made no reference to tribal sovereignty. House Speaker Dennis Hastert, after a visit with several Indian tribes and a discussion with the party's ad hoc Native American Caucus, amended the platform to include an endorsement of tribal sovereignty and a government-to-government relationship (Adams 2004b).

Republicans in Arizona initiated a Native get-out-the-vote drive that the state Republican chair described as "unprecedented" (House 2004). Paul DeMain, an Indian newspaper editor, claimed that "Most Indians share Republican values" (Glionna 2004).

The Republican campaign for Indian voters has met with some success. In 2002, significant Indian campaign donations went to Republicans (Glionna 2004). Some prominent Indians have endorsed Republicans. John Gonzales, the former governor of San Ildefonso Pueblo, stated that he thought the Republican Party "represents empowerment to tribes" (Hoffman 2004). Congressman Rick Renzi, a Republican representing northern Arizona, received endorsements from several prominent Navajos, including former chairman Peter McDonald and Kathy Kitcheyan, the chairwoman of the San Carlos Apache Tribe (Kraker 2004c).

Like the Democrats, the Republicans paid special attention to the Navajo Reservation. In September 2004, the party opened an office in Shiprock, New Mexico (Mayeux 2004). At the height of the campaign, Department of Health and Human Services Secretary Tommy Thompson made a campaign trip to the reservation, and campaign literature was published in the Navajo language. The Sioux in South Dakota also received special attention; both parties knew that the race between Senator Tom Daschle and John Thune would be very close. In April 2004 Representative Richard Pombo, a prominent Republican, visited the Rosebud Reservation for a ceremonial buffalo hunt. Thune himself met with numerous tribal leaders, including the controversial former AIM leader Russell Means (Woster 2004a).

Not all went well between the Republicans and Indians, however. Televangelist Pat Robertson, who strongly supported John Thune in South Dakota, made erroneous accusations about Indian voters: "The thing that I think is concerning many is the fraud on the Indian reservations. People go in there, and they . . . take advantage of people that are not totally literate or, I don't know what they do, but there has been massive fraud" (quoted in *Indian Country Today* October 22, 2004). Still, Republicans made significant overtures to Indian voters in 2004.

The get-out-the-vote campaigns of both parties helped increase Indian turnout, but neither party got everything it wanted from native voters (Norrell 2004). The Indian vote did not decide the presidential election, and it was not enough to save Tom Daschle in South Dakota, as it had saved Tim Johnson in 2002. However, it did make the difference in the race to replace South Dakota Representative William Janklow, who resigned after being convicted of manslaughter. The Democratic candidate for that office, Stephanie Herseth, won narrowly with a large Indian vote. A Republican leader noted that their candidate would have won "[i]f you take out the Indian reservation . . ." (Democratic Policy Committee 2004; Melmer 2004a).

A systematic analysis of the impact of Indian voters in the 2004 elections was conducted by the First American Education Project and the Center for Civic Participation. The report began by noting that "Never before had Indian Country experienced such attention. Never before had such a commitment of time, energy and resources been expended in an effort to increase Native participation in American politics" (Lehman and Macy 2004, 6). The report found that "in many parts of the country, many Native communities saw increases of 50 percent to 150 percent in their turnout," and there was a "direct correlation between focused localized commitments to increasing participation rates in Native communities and the actual increases that result" (7).

NCAI also evaluated the success of the 2004 vote campaign by holding a debriefing meeting with their project coordinators and organizers. That meeting yielded a frank assessment of the successes and weaknesses of their efforts. Of particular note was their emphasis on voter apathy: "voter apathy was an expected obstacle, but the extent of the apathy in some communities was shocking to some of the Native Vote projects. This was mostly true in the urban Indian communities and the extremely remote reservations" (NCAI/National Voice. 2004, 2). Despite the problems, the debriefing report trumpeted the dramatic gains made in 2004 and recommended changes for improving the Native Vote effort in 2006. In the meantime, NCAI launched its "Native Vote 2006" campaign (*NCAI Sentinel* 2005).

Procedural Problems and Resistance

Even though Natives' voting has increased and dozens of VRA cases have been litigated on their behalf, it would be a mistake to conclude that all procedural problems have been solved and Indians are welcomed at the polls with open arms. During the 2004 election cycle, a number of difficulties arose.

In New Mexico, the issue was the legality of registering Indians to vote at an Indian Health Service facility. The facility's director told employees that they were not allowed to do a nonpartisan voter registration drive on federal property. However, such drives occur in other federal facilities, including military bases, and have been authorized by the General Accounting Office (Becker 2004).

On the Red Lake Reservation in Minnesota, a partisan poll watcher became so aggressive and threatening that the tribal police were called and the individual was escorted off the reservation (Lehman and Macy 2004, 21).

A boundary issue became contentious in the South Dakota town of Lake Andes. The city conducted a review of the city's boundaries and determined that some residents, mostly Native Americans, who had been thought to be city residents, actually lived outside the city limits. Some Indians felt that the action was racially motivated and filed suit. According to *Indian Country Today*, "Tension between the American Indian residents and the non-Indian power structure of the city continues. American Indian residents, who make up more than half of the population of the city, do not have representation on the city council or on the county commission" (Melmer 2004b). The case was later dismissed on a procedural issue (*Zephier v. Cihak* 2004*).

Problems at the polls were anticipated, and a number of Indian organizations put together teams of lawyers and poll watchers in an effort to avoid them. The "Election Protection Project" placed poll observers in twelve states, relying on an army of 400 to 500 volunteers (*Arizona Daily Sun* 2004; Native Vote 2004). In Montana the effort was coordinated by a group called Native Action, which placed nearly fifty lawyers and student volunteers at polling places on the state's seven Indian reservations (Rave 2004). In South Dakota, the only state where extensive poll watching had taken place in earlier elections, native poll watchers again covered critical precincts. Republicans also sent out non-Indian poll watchers. In just one precinct on the Pine Ridge Reservation, seven attorneys from both parties showed up to monitor the voting (Melmer 2004c).

On election day, several Republican poll watchers in South Dakota claimed that Indian people were being paid to vote. The Democrats charged that the Republicans had started the rumor, and claimed that it was unfounded. The rumor may have originated from the fact that some Indians who had cars were asked to drive other Indians to the polls and were reimbursed for their time and expenses, which is legal (Woster 2004b).

After the election, the Native Vote 2004–Election Protection Project released a report that cataloged the alleged problems on election day involving Indians. They recorded 300 specific "incidents," nearly 60 percent of which were related to registration problems. There were relatively few instances of overt race-based intimidation (Thompson 2005).

Beyond Voting

Recent elections have made it clear that Indian voters have a voice and are willing to use it. But voting is just one form of political activity; real political power requires other activities, such as lobbying, making campaign contributions, and running for office. Historically, Indian tribes have been too poor to make campaign contributions or organize national lobbying efforts, but that situation began to change with the advent of Indian gaming. Recent years have seen a dramatic increase in campaign contributions from Indian tribes, primarily those with gaming revenues. In fiscal year 2004, Indian gaming revenues totaled $19.4 billion, according to the National Indian Gaming Commission (2005).

An analysis by the Associated Press found that Indian tribes gave $7 million during the 2001–2 election cycle, most of it from thirty tribes with casinos (Associated Press 2003). According to another source, tribes in just three states – California, Connecticut, and Michigan – gave close to $5 million to both parties by September 2004 (Kershaw 2004). Nearly all large tribal donations came from gaming tribes.

The most comprehensive analysis of Indian gaming contributions at the federal level is from the Center for Responsive Politics. During the 1995 election cycle, Indian gaming interests (i.e., political action committees, soft money, individual contributions) contributed $1.6 million – a significant increase over previous years; Democrats received 87 percent. Since then, two trends have become evident. First, total contributions have dramatically increased. In 2004, Indian gaming provided $7.2 million in contributions. For the 2005–6 election cycle, gaming tribes had contributed over $2 million at this writing – and the campaign season had barely begun.

The second trend is that Republican candidates are receiving increasing donations from Indian gaming. In 2004, there were eight Republicans among the top twenty recipients of Indian gaming at the national level. During that election cycle, Indian tribes gave $1.8 billion to Democrats running for Congress and just under $1 billion to Republican candidates. The top Democratic candidates were Tom Daschle in the Senate and Kalyn Free, who was running for a House seat (both lost). Senator Ben Nighthorse Campbell was the top Republican recipient of Indian gaming money even though he was not running for office (he decided to retire in March 2004). So, these contributions did not buy a lot of access. Thus far in the 2005–6 election cycle, Indian gaming donations have been evenly split between the parties; the top recipient at this writing is Representative Richard Pombo of California; this certainly belies the notion that Indians only support liberal Democrats (Center for Responsive Politics 2005).

Big campaign contributions can potentially have a direct impact on Indian voting, in three ways. First, they make candidates more responsive to Indian interests and help buy access. This could make at least some politicians more sensitive to Indian needs, which in turn may help convince Indians that elections at all levels of government truly do "belong" to them. In effect, political participation via campaign spending gives Indians a stake in the system. Second, although most donations appear to go to candidates for national office, the efficacy of such efforts may lead to increasing donations to state and local races, thus bringing Indians even further into the electoral contests in and around Indian Country. And third, Indian donations go to both parties, giving them access no matter who wins; this in effect puts the parties in competition for both Indian votes and Indian dollars. A case in point: during the 2004 campaign, the

National Indian Gaming Association hosted a fund-raiser for Democratic Senator Patty Murray; at about the same time, the San Carlos Apache and San Manuel Mission Indians – two big gaming tribes – hosted a fund-raiser for Republican Congressman Rick Renzi (Baldor 2004). As one Republican lobbyist put it, "The Native American community has realized it's important not to put all their eggs in one basket" (*National Journal* 2002).

One of the goals of the VRA was to give Indians an opportunity to elect candidates of their choice. That law, combined with a significant amount of campaign money, spread widely, will increase the probability that candidates with a pro-Indian stance will win at least some elections. A statement by South Dakota Senator Tim Johnson is instructive; "when I first came into politics, it was rare for a tribal chairman to want to be seen on the stage with a white politician. They viewed these as white man's elections.... Today, they are a force to be reckoned with" (Kershaw 2004). Johnson should know; he owed his political survival in 2002 to late returns from Indian precincts.

In addition to voting and making campaign contributions, a third form of political activity, lobbying, is increasing. Tribes, especially those with gaming revenue, now have the money to hire high-powered lobbyists to represent them in Washington and the state capitals. A journalist familiar with the politics of the pueblos in New Mexico wrote that "Indian have developed one of the fastest growing and most respected lobbies in federal politics...." (Hargrove 2004). However, Indian people do not always hire others to do their lobbying for them; they have become quite adept at playing the game themselves (see Wilkins 2002, 201–15). The NCAI recently initiated a fund-raising campaign to construct its own building in Washington, D.C., to be called the American Indian Hall of Nations. Former NCAI President Tex Hall said that with the new building, tribes will have "an emerging presence" in the Capital (Sarasohn 2004). The NCAI has also embarked on an ambitious partnership with the National Conference of State Legislatures to "help legislators and tribal leaders gain a greater understanding of the issues affecting each constituency and to identify methods for cooperative policymaking" (National Conference of State Legislatures 2005). It remains to be seen whether that cooperation will extend to Indian voting issues.

Lobbying is not without pitfalls, however. When large amounts of money are tossed into the political arena, it is sometimes difficult to control who gets it and how it is used. Lobbyist Jack Abramoff and his partners collected $82 million in lobbying fees from Indian tribes and used at least some of it to lobby against another Indian tribe that wanted to open a new casino. Abramoff used some of the money to enrich himself through a kickback scheme. His protégé, Michael Scanlon, pleaded guilty in November 2005 to defrauding Indian tribes and attempting to bribe public officials, and agreed to pay back $19 million to the Indian tribes he defrauded (*U.S. v. Scanlon* 2005; Weisman and Willis 2005). In January 2006, Abramoff pleaded guilty to fraud, tax evasion, and conspiracy to bribe public officials. He will be required to make restitution to the Indian tribes he defrauded (Mabeus 2005; Schmidt and Grimaldi, 2005a, 2005b, 2006). The fallout from the Abramoff scandal immediately led to calls to curb the political influence of gaming tribes (Drinkard 2006; Florio 2006; Rave 2006). The tribes' experience with Abramoff is reminiscent of past relationships in which non-Indians professing to be working on behalf of Indians instead enriched themselves at the expense of Indians. This reinforces an important lesson from history; Indians are their own best advocates.

A fourth form of political activism goes right to the heart of politics; increasingly, Indian candidates are running for office. To assist in that effort, a new candidate-support organization was started by Kalyn Free soon after her unsuccessful 2004 bid for a House seat. Free, a Choctaw from Oklahoma, modeled her organization on Emily's List and called it INDN's List, short for the Indigenous Democratic Network. The objective of the new organization is to recruit and elect Native American candidates and mobilize Indian voters on behalf of those candidates (INDN's List 2005). According to Free, "We've already been the determining factor in so many elections. It's time for us to be on the ballot" (Marrero 2005). In October 2005 the group organized its first "campaign camp." Democratic National Committee Chairman Howard Dean and humorist Al Franken were among the speakers (Adams 2005). Another Indian activist program, called "Empowering the Hoop," hopes to provide "the tools and resources necessary for communities to develop, implement, and assess homegrown civic engagement initiatives" (Center for Civic Participation 2005). Such efforts have already paid off. Currently, forty-eight Indians sit in state legislatures, including ten in Oklahoma and eight in Montana (Lehman and Macy 2004, 27; Lohn 2005). Dozens more hold elective offices at the local level. But with the retirement of Senator Ben Nighthorse Campbell, only one Indian, Representative Tom Cole of Oklahoma, is in the U.S. Congress.

Not everyone is pleased with the Indians' newfound political power. According to one lobbyist for an Indian gaming tribe, "Now that there's some money coming into Indian country, the pressures against us are actually mounting" (Kosseff 2005). Several interest groups have formed to challenge Indian tribes and what they perceive to be abuses of power. United Property Owners, based in Redmond, Washington, was formed in 1989 to "bring more balance to federal Indian policy." According to them, "Across the United States, certain Indian tribal leaders, emboldened by seriously flawed and often corrupt Federal policies, are using their extreme wealth from gambling to rapidly expand their self-declared authority and to encroach on the rights of private citizens, small businesses, and local and state governments" (United Property Owners 2004).[2] That organization recently combined with another anti-Indian group and formed a new organization called One Nation United. According to the group's executive director, "We've got truth, justice and the American way on our side" (Turnbull 2004).

Another group, the Citizens Equal Rights Alliance, claims that federal Indian policy is unconstitutional and that "The excessive authority of tribal governments can only be exercised at the expense of state and local jurisdictions, and the constitutional rights of individual citizens" (Citizens Equal Rights Alliance 2004). The American Land Rights Association is part of a coalition of groups attempting to stop Indian gaming, claiming that "There are many people nationally who are concerned about the abuse of Indian reservations as a tool to ignore local land use laws" (American Land Rights Association 2005).

As American Indians become more involved in extratribal politics through voting, campaigning, and lobbying, there will be shifts in political power, which is always a complex and conflicted process (see Wilkinson 2005). The VRA will remain a part of that process as tribes attempt to gain opportunities to elect candidates that reflect their interests.

The Future of the Voting Rights Act

The future role of American Indians in the electoral process depends in part on the strength and enforcement of the VRA. The act's renewable sections were set to expire in 2007 and had to be reauthorized by Congress to remain in effect (Section 2 is permanent and does not require reauthorization). In 2005 Congress began debating the fate of the preclearance provisions of Section 5, the federal observer provisions of Sections 6

[2] This organization was influential in getting the Republican Party of Washington state to write a plank into its 2000 platform calling for the termination of all tribal governments. The plank was later withdrawn (Lehman 2003).

through 9, and the language provisions of Sections 203 and 4(f). According to proponents, these sections of the act have played a pivotal role in the development of Indian voting rights and have assisted Indian people in their efforts to play an active part in our democratic form of government (see Jackson 2004; McDonald 2005b, 2005c). Indeed, about a third of the cases covered in this book were based on the renewable sections of the act. The VRA, including these renewable provisions, has significantly helped Indian people to become part of "government by the people."

The debate over VRA reauthorization emphasized the importance of the act in Indian Country. In 2005 the National Commission on the Voting Rights Act held hearings throughout the United States, including one in Rapid City, South Dakota, that focused exclusively on American Indian voters.[3] Raymond Uses the Knife, the vice chairman of the Cheyenne River Sioux Tribe, told of difficulties encountered by Indian people when they tried to vote and said, "Things like this are going on on the reservations" (Gease 2005). Several other tribal members also testified (see: Lawyers' Committee for Civil Rights Under Law 2006).

The U.S. House of Representatives began holding reauthorization hearings in the fall of 2005. By the summer of 2006 bills had been introduced in both houses, titled the "Fannie Lou Hamer, Rosa Parks and Coretta Scott King Voting Rights Act Reauthorization and Amendments Act of 2006" (U.S. Congress, House, 2006). Jacqueline Johnson, executive director of the NCAI, testified on the importance of Section 203 – the language assistance provision: "The value of Section 203 to Indian country cannot be overstated. Today, according to the new determinations released by the Census Bureau in July 2002, eighty-eight (88) jurisdictions in seventeen (17) states are covered jurisdictions that need to provide language assistance to American Indians and Alaskan Natives" (Johnson 2005b, also see Securing the Native Voice 2005). Penny Pew, the elections director for Apache County, Arizona, which is 77 percent Native American, spoke in favor of Sections 6 and 8, the provisions for federal examiners and observers: "The observer program has proven successful for us and has given us insight[into] the happenings at each polling place that may otherwise go unnoticed" (Pew 2005). In regard to Section 203, she described

[3] This commission is not a government agency. It was established by the Lawyers' Committee for Civil Rights Under Law and other civil rights organizations to "write a comprehensive report detailing discrimination in voting since 1982" (Lawyers' Committee for Civil Rights Under Law 2005)

how the county had created a "Navajo Language Election Glossary," and she quoted from a letter to her written by a Navajo constituent: "...the language program has been positive for our county in educating and promoting our most fundamental right...the power of our vote." Laughlin McDonald, the director of the ACLU's Voting Rights Project, spoke in favor of renewing all the special provisions in the act. In regard to Section 5, he said, "Recent voting rights litigation throughout the South and in Indian Country, as well as Court findings of widespread and systematic discrimination against minority voters underscores the need for continuing Section 5." He made specific references to the *Bone Shirt* and *Quick Bear Quiver* cases (McDonald 2005b).

Reauthorization of the renewable provisions of the VRA also sparked considerable opposition. In congressional testimony, Edward Blum of the American Enterprise Institute's Project on Fair Representation argued that Section 5 had "degenerated into an unworkable, unfair, and unconstitutional mandate that is bad for our two political parties, bad for race relations, and bad for our body politic" (Blum 2005). The popular columnist George Will called the renewable sections of the VRA "antiquarian nonsense" that gives "a few government-favored groups entitlements to elective office" (Will 2005). In June 2006 opponents of the act's renewal, led by Congressman Lynn Westmoreland of Georgia, managed to stop the bill's progress, arguing that Section 5 was based on "outdated standards" (Voting Rights Renewal Update 2006a). Westmoreland was joined by eighty other Republicans, who also objected to Section 203, arguing that it encouraged "linguistic division" and that "the American people want to be an English-speaking nation" (Babington 2006, A07). Despite this opposition, the bill passed the House of Representative on July 13, 2006, by a vote of 390–33 (Hernandez 2006).

The hearings in South Dakota sponsored by the National Commission on the Voting Rights Act provided an opportunity for both pro and con positions on reauthorization. Chris Nelson, secretary of state for South Dakota and a guest commissioner at the hearings, noted that all of the South Dakota laws that were reviewed by the Justice Department under Section 5 were accepted without objection or suggestions for change: "Not one of the laws that were not filed were retrogressed," and suggested there was no need for Section 5 of the VRA (Melmer 2005b). Press coverage of the hearings prompted a blog response regarding the ACLU and former Senator Tom Daschle – both participated in the hearing: "Why would it surprise anyone that two well known socialist entities, both looking forward to the downfall of America, both contributing to the Marxist cause, the ACLU and Tom Daschle would team up together" (Mount Blogmore 2005).

Obviously, passions ran high in South Dakota and other states that were subject to the special provisions of the VRA, and the debate over reauthorization gave vent to some of those feelings. However, supporters of the act were pleased when President George W. Bush indicated support for reauthorization (Loven 2005) and subsequently signed the extension into law on July 27, 2006. At a press conference in June 2006, President Bush reiterated his support for reauthorization: "I am working very carefully with members of Congress to implement that which I said when I signed the proclamation for Rosa Parks, is I want this Voting Rights Act extended" (Voting Rights Renewal Update 2006b). One of the lessons from this debate is that, while nearly everyone supports the ideal of democracy, there is still a wide range of opinions regarding the process of democracy.

Conclusion

In the watershed case of *Harrison v. Laveen* in 1948, Arizona Supreme Court Justice Levi Udall succinctly characterized the challenge that is the focus of this book:

> In a democracy suffrage is the most basic civil right, since its exercise is the chief means whereby other rights may be safeguarded. To deny the right to vote, where one is legally entitled to do so, is to do violence to the principles of freedom and equality. (342)

For American Indians, suffrage is an unfinished agenda, but stunning progress has been made since that Denver crowd screamed "exterminate them, exterminate them" in 1866. Much of that progress has been due to the VRA. The Democratic National Committee's report "The American Indian Vote: Celebrating 80 Years of U.S. Citizenship," issued at the height of the 2004 election campaign, noted that the VRA "has provided Native communities with a very powerful tool to ensure that the past practices of discrimination cease" (Democratic Policy Committee 2004, 4). As a result, Indian people now have a greater opportunity to express their political will, to participate in politics from a position of equality with non-Indians, and occasionally to elect one of their own, or at least someone who is sensitive to their unique status and needs.

The impact of the VRA, combined with that of other civil rights and voting legislation, has greatly expanded Indian opportunities to participate. This, and earlier efforts to end the denial of voting rights, have helped make possible the unprecedented level of Indian voting in the 2004 elections. Tex Hall, then president of NCAI, praised the electoral involvement of American Indians in his 2004 "State of the Indian Nations" address:

> 2004 stands out for another reason. As you may know, Indian people have a historical record of very low participation in federal and state elections. However, last year the NCAI's Native Vote campaign energized Indian voters like no other time in history. Last year I promised the highest level of involvement ever in the political election process and I am happy to tell you that we achieved our goal. From Alaska to Oklahoma and Oregon to Minnesota, Indian voters turned out to the election polls in greater numbers than [for] any other election in history. (Hall 2005).

The power and promise of the VRA have been enhanced by two other recently enacted laws, both of which have the potential to increase Indian voting. The Help America Vote Act (HAVA) requires that states provide provisional ballots and place limits on the kinds of identification that can be required by states. The National Voter Registration Act of 1993, known as the "motor voter" law, requires state departments of motor vehicles and various other state agencies to offer to register citizens and allow voters to use mail-in ballots.

The voting rights of American Indians hold great promise. As former NCAI president Tex Hall put it, "We have the power to shape the political landscape in key states. When Indian people vote, Indian issues are addressed" (Hall 2004). At least some politicians are listening; President George W. Bush, two days after his reelection in 2004, released a proclamation recognizing National American Indian Heritage Month and claiming his government's commitment to "recognize tribal sovereignty and self-determination" and a "government-to-government relationship" with the tribes (Bush 2004). Congressman Richard Pombo, a Republican from California, told Indians that "The biggest influence you can have on this town [Washington, D.C.] is by what you do in November and turning out to vote" (quoted in *NCAI Sentinel* 2004b). With the help of the VRA, American Indians have the opportunity to do just that.

However, there are still significant limitations. Indian people, despite the impact of gaming on some reservations, remain poor, and poverty correlates strongly with political apathy. In 1993 the Census Bureau issued a report titled "We the First Americans." According to it, the national poverty rate in 1989 was 13 percent; the rate for Indians was 31 percent. In 1990, unemployment on Indian reservations averaged a staggering 74.4 percent. The per capita income for the reservations was $4,478 (U.S. Census 1993). According to the 2000 census, the poverty rate for American Indians and Alaska Natives was 24.5 percent (compared to 9.9 percent for whites). Furthermore, Indians "were the only group to show a decline when the 2000–2001 average was compared with 1999–2000" (U.S. Census 2001). Thus, tribal political gains have not translated into economic equality with non-Indians.

However, there are signs of improvement. A study by the Harvard Project on American Indian Economic Development found substantial increases in income and decreases in unemployment and poverty rates from 1990 to 2000. During those ten years, Indian income rose by 20 percent – considerably more than the 11 percent increase for the population as a whole. The improved economic picture is due in part to Indian gaming. But despite these gains, there are still "substantial gaps" between Indian and non-Indian measures of economic well-being (Harvard Project 2005).

The improved economic picture for Indians comes at a time of significant cuts in federal Indian programs (Harden 2004; Nieves 2004; U.S. Department of the Interior 2004). President Bush's proposed fiscal year (FY) 2006 budget reduced the BIA budget by $110 million. (Fogarty 2005). The proposed cuts prompted Senator Tim Johnson to protest budget reductions that are "an outrage and will hurt those with the greatest need: communities served by the weakest infrastructures with the least access and economic opportunity and basic government services" (Melmer 2005a). Recall that Senator Johnson was reelected by a razor-thin margin in 2002, thanks in part to the Indian vote. Congress restored much of the BIA buget but still cut $22 million. For FY 2007, President Bush again proposed cutting BIA funding, this time by $52 million (Budget of the U.S. Government for FY 2007). The president's budget also zero-funded urban Indian programs. Once again Senator Johnson led the effort to restore nearly $1 billion to Indian programs, but his measure was defeated, with the vote following party lines (Melmer 2006: 1).

In addition, conflicts over voting rights continue, as pointed out in Chapter 3. In January 2005, the ACLU's Voting Rights Project filed a lawsuit on behalf of Indian plaintiffs in Charles Mix County, South Dakota, alleging malapportionment, Section 2 vote dilution, and racial discrimination (*Blackmoon v. Charles Mix County* 2005). In Wyoming, the case of *Large v. Fremont County* (2005*) raises similar issues. Commenting on the continuing problems, former Senator Ben Nighthorse Campbell said, "There's no question that there still is some subtle discouragement. We've come a long way but we have a long way to go" (Jalonick 2006, 1).

Despite persistent poverty, budget cuts, and continuing conflicts over voting rights, there are reasons for optimism. Many of the VRA cases are fairly recent, so their full impact on Indian voting may not appear for several years. Many tribal members are novices at extratribal politics and need time to learn how to participate effectively. And states need time to adjust to the new realities of Indian voting. Some non-Indians will welcome them with open arms; others will be resentful and fearful of new political competitors, and a few will view the changes in purely racist terms. But the clock cannot be turned back.

To a great extent, the potential of the VRA will be determined by the Indian people themselves. It is important to reiterate that the cases discussed in this book do not compel anyone to participate in state and local elections. Many Indian people still believe that voting in state and local elections will lead to the demise of tribal sovereignty; that participation in nontribal government implies a preference for nontribal government, or at least a tacit consent to be governed from outside the reservation. But others understand that the best way to prevent state and local governments from threatening tribal autonomy is to have influence and power from within the system. Political scientist David Wilkins notes that many Indians believe that "in order to protect their sovereign rights, they must participate in the American electoral process" (Wilkins 2002, 191). This is true not only for state and local government, but especially at the federal level, which is charged with the responsibility of upholding treaties.

The power of the Indian vote will also be determined by the extent to which Indians vote as a cohesive group. Small groups within the electorate can command great influence when the rest of the electorate is divided roughly equally and the small group votes as a bloc. Recent elections indicate that America is a divided nation, and that division has resulted in many very close elections. In such situations, the Indian vote can make the difference between victory and defeat, but only if it too is not divided. The 2004 elections indicated that no party can take the Indian vote for granted, and that Indian unity could become a casualty of the internecine partisan struggles that have been so evident in recent elections. Comprising less than 1 percent of the population, American Indians must use their franchise in a sophisticated manner if they hope to wield significant influence in the electoral system. At the national level, that will be a difficult task, but in state and local elections, American Indians have the potential to dramatically affect voting outcomes. And, as suggested in Chapter 7, that in turn has a direct impact on policy.

Finally, the future of Indian voting will depend in part on continued litigation, or the threat of litigation, under the VRA. This assumes that the Department of Justice will continue to enforce the act aggressively; not everyone agrees that the department is currently performing that role effectively (see Eggen 2006). Future litigation will also depend on the continued activity of the ACLU's Voting Rights Project and possibly on other sources of assistance to Indian voters such as the Native American Rights Fund.

The litigation that ultimately overcame the denial of Indian suffrage, and is currently overcoming abridgments of that suffrage, has the potential to empower Indian voters on a par with Anglos. These cases have articulated the inadequacies of the electoral system and validated Indian participation in that system. Such articulation can build faith in the election process and convince alienated citizens that they have a place in the democratic process. But, newly won rights are rarely self-implementing. After all the briefs have been filed and the lawyers go home, a persistent effort is required to make VRA victories more than mere courtroom drama. If Indian people choose to participate in nontribal elections – and the choice is theirs alone – it will be necessary to organize voter registration drives, educate tribal members, instill a sense of civic duty that goes beyond tribal boundaries, and engage in the full panoply of political activities. Voting is just one component of civic engagement. Ultimately, the impact of the VRA in Indian Country is dependent on the will of Indian citizens, which is, after all, the essence of democracy.

References

Articles, Books, Hearings, Interviews

ACLU Pushing Plans to Increase Odds of Indian at State House, *Native American Law Digest*, 2001, 11–12.

Adams, Jason. 2004. School board member, Ronan School District, Montana. Phone interview, December 29.

Adams, Jim. 2004a. Kerry's election hopes hinge on Native vote. *Indian County Today*, Oct. 5. www.Indiancountry.com

Adams, Jim. 2004b. House Speaker Hastert intervenes to strengthen GOP Indian plank. *Indian Country Today*, Aug. 30. www.Indiancountry.com

Adams, Jim. 2005. Betting on themselves. *Indian Country Today*, Dec. 1. www.Indiancountry.com

Allen, Jessie. 2004. Symposium on race, crime, and voting: Social, political, and philosophical perspectives on felony disenfranchisement in America. *Columbia Human Rights Law Review* 36 (Fall): 1–286.

Allen, John H. 1956. Denial of voting rights to reservation Indians. *Utah Law Review* 5(2): 247–56.

Alt, James E. 1994. "The impact of the Voting Rights Act on Black and White registration in the South." In *Quiet Revolution in the South: The Impact of the Voting Rights Act, 1965–1990*, ed. Chandler Davidson and Bernard Grofman, pp. 351–77. Princeton, NJ: Princeton University Press.

American Land Rights Association. 2005. www.landrights.org.

Andrews Davis (law firm) 2004. Press Release: "Indian Attorney Association to Help Voters." Oct. 18. Tulsa, OK.

Arizona Daily Sun. 2004. Indian group to put poll watchers in 12 states. Sept. 12. www.azdailysun.com

Arizona Native Voter. 2004. Call to action. Moving America Forward Foundation. Sept. 1. http://lrm102.securednshost.com

Arrington, Theodore. 2000. "Declaration of Theodore S. Arrington, Ph.D." *U.S. v. Blaine County*. Civ. No. 99-122-GF.

Arrington, Theodore. 2001. "Rebuttal Declaration of Theodore S. Arrington." *U.S. v. Blaine County*. Civ. No. 99-122-GF.

Associated Press. 2002. Thune supporters called "sore losers." *Lakota Journal*, Dec. 13, 1.

Associated Press. 2003. Indian tribes contributed at least $7 million. May 18.

Associated Press. 2005. ACLU challenging ABQ voter ID ordinance. *Albuquerque Journal*, oct. 27. www.abqjournal.com

Babbitt, Bruce. 1975. Report of the 3rd Annual Indian Town Hall, "Arizona's Indian Participation in the Political Process," Oct. 20–1. Sponsored by the Arizona Commission of Indian Affairs. Phoenix, AZ.

Babington, Charles. 2006. Rebellion stops Voting Rights Act. *Washington Post*, June 22, A07.

Bailey, Garrick and Roberta G. Bailey. 1986. *A History of the Navajos: The Reservation Years*. Sante Fe, NM: School of American Research Press.

Baker, Deborah. 2004. Dems court Indian vote. *Farmington Daily Times*, July 28. www.daily-times.com

Baldor, Lolita. 2004. Flush with casino cash, Indian tribes placing bets in key races. *Santa Fe New Mexican*, Sept. 28. www.santafenewmexican.com

Ball, Howard, Dale Krane, and Thomas P. Lauth. 1982. *Compromised Compliance: Implementation of the 1965 Voting Rights Act*. Westport, CT: Greenwood Press.

Becker, Joe. 2004. Indian Health Service Agency barred new-voter drive. *Washington Post*, Oct. 6. www.washingtonpost.com

Benally, Clyde, Andrew O. Wiget, John R. Alley, and Garry Blake. 1983. *Dineji Nakee Naahane: A Utah Navajo History*. Salt Lake City: University of Utah Printing Service.

Berman, David R. and Tanis J. Salant. 1998. Minority representation, resistance, and public policy: The Navajos and the counties. *Publius: The Journal of Federalism* 28(4): 83–104.

Bernstein, Alison. 1991. *American Indians and World War II*. Norman: University of Oklahoma Press.

Bick, Ron. 2001. Stevens is first tribal member to chair Ronan School Board. *Char-Koosta News*, July 12, 3.

Bilosi, Thomas. 2001. *Deadliest Enemies*. Berkeley: University of California Press.

Black, Zenos L. 1983. "Education in San Juan County." In *San Juan County, Utah: People Resources, and History*, ed. Allan Kent Powell, pp. 337–52. Salt Lake City: Utah State Historical Society.

Blum, Edward J. 2005. Oversight Hearings on the Voting Rights Act, Testimony Before the House Judiciary Committee's Subcommittee on the Constitution, Oct. 25. 109th Cong., 2d sess.

Bobo, Lawrence and Franklin Gilliam. 1990. Race, sociopolitical participation, and Black empowerment. *American Political Science Review* 84(2): 377–93.

Bork, Jeffrey Holt. 1973. Income and Employment Status of the Navajo Indian in San Juan County, Utah. M.S. thesis, University of Utah.

Bosser, L. Joy. 1976. DeConcini defeats Steiger. *Navajo Times*, Nov. 11, 1.

Brady, H., S. Verba, and K. Schlozman. 1995. Beyond SES: A resource model of political participation. *American Political Science Review* 89(2): 271–94.

Brischetto, Robert R. and Richard L. Engstrom. 1997. Cumulative voting and Latino representation: Exit surveys in fifteen Texas communities. *Social Science Quarterly* 78(4): 973–91.

Brockington, David and Todd Donovan. 1998. Minority representation under cumulative and limited voting. *Journal of Politics* 60(4): 1108–29.

Browning, Rufus P., Dale Rogers Marshall, and David H. Tabb. 1984. *Protest Is Not Enough: The Struggle of Blacks and Hispanics for Equality in Urban Politics*. Berkeley: University of California Press.

Buckanaga, Celine. 2005. Plaintiff, *Buckanaga v. Sisseton School District, South Dakota*. Phone interview, Jan. 14.

Budget of the U.S. Government for FY 2007. www.whitehouse.gov/omb/budget/fy2007

Bush, George W. 2004. "National American Indian Heritage Month, 2004." By the President of the United States of America, a Proclamation. Office of the Press Secretary. Nov. 4.

Caldeira, Gregory A. 1992. "Litigation, Lobbying, and the Voting Rights Bar." In *Controversies in Minority Voting: The Voting Rights Act in Perspective*, ed. Bernard Grofman and Chandler Davidson, pp. 230–57. Washington, DC: The Brookings Institution.

Cameron, Charles, David Epstein, and Sharyn O'Halloran. 1996. Do majority-minority districts maximize substantive Black representation in Congress? *American Political Science Review* 90: 794–812.

Campbell, David, and Joe R. Feagin. 1975. Black politics in the South: A descriptive analysis. *Journal of Politics* 37(1): 129–62.

Canon, David T. 1999. *Race, Redistricting, and Representation*. Chicago: University of Chicago Press.

Cavanagh, Sean. 2002. S.D. district sued over at-large election system. *Education Week*, May 1, 6.

Center for Civic Participation. 2005. Empowering the Hoop. www.centerforcivicparticipation.org/organizing/groups/nativeamerican

Center for Responsive Politics. 2005. Indian gaming. www.opensecrets.org

Charley, Wallace. 2005. Commissioner, San Juan County, New Mexico. Phone interview, Mar. 17.

Chavez, Ervin. 2005. Commissioner, San Juan County, New Mexico. Phone interview, Feb. 22.

Citizens Equal Rights Alliance. 2004. www.citizensalliance.org

Cohen, Adam. 2004. Indians face obstacles between the reservation and the ballot box. *New York Times*, June 21. www.nytimes.com

Cohen, Felix. 1942. *Handbook of Federal Indian Law*. Washington, DC: U.S. Government Printing Office.

Cole, Leonard. 1974. Electing blacks to municipal office. *Urban Affairs Quarterly* 10(1): 17–39.

Cole, Leonard. 1976. *Blacks in Power: A Comparative Study of Black and White Elected Officials*. Princeton, NJ: Princeton University Press.

Cole, Steven. 2003. "Report of Steven P. Cole, Ph.D. *Bone Shirt v. Hazeltine*, January 21, 2003." 2001. CIV. 01–3032.

Congressional Globe. 1866. Vol. 36, 39th Cong., 1st. sess. May 30.

Congressional Quarterly Almanac. 1975. Washington, DC: Congressional Quarterly, Inc.

Congressional Record. 1924. House. May 23, 1924, 68th Cong., 1st. sess.

Connell, Evan. 1985. *Son of the Morning Star*. New York: Harper Perennial.

Cooper, William. 2004. Trial Exhibit 358. *Bone Shirt v. Hazeltine*. 2001. CIV. 01–3032.

Coulter, Robert T. 2001. Racial justice lawyering on behalf of Indians and other indigenous peoples. www.indianlaw.org/body_default.htm

Council of State Governments. 1940. Voting in the United States: Qualifications and disqualifications, absentee voting, voting rights of persons in military service. August 1940. Washington, DC: Council of State Governments.

Cowger, Thomas W. 1999. *The National Congress of American Indians: The Founding Years*. Lincoln: University of Nebraska Press.

Cunningham, Maurice T. 2001. *Maximization, Whatever the Cost: Race, Redistricting, and the Department of Justice*. Westport, CT: Praeger.

Custer, Geraldine. 2005. Clerk and Recorder, Rosebud County, Montana. Phone interview, May 26.

Dakota-Lakota-Nakota Human Rights Advocacy Coalition. 2002. South Dakota settles largest-ever voting rights lawsuit brought by ACLU on behalf of Native Americans. (Nov. 7). www.dlncoalition.org/dln_issues/nov082002aclu.htm

Dalton, Gail. 1983. Letter to San Juan County Commisioner Cal Black. Nov. 2.

Daniels, Robert E. 1970. "Cultural Identities Among the Oglala Sioux." In *The Modern Sioux: Social Systems and Reservation Culture*, ed. Ethel Nurge, pp. 198–245. Lincoln: University of Nebraska Press.

Danner, Jade. 2004. Native Hawaiian voters targeted. *NCAI Sentinel 2004 Special Edition*, 13. www.NCAI.org

Davidson, Chandler. 1992. "The Voting Rights Act: A Brief History." In *Controversies in Minority Voting: The Voting Rights Act in Perspective*, ed. Bernard Grofman and Chandler Davidson, pp. 7–51. Washington, DC: The Brookings Institution.

Davidson, Chandler, and Bernard Grofman. 1994. "The Voting Rights Act and the Second Reconstruction." In *Quiet Revolution in the South: The Impact of the Voting Rights Act, 1965–1990*, ed. Chandler Davidson and Bernard Grofman, pp. 378–87. Princeton, NJ: Princeton University Press.

Davidson, Chandler, and George Korbel. 1984. "At-Large Elections and Minority Group Representation." In *Minority Vote Dilution*, ed. Chandler Davidson, pp. 65–81. Washington, DC: Howard University Press.

Davis, James. 1983. Native-Americans in Oklahoma: Political attitudes and behavior. Paper presented at the annual meeting of the American Political Science Association, Chicago.

Days, Drew S., III. 1980. Letter as Assistant Attorney General, Civil Rights Division, to David Silva, Superintendent of Schools, St. Johns, Arizona. Mar. 20, 1980, and May 7, 1980.

Days, Drew S., III. 1992. "Section 5 Enforcement and the Department of Justice." In *Controversies in Minority Voting: The Voting Rights Act in Perspective*, ed. Bernard Grofman and Chandler Davidson, pp. 52–65. Washington, DC: The Brookings Institution.

Deloria, Vine, Jr., and Clifford Lytle. 1983. *American Indians, American Justice*. Austin: University of Texas Press.

Deloria, Vine, Jr., and David Wilkins. 1999. *Tribes, Treaties, and Constitutional Tribulations*. Austin: University of Texas Press.

Democratic Policy Committee. 2004. Special Report. The American Indian Vote: Celebrating 80 years of U.S. Citizenship. Democratic Policy Committee of the U.S. Senate, Senator Byron Dorgan, Chairman. Oct. 7.

Derfner, Armand. 1973. Racial discrimination and the right to vote. *Vanderbilt Law Review* 26(3): 523–84.

Deyhle, Donna. 1993. Affidavit in *Sinajini et al. v. Board of Education of the San Juan School District*, Civ. No. 74-C-346A. Oct. 22, 1993.

Deyhle, Donna. 1995. Navajo youth and Anglo racism: Cultural integrity and resistance. *Harvard Educational Review* 65(3): 403–44.

Doyle, John. 2005. Commissioner, Big Horn County, Montana. Phone interview, Jan. 20.

Drinkard, Jim. 2006. Tribes' political giving targeted. *USA Today*, Feb. 6. www.usatoday.com

Dye, Thomas R., and James Renick. 1981. Political power and city jobs: Determinants of minority employment. *Social Science Quarterly* 62(3): 475–86.

Eggen, Dan. 2005a. Civil rights focus shift roils staff at Justice: Veterans exit division as traditional cases decline. *Washington Post*, Nov. 13, A01.

Eggen, Dan. 2005b. Criticism of voting law was overruled: Justice Dept. backed Georgia measure despite fears of discrimination. *Washington Post*, Nov. 17, A01.

Eggen, Dan. 2005c. Staff opinions banned in voting rights cases. *Washington Post*, Dec. 10, A03.

Eggen, Dan. 2006. Politics alleged in voting cases. *Washington Post*, Jan. 23, A01.

Eisinger, Peter K. 1982. Black employment in municipal jobs: The impact of black political power. *American Political Science Review* 76(2): 380–92.

Ellingson, Marilyn. 2005. Interview. Mar. 1.

Ely, John Hart. 2002. Confounded by *Cromartie*: Are racial stereotypes now acceptable across the board or only when used in support of partisan gerrymanders? *University of Miami Law Review* 56: 489–506.

Engstrom, Richard L., and Charles J. Barrilleaux. 1991. Native Americans and cumulative voting: The Sisseton-Wahpeton Sioux. *Social Science Quarterly* 72(2): 388–92.

Engstrom, Richard L., and Michael E. McDonald. 1981. The election of Blacks to city councils: Clarifying the impact of electoral arrangements on the seats/population relationship. *American Political Science Review* 75(2): 344–54.

Epp, Charles R. 1996. Do bills of rights matter? The Canadian Charter of Rights and Freedoms. *American Political Science Review* 90(4): 765–79.

Epp, Charles R. 1998. *The Rights Revolution: Lawyers, Activists, and Supreme Courts in Comparative Perspective*. Chicago: University of Chicago Press.

Epstein, David, and Sharyn O'Halloran. 1999a. A social science approach to race, redistricting, and representation. *American Political Science Review* 93: 187–91.

Epstein, David, and Sharyn O'Halloran. 1999b. Measuring the electoral and policy impact of majority-minority voting districts. *American Journal of Political Science* 43(2): 367–95.

Epstein, Lee. 1985. *Conservatives in Court*. Knoxville: University of Tennessee Press.

Felipe, Lloyd. 2005. School Board Vice President, Grants-Cibola County School District, New Mexico. Phone interview, Feb. 17.

Flagg, Ellen. 1990. Did "outsider" stir race-relations stew in San Juan? *Deseret News*, Nov. 14, B1.

Florio, Gwen. 2006. Abramoff scandal irks Montana Indians. *Great Falls Tribune*, Jan. 3. www.greatfallstribune.com

Fogarty, Mark. 2004. Democrats court Native vote. *Indian Country Today*, Oct. 26. www.Indiancountry.com

Fogarty, Mark. 2005. 2006 housing aid targeted for draconian cuts. *Indian Country Today*, Mar. 16. www.Indiancountry.com

Fort Belknap Community Council. 1985. Letter to Senator John Melcher. May 28, 10.

Fraga, Luis Ricardo, Kenneth J. Meier, and Robert E. England. 1997. "Hispanic Americans and Educational Policy: Limits to Equal Access." In *Pursuing Power: Latinos and the Political System*, ed. F. Chris Garcia, pp. 279–85. Notre Dame, IN: University of Notre Dame Press.

Gease, Heidi Bell. 2005. Indian voters face hurdles. *Rapid City Journal*, Sept. 12, 1.

Glionna, John. 2004. Finding a voice in politics. *Los Angeles Times*, May 22, A-1.

Goodrich, Thomas. 1997. *Scalp Dance: Indian Warfare on the High Plains, 1865–1879*. Mechanicsburg, PA: Stackpole Books.

Greene, Eric. J. 2000. Blaine County resists federal effort to build Indian representation. *Great Falls Tribune*, Feb. 20, 1A.

Greene, Jerome. 1993. *Battles and Skirmishes of the Great Sioux War, 1876–1877*. Norman: University of Oklahoma Press.

Grofman, Bernard. 1992. "Expert Witness Testimony and the Evolution of Voting Rights Case Law." In *Controversies in Minority Voting: The Voting Rights Act in Perspective*, ed. Bernard Grofman and Chandler Davidson, pp. 197–229. Washington, DC: The Brookings Institution.

Grofman, Bernard, and Chandler Davidson. 1994. "The Effects of Municipal Election Structure on Black Representation in Eight Southern States." In *Quiet Revolution in the South: The Impact of the Voting Rights Act, 1965–1990*, ed. Chandler Davidson and Bernard Grofman, pp. 301–34. Princeton, NJ: Princeton University Press.

Grofman, Bernard, Lisa Handley, and David Lublin. 2001. Drawing effective minority districts: A conceptual framework and some empirical evidence. *North Carolina Law Review* 79: 1383–430.

Grofman, Bernard, Lisa Handley, and Richard Niemi. 1992. *Minority Representation and the Quest for Voting Equality*. Cambridge, MA: Cambridge University Press.

Guinier, Lani. 1997. "Groups, Representation, and Race-Conscious Districting: A Case of the Emperor's Clothes." In *Affirmative Action and Representation:*

Shaw v. Reno and the Future of Voting Rights, ed. Anthony A. Peacock, pp. 223–84. Durham: Carolina Academic Press.

Hall, Tex. 2004. Don't be silent on election day. *NCAI Sentinel: Native Vote 2004 Special Edition*. www.NCAI.org

Hall, Tex. 2005. Healthy communities: Strong tribal self-governance. 2005 State of the Indian Nations Address. National Congress of American Indians, Feb. 3. www.ncai.org

Hancock, Paul F., and Lora L. Tredway. 1985. The bailout standard of the Voting Rights Act: An incentive to end discrimination. *The Urban Lawyer* 17(3): 379–425.

Handley, Lisa, and Bernard Grofman. 1994. "The Impact of the Voting Rights Act on Minority Representation: Black Officeholding in Southern State Legislatures and Congressional Delegations." In *Quiet Revolution in the South: The Impact of the Voting Rights Act, 1965–1990*, ed. Chandler Davidson and Bernard Grofman, pp. 335–50. Princeton, NJ: Princeton University Press.

Harden, Blaine. 2004. Walking the land with pride once more. *Washington Post*, Sept. 19. www.washingtonpost.com.

Hargrove, Tom. 2004. American Indians see gains in political clout. *Albuquerque Tribune*, Sept. 16, 1.

Harriman, Peter. 2006. Panel, tribe going after voters. *Argus Leader*, Jan. 23. www.argusleaderonline.com

Harvard Project on American Indian Economic Development. 2005. American Indians on reservations: A databook of socioeconomic change between the 1990 and 2000 censuses. Jan. 5. www.ksg.harvard.edu/hpaied/nev_main.htm

Hasen, Richard. 2005. Congressional power to renew the preclearance provisions of the Voting Rights Act after *Tennessee v. Lane*. *Ohio State Law Journal* 66: 177–207.

Henderson, Gordon. 1985. Letter to Stanley Halpin and John Petoskey [NIYC attorneys]. Dec. 5. Albuquerque, NM: NIYC archives, University of New Mexico Library.

Hennessey, Jack. 1973. Testimony before the United States Commission on Civil Rights. Window Rock, AZ, Oct. 22–4.

Hernandez, Raymond, 2006. After challenges, House approves renewal of Voting Act. *New York Times*, July 14.

Hewes, Brooke. 2005. A Place at the Table. *Perceptions*. A Special Report on Race in Montana by the University of Montana School of Journalism. www.umt.ed/journalism/student_work/Native_News_2005

Hoffman, Leslie. 2004. Endorsements pit Navajo leader against Senator. *Farmington Daily Times*, Oct. 28. www.daily-times.com

Hogen, Philip. 1978. Attorney, Jackson County, testimony before the U.S. Commission on Civil Rights, "American Indian Issues in the State of South Dakota." Hearing held in Rapid City, SD, July 27–8, 91.

Holm, Tom. 1985. "Fighting a White Man's War: The Extent and Legacy of Indian Participation in World War II." In *The Plains Indians of the Twentieth Century*, ed. Peter Iverson, pp. 149–65. Norman: University of Oklahoma Press.

Holmes, Jack. 1967. *Politics in New Mexico*. Albuquerque: University of New Mexico Press.

Houghton, Neil. 1945. Wards of the United States: Arizona applications. *University of Arizona Bulletin/Social Science Bulletin* No. 14 (Vol. XVI, No. 3, July 1): 4–19.

Hoxie, Frederick. 1985. "From Prison to Homeland: The Cheyenne River Indian Reservation Before World War I." In *The Plains Indians of the Twentieth Century*, ed. Peter Iverson, pp. 55–76. Norman: University of Oklahoma Press.

Hoxie, Frederick. 2000. "Declaration of Frederick E. Hoxie, Ph.D." Expert witness report prepared for the plaintiffs in *U.S. v. Blaine County.*

Huff, Delores. 1997. *To Live Heroically*. New York: SUNY Press.

Indian Country Today. 1984. Judge hears arguments on suit filed by four Sisseton Indians. Oct. 24, 2.

Indian Country Today (*Lakota Times*). 1985. Indian law firm to study illegalities in voting system. Feb. 27, 18.

Indian Country Today. 1986. Jan. 18, B1.

Indian Country Today. 2002. Largest voting rights lawsuit filed against South Dakota. Aug. 12, 1.

Indian Country Today. 2004. John Kerry is conservative choice for President. Oct. 22. www.Indiancountry.com

Indian Law Resource Center. 1999. ACLU and Indian rights group seek to secure voting rights for Montana's Native Americans. July 7. www.indianlaw.org/body_voting_rights.htm

Indian Law Resource Center. 2005. www. indianlaw.org/index.html

INDN's List. 2005. Indigenous Democratic Network: Who we are. www.indinslist.org

Issacharoff, Samuel. 2004. Is Section 5 of the Voting Rights Act a victim of its own success? *Columbia Law Review* 104: 1710–31.

Jackson, Danna. 2004. Eighty years of Indian voting: A call to protect Indian voting rights. *Montana Law Review* 65(1): 269–88.

Jalonick, Mary Clare. 2006. "Indians Still Face Obstacles in Voting." *Rapid City Journal*. March 27.

James, Zane. 2004. Native American Election Coordinator, Secretary of State's Office, New Mexico. Interview, Nov. 10.

James, Zane. 2005. Native American Election Coordinator, Secretary of State's Office, New Mexico. Interview, Feb. 10.

Johnson, Jacqueline. 2004a. *Indian Vote 2004*. Washington, DC: National Congress of American Indians.

Johnson, Jacqueline. 2004b. "'Vote and Tell' – NV04 Needs Your Numbers." Washington, DC: National Congress of American Indians.

Johnson, Norman. 2004a. County Clerk, San Juan County, Utah. Interview, Feb. 16.

Johnson, Norman. 2004b. County Clerk, San Juan County, Utah. E-mail correspondence, Mar. 5.

Johnson, Norman. 2005a. County Clerk, San Juan County, Utah. E-mail correspondence, May 23.

Johnson, Norman. 2005b. County Clerk, San Juan County, Utah. E-mail correspondence, Dec. 13.

Jones-Correa, Michael, and Karthick Ramakrishnan. 2004. Studying the effects of language provisions under the Voting Rights Act. Paper presented at the annual meeting of the Western Political Science Association, Mar. 11–13, Portland, OR.

Karlan, Pamela S. 2002. Exit strategies in constitutional law: Lessons for getting the least dangerous branch out of the political thicket. *Boston University Law Review* 82: 667–98.

Karnig, Albert K. 1976. Black representation on city councils: The impact of district elections and socioeconomic factors. *Urban Affairs Quarterly* 12(2): 223–42.

Karolevitz, Robert. 1975. *Challenge: The South Dakota Story*. Sioux Falls, SD: Brevet Press.

Karst, Cheryl. 2005. Business Manager, Sisseton School District, South Dakota. Phone interview, Jan. 14.

Keech, William R. 1968. *The Impact of Negro Voting: The Role of the Vote in the Quest for Equality*. Chicago: Rand McNally.

Kent, Jim. 2002. Yankton tribal members sue Wagner School District. *News from Indian Country*, Apr. 30, 15A.

Kernell, Chebon. 2004. Oklahoma rocks young native voters. *NCAI Sentinel 2004 Special Edition*, 8.

Kershaw, Sarah. 2004. Politicians go courting on Indian reservations. *New York Times*, Sept. 23. www.nytimes.com

Kettle, Sheila. 2004. Seneca Nation: Working for a record voter turnout in '04. *NCAI Sentinel 2004 Special Edition*, 5. www.NCAI.org

Kilborn. Peter T. 1992. Life at the bottom: America's poorest county/A special report. *New York Times*, Sept. 20, 1–1.

Kosseff, Jeff. 2005. Tribes buy into political process. *The Oregonian*, May 9. www.oregonlive.com

Kousser, J. Morgan. 1999. *Colorblind Injustice: Minority Voting Rights and the Undoing of the Second Reconstruction*. Chapel Hill: University of North Carolina Press.

Kousser, J. Morgan. 2001. Ecological inference from Goodman to King. *Historical Methods* 34 (Summer, no. 3): 101–26.

Kraker, Daniel. 2004a. "Native Americans could decide tight races in key western states." Native Radio, KNAU, Flagstaff, AZ, Aug. 25. www.alternet.org/election04/19670

Kraker, Daniel. 2004b. Tribes turn out to vote. *High Country News*, Aug. 16, 7.

Kraker, Daniel. 2004c. Dems stumble in Arizona race. *High Country News*, Oct. 25, 4.

KTUU. 2004. Push is on to "Get Out the Native Vote." Sept. 27. www.ktuu.com

Lakota Times. 1990. "Indian Votes," Sept. 25, A1.

Lamar, Howard Roberts. 1956. *Dakota Territory, 1861–1889*. New Haven, CT: Yale University Press.

Landsberg, Brian K. 1997. *Enforcing Civil Rights: Race Discrimination and the Department of Justice*. Lawrence: University of Kansas Press.

Laney, Garrine P. 2003. *The Voting Rights Act of 1965: Historical Background and Current Issues*. New York: Novinka Books.

Lawson, Michael, and James Muhn. 2003. The Political History of the Oglala Sioux Tribe of the Pine Ridge Reservation and the Rosebud Sioux Tribe of the Rosebud Reservation from Prehistory to the Present. Prepared for the state of South Dakota, Office of the Attorney General, in connection with *Bone Shirt v. Hazeltine*.

Lawyers' Committee for Civil Rights Under Law. 2005. Goals of the National Commission on the Voting Rights Act. www.votingrightsact.org

Lawyers' Committee for Civil Rights Under Law. 2006. *Protecting Minority Voters: The Voting Rights Act at Work, 1982–2005*. New York: A Report by the National Commission on the Voting Rights Act.

Lee, Valerie. 2004. Navajos invited to voting forum. *Farmington Daily Times*, Sept. 17. www.daily-times.com

Leech, Beth L. 2002. Asking questions: Techniques for semi-structured interviews. *PS: Political Science and Politics* 34(4): 665–8.

Lehman, Russ. 2003. "The Emerging Role of Native Americans in the American Electoral Process." First American Education Project, sponsored by the Evergreen State College Native American Applied Research Institute. Jan. www.first-americans.net

Lehman, Russ, and Alyssa Macy. 2004. "Native Vote 2004: A National Survey and Analysis of Efforts to Increase the Native Vote in 2004 and the Results Achieved." Minneapolis: First American Education Project and the Center for Civic Participation.

Lewis, Ty. 2004. County commissioner, San Juan County, UT. Interview, Feb. 16.

Lohn, Martiga. 2005. American Indians are getting more involved in state politics. *Free New Mexican*, Dec. 29. www.freenewmexican.com/story

Lonetree, Anthony. 2005. Minneapolis City Council picks up five newcomers. *Minneapolis Star Tribune*, Nov. 9, 1B.

Loven, Jennifer. 2005. Bush OKs parks statue, urges renewal of Voting Rights Act. Associated Press, Dec. 2. www.chicagotribune.com/news

Lublin, David. 1998. Racial redistricting and African-American representation: A critique of "Do majority-minority districts maximize substantive Black representation in Congress?" *American Political Science Review* 93: 183–5.

Lublin, David, and D. Stephen Voss. 2000. Racial redistricting and realignment in southern state legislatures. *American Journal of Political Science* 44: 792–810.

Mabeus, Courtney. 2005. With friends like these. *Capital Eye*, Nov. 21. www.capitaleye.org

MacManus, Susan A. 1978. City council election procedures and minority representation: Are they related? *Social Science Quarterly* 59(1): 153–61.

Marerro, Diana. 2005. Woman hopes to buff up Indian political clout. *Great Falls Tribune*, Nov. 28. www.greatfallstribune.com/apps

Marshall, Catherine, and Gretchen B. Rossman. 1999. *Designing Quality Research*, 3rd ed. Thousand Oaks, CA: Sage Publications.

Maryboy, Mark. 2005. Former Commissioner, San Juan County, Utah. Interview, Feb. 21.

Mayeux, Debra. 2004. GOP office lands in Shiprock. *Farmington Daily Times*, Sept. 19. www.daily-times.com

McCool, Daniel. 1982. Voting patterns of American Indians in Arizona. *Social Science Journal* 19(3): 101–13.

McCool, Daniel. 1985. "Indian Voting." In *American Indian Policy in the Twentieth Century*, ed. Vine Deloria, Jr., pp. 105–33. Norman: University of Oklahoma Press.

McCool, Daniel. 1987. *Command of the Waters: Iron Triangles, Federal Water Development, and Indian Water*. Berkeley: University of California Press.

McCool, Daniel. 2000. Expert witness report regarding *U.S. v. Blaine County, Montana*. C. A. No. CV 99-122-GF-DWM (D. Mont.), DJ.

McCool, Daniel. 2003a. "Expert witness report re: *Bone Shirt v. Hazeltine* (Civil Action No. CIV OI-3032, U.S. District Court, District of South Dakota.

McCool, Daniel. 2003b. Report filed by Professor Daniel McCool, Ph.D., in Rebuttal to "The Political History of the Oglala Sioux Tribe of the Pine Ridge Reservation and the Rosebud Sioux Tribe of the Rosebud Reservation from Prehistory to the Present" by Michael Lawson, Ph.D., and James Muhn, M.A. In the case of *Bone Shirt* v. *Hazeltine* (U.S. Dist. Ct. SD Civ. Act. 01-3032), Feb. 5.

McDonald, Gary. 2005. Commissioner, Roosevelt County, Montana. Phone interview. Mar. 1.

McDonald, Laughlin. 1989. The quiet revolution in minority voting rights. *Vanderbilt Law Review* 42: 1249–97.

McDonald, Laughlin. 1992. "The 1982 Amendments of Section 2 and Minority Representation." In *Controversies in Minority Voting: The Voting Rights Act in Perspective*, ed. Bernard Grofman and Chandler Davidson, pp. 66–84. Washington, DC: The Brookings Institution.

McDonald, Laughlin. 2003a. *A Voting Rights Odyssey: Black Enfranchisement in Georgia*. Cambridge: Cambridge University Press.

McDonald, Laughlin. 2003b. Director, Southern Regional Office, ACLU. Interview, Atlanta, July 24–5.

McDonald, Laughlin. 2004. The Voting Rights Act in Indian Country: South Dakota, a case study. *American Indian Law Review* 29: 43–74.

McDonald, Laughlin. 2005a. Personal communication, Jan. 26.

McDonald, Laughlin. 2005b. Testimony before the House Judiciary Committee's Subcommittee on the Constitution. Oct. 25, 109th Cong., 2d Sess.

McDonald, Laughlin. 2005c. Testimony before the House Judiciary Committee's Subcommittee on the Constitution. Hearings to Examine the Impact and Effectiveness of the Voting Rights Act. Nov. 9, 109th Cong., 2d Sess.

McDonald, Laughlin, Janine Pease, and Richard Guest. 2006. "Voting Rights in South Dakota 1982–2006." A report commissioned by the Leadership Conference for Civil Rights Education Fund. March. www.renewtheVRA.org/

McPherson, Robert S. 1995. *A History of San Juan County: In the Palm of Time*. Salt Lake City: Utah State Historical Society.

McPherson, Robert S. 2001. *Navajo Land, Navajo Culture: The Utah Experience in the Twentieth Century*. Norman: University of Oklahoma Press.

Melmer, David. 2004a. Special report: On the campaign trail in South Dakota. *Indian Country Today*, May 7. www.Indiancountry.com

Melmer, David. 2004b. Indian voters ousted from city in South Dakota. *Indian Country Today*, Sept. 10. www.Indiancountry.com

Melmer, David. 2004c. Campaign 2004: Voting goes smoothly on Pine Ridge. *Indian Country Today*, Nov. 2. www.Indiancountry.com

Melmer, David. 2005a. Senator upset over BIA budget. *Indian Country Today*, Feb. 28. www.Indiancountry.com

Melmer, David. 2005b. American Indian voters face hostility in South Dakota. *Indian Country Today*, Sept. 26. www.Indiancountry.com

Melmer, David. 2005c. ACLU files another suit in South Dakota. *Indian Country Today*, Feb. 15. www.Indiancountry.com

Melmer, David. 2006. Indian programs to take a hit in proposed Bush budget. *Indian Country Today*, Apr. 17. www.indiancountrytoday.com

Mendoza, Greg. 2004. Gila River community program educates youth on political involvement. *NCAI Sentinel 2004 Special Edition*, 9. www.NCAI.org

Mickelson, George. 1990. Executive Proclamation, State of South Dakota, Office of the Governor, "Year of Reconciliation." Quoted in Mario Gonzalez and Elizabeth Cook-Lynn, *The Politics of Hallowed Ground*. Champaign: University of Illinois Press, 1998.

Miller, Jared. 2004. Indian leader rallies voters at Fort Belknap. *Great Falls Tribune*, Jan. 28. www.greatfallstribune.com

Miller, Jared. 2005. Federal race mediator back at work in Havre. *Great Falls Tribune*, Oct. 26. www.greatfallstribune.com

Miniclier, Kit. 1990. Indian vote puts whites on notice in Utah county. *The Denver Post*, Nov. 11, 1C.

Mladenka, Kenneth R. 1989. Blacks and Hispanics in urban politics. *American Political Science Review* 83(1): 165–91.

Montana Human Rights Network. 2000. Drumming up resentment: The anti–Indian movement in Helena, Montana.

Moore, Tammy. 2005. County Clerk, Thurston County, Nebraska. Phone interview, Feb. 7.

Morgan, Manuel. 2004. Commissioner, San Juan County, Utah. Interview, Feb. 16.

Morris, Milton, D. 1984. "Black Electoral Participation and the Distribution of Public Benefits." In *Minority Vote Dilution*, ed. Chandler Davidson, pp. 271–85. Washington, DC: Howard University Press.

Mount Blogmore. 2005. Voting Rights Commission hearing. Sept. 9. www.rapidcityjournal.com/politicalblog/?=831#comments.

Mountain States Legal Foundation. 2004. www.mountainstateslegal.org/mission.cfm

Muskrat, Joseph. 1973. Thoughts on the Indian dilemma. *Civil Rights Digest* 6: 46–7.

National Commission on the Voting Rights Act. 2005. www.votingrightsact.org

National Conference of State Legislatures. 2005. States and tribes building new traditions series. www.ncsl.org/programs/statetribe/2005triblg.htm

National Congress of American Indians. 2004a. Knowing your rights: The Voting Rights Acts of 1965 and 1973 and their implementation. www.NCAI.org

National Congress of American Indians. 2004b. Native Vote 2004 Survey. www.NCAI.org

National Indian Gaming Commission. 2005. National Indian Gaming Commission tribal gaming revenues. www.nigc.gov/nigc/tribes/trigamrev2004to2003.jsp

National Journal. 2002. The K Street jackpot from Indian casinos. Apr. 20, 8.

National Office News 2004. www.fex.org/national_news.shtml#motivate

Native Action Network. 2004. www.nwnativeinfo.com

Native American Rights Fund. 2003. www.narf.org/intro/history.html

Native American Rights Fund. 2005. www.narf.org/cases/index.html

Native Vote 2004–Election Protection Project. February 2005. Special Report. Washington, DC: National Congress of American Indians and the DC Native American Bar Association.

Navajo Times. 2004. Ruling may raise Dine voter turnout. Oct. 28, 1.

NCAI/National Voice. 2004. "Native Vote: Learning from 2004 and preparing for the future: A report from the Native Vote Project leads debriefing." Washington, DC: National Congress of American Indians.

NCAI News, 2004a. Hearing scheduled in voting rights lawsuit filed by National Congress of American Indians and the Minnesota ACLU. www.NCAI.org

NCASL News. 2004b. "State-Tribal issues a focus of Native American rally. National Conference of State Legislatures, Sept. 20. www.ncsl.org

NCAI Sentinel. 2004a. *Native Vote 2004 Special Edition*. National Congress of American Indians. www.NCAI.org

NCAI Sentinel. 2004b. National leaders sound off on native vote 2004. *NCAI Sentinel: Native Vote 2004 Special Edition*. National Congress of American Indians. www.NCAI.org

Newsweek. 2004. Politics: Native power. Sept. 6, 12.

Nieves, Evelyn. 2004. On Pine Ridge, a string of broken promises. *Washington Post*, Oct. 21. www.washingtonpost.com

Norrell, Brenda. 2004. American Indians in Southwest rush to vote. *Indian Country Today*, Nov. 2. www.indiancountry.com

O'Brien, Sharon. 1989. *American Indian Tribal Governments*. Norman: University of Oklahoma Press.

Office of Indian Affairs. 1922. Indian citizenship. Bulletin 20. Washington, DC: U.S. Government Printing Office.

Pachon, Harry, and Louis DeSipio. 1992. Latino elected officials in the 1990s. *PS: Political Science and Politics* 25(2): 212–17.

Parker, Frank R. 1984. "Racial Gerrymandering and Legislative Reapportionment." In *Minority Vote Dilution*, ed. Chandler Davidson, pp. 85–117. Washington, DC: Howard University Press.

Peterson, Helen L. 1957. American Indian political participation. *Annals of the American Academy of Political and Social Science* 311 (May): 116–26.

Pettinger, Ann. 2005. Bordering on racism. *Perceptions*. A Special Report on Race in Montana by the University of Montana School of Journalism. www.umt.ed/journalism/student_work/Native_News_2005

Pew, Penny. 2005. Testimony before the House Judiciary Committee's Subcommittee on the Constitution. Hearing on the Voting Rights Act: Sections 6 and 8 – The Federal Examiner and Observer Program. Nov. 15. 109th Cong., 2d. Sess.

Phelps, Glenn A. 1985. Representation without taxation: Citizenship and suffrage in Indian Country. *American Indian Quarterly* 9(2): 135–48.

Phelps, Glenn A. 1991. Mr. Gerry goes to Arizona: Electoral geography and voting rights in Navajo Country. *American Indian Culture and Research Journal* 15(2): 63–92.

Phillips, Barbara Y. 1995. Reconsidering *Reynolds v. Sims*: The relevance of its basic standard of equality to other vote dilution claims. *Howard Law Journal* 38 (Summer): 561–85.

Pildes, Richard H. 2002. Is voting-rights law now at war with itself? Social science and voting rights in the 2000's. *North Carolina Law Review* 80 (June): 1517–73.

Pitts, Michael J. 2003. Section 5 of the Voting Rights Act: A once and future remedy? *Denver University Law Review* 81: 225–88.

Plumage, Jack. 1985. Statement to the Montana Advisory Committee to the U.S. Commission on Civil Rights, "Hearings on Grievances of Fort Belknap Community Concerning School District No. 12, Harlem, Montana." Sept. 21, 6.

Pommersheim, Frank. 1995. *Braid of Feathers*. Berkeley: University of California Press.

Porter, Kirk. 1918. *A History of Suffrage in the United States*. Chicago: University of Chicago Press.

Porterfield, K. Marie. 1997. North Dakota school district elects two American Indians. *Indian Country Today*, July 14, B1.

President's Committee on Civil Rights. 1947. "To Secure These Rights." Washington, DC: U.S. Government Printing Office.

Pretty-on-Top, John. 2005. Commissioner, Big Horn County, Montana. Phone interview, Mar. 8.

Prucha, Francis Paul. 1984. *The Great Father: The United States Government and the American Indians*, Vols. I and II. Lincoln: University of Nebraska Press.

Raines, Howell. 1977. *My Soul Is Rested: Movement Days in the Deep South Remembered*. New York: Putnam.

Rambow, Charles. 1973. Ku Klux Klan in the 1920s: A concentration on the Black Hills. *South Dakota History – SD State Historical Society and Board of Cultural Preservation Quarterly* (Winter). www.geocities.com/crazyoglala/pahasapa_KKK1920s.html

Rave, Jodi. 2004. Volunteers fight for native voters. *The Missoulian*, Nov. 2, 1.

Rave, Jodi. 2006. Tribes to feel lingering effects of Abramoff scandal. *The Missoulian*, Jan. 8. www.missoulian.com

Rawls, James. 1996. *Chief Red Fox Is Dead: A History of Native Americans Since 1945*. New York: Harcourt Brace.

Redd, Bill. 2004. Former Commissioner, San Juan County, Utah. Interview, Feb. 15.

Reynolds, Jerry. 2004a. NCAI, ACLU ask courts to intervene for Indian voters in Minnesota. *Indian Country Today*, Oct. 29. www.indiancountry.com

Reynolds, Jerry. 2004b. Court: Tribal IDs valid to vote with in Minnesota. *Indian Country Today*, Nov. 1. www.indiancountry.com

Riley, Michael. 2005. Montana town confronts racist label. *Denver Post*, Sept. 18. www.denverpost.com/portlet

Ritt, Leonard. 1979. Some social and political views of American Indians. *Ethnicity* 6: 45–72.

Robertson, Paul. 2002. *The Power of the Land*. New York: Routeledge Press.

Robinson, Theodore P. and Thomas Dye. 1978. Reformism and Black representation on city councils. *Social Science Quarterly* 59(1): 133–41.

Rodriguez, Victor Andres. 2003. Section 5 of the Voting Rights Act of 1965 after *Boerne*: The beginning of the end of preclearance? *California Law Review* 91 (May): 769–826.

Roosevelt, Theodore. 1901. *Messages and Papers of the Presidents*, Vol. XV. Washington, DC: U.S. Government Printing Office.

Rosebrough, Bob. 2005. Mayor, Gallup City, New Mexico. Phone interview, Mar. 1.

Sage Council. 2004. www.sagecouncil.org

Sarasohn, Judy. 2004. Indians build "emerging presence" in capital. *The Washington Post*, Oct. 28. www.washingtonpost.com

Schell, Herbert. 1975. *History of South Dakota*. Lincoln: University of Nebraska Press.

Schermerhorn, James. 2004. Former Attorney, U.S. Department of Justice. Phone interview, Sept. 26.

Schermerhorn, James M., and Michael A. Stoto. 1984. Measuring a redistricting plan's deviation from population equality and its effect on minorities: New Mexico's experiment with a "votes cast" formula. *U.C. Davis Law Review* 17(2): 591–610.

Schmidt, Steve. 2004. Getting out vote in Indian Country. *San Diego Union-Tribune*, Sept. 26. www.signonsandiego.com

Schmidt, Susan, and James Grimaldi. 2005a. Panel says Abramoff laundered tribal funds. *Washington Post*, June 23, A1.

Schmidt, Susan, and James Grimaldi. 2005b. Plea deal near with 2nd Abramoff associate. *Washington Post*, Dec. 9, A8.

Schmidt, Susan, and James Grimaldi. 2006. Abramoff pleads guilty to 3 counts. *Washington Post*, Jan. 4. www.washingtonpost.com

Securing the Native Voice: Reauthorization of the Minority Language Provisions (Section 203) of the Voting Rights Act. 2005. Joint Testimony of the National Congress of American Indians and the Native American Rights Fund before the House Judiciary Committee, Subcommittee on the Constitution. Washington, DC., Nov. 9. Report available from the National Congress of American Indians.

Sells, Bryan. 2003. Staff Attorney, Southern Regional Office, ACLU. Interview, July 25.

Shaffer, Mark. 2004. Campaign 2004: Southwest primaries attract native pollsters. *Indian Country Today*, Feb. 13. www.indiancountry.com

Shaw, Bill. 1986. Whites vs. Indians in Montana, where racism still reigns. *San Francisco Examiner*, Oct. 5, A-4.

Sho-Ban News. 1986a. At-large voting challenged by NIYC. Dec. 31, 16.

Sho-Ban News. 1986b. Violation of 1965 Voting Rights Act. June 5, 15.

Sho-Ban News. 1987. Judge stalls discriminatory election. Feb. 5, 6.

Sioux Falls Argus Leader. 1989. Feb. 13, A1.

Sisco, Carol. 1990a. Navajos build pathway to added clout. *The Salt Lake Tribune*, June 24, B1.

Sisco, Carol. 1990b. Navajos flock to polls in historic San Juan vote. *The Salt Lake Tribune*, Nov. 7, B1.

Sleight, Ken. 1998. The political Mark Maryboy: Utah's only Native American county commissioner. *The Zephyr*, Oct.–Nov. 18–19.

Smith, Constance. 1960. *Voting and Election Laws*. New York: Oceana Publications.

Smith, Stephen Samuel, Karen M. Kedrowski, and Joseph M. Ellis. 2004. Electoral structures, venue selection, and the (new?) politics of school desegregation. *Perspectives on Politics* 2(4): 795–801.

Smith, Susan. 2005, Superintendent, Wagner School District, South Dakota. Phone interview, Feb. 4.

Snowball, Paul. 2005. Commissioner, Thurston County, Nebraska. Phone interview, Jan. 13.

South Dakota Advisory Committee to the U.S. Commission on Civil Rights. 1981. Native American participation in South Dakota's political system. Washington, DC.

South Dakota Advisory Committee to the U. S. Commission on Civil Rights. 2000. Native Americans in South Dakota: An erosion of confidence in the justice system. Washington, DC.

South Dakota Equal Justice Commission. 2006. Final Report and Recommendations. Pierre: South Dakota Supreme Court.

Steiner, Stan. 1968. *The New Indians*. New York: Harper & Row.

Stephenson, Donald Grier, Jr. 2004. *The Right to Vote: Rights and Liberties Under the Law*. Santa Barbara, CA: ABC-CLIO.

Stevens, Lynn. 2004. Commissioner, San Juan County, Utah. Interview, Feb. 16.

Stevens, Patty. 2005a. School Board Member, Ronan School District, Montana. Phone interview, Jan. 5.

Stevens, Patty. 2005b. School Board Member, Ronan School District, Montana. Phone interview, Feb. 16.

Swenson, Eric. 2004a. Attorney. Phone interview, Feb. 10.

Swenson, Eric. 2004b. Interview, Sept. 14.

Taebel, Delbert. 1978. Minority representation on city councils: The impact of structure on Blacks and Hispanics. *Social Science Quarterly* 59(1): 142–52.

Tapaha, Edward. 2004. Election Coordinator, San Juan County, Utah. Interview, Feb. 16.

Thompson, Gregory C. 1983. "Utah's Indian Country: The American Indian Experience in San Juan County, 1700–1980." In *San Juan County, Utah: People, Resources, and History*, ed. Allan Kent Powell, pp. 51–71. Salt Lake City: Utah State Historical Society.

Thompson, Heather Dawn. 2005. Special Report: Native Vote 2004 Election Protection Project. Washington, DC: National Congress of American Indians and the DC Native American Bar Association.

Thompson, Linda. 1998. Selection of juries is racist, lawyer says. *Deseret News*, May 13, B1.

Tobar, Hector. 1990. Navajos try to seize power in sweeping bid for office politics: An all Indian slate runs in county election in southern Utah, with the goal of redistributing funds. *Los Angeles Times*, Aug. 27, 1.

Toobin, Jeffrey. 2004. Poll position. *New Yorker* 80(27): 56–61.

Trahant, M. N. and Mary Jo Pitzl. 1988. Rights suit could boost school-board minorities. *Arizona Republic*, Jan. 31, A1.

Treaty of Fort Laramie. 1868. Signed Apr. 28. www.archives.gov/education/lessons/sioux-treaty.

Turnbull, Lornet. 2004. Indian policy comes under fire. *Seattle Times*, Dec. 19, A-1.

Tyler, Lyman. 1973. *A History of Indian Policy*. Washington, DC: U.S. Department of the Interior, Bureau of Indian Affairs, U.S. Government Printing Office.

United Property Owners. 2004. Grassroots strength and information on the protection of private property rights. www.unitedpropertyowners.org

U.S. Census. 1980a. Advanced estimates of social, economic, and housing characteristics, Utah. www.census.gov

U.S. Census. 1980b. American Indians, Eskimos, and Aleuts on identified reservations and in the historic areas of Oklahoma. www.census.gov

U.S. Census. 1993. We the first Americans: A special analysis. Sept. www.census.gov/specialreports.

U.S. Census. 2000. Data Set: Census 2000 Summary File 3 (SF 3)–Sample Data. www.census.gov

U.S. Census. 2001. Poverty in the United States: 2001. Special Report. www.census.gov/specialreports

U.S. Census. 2002. Department of Commerce: State and County QuickFacts. www:quickfacts.census.gov/qfd/states/46/46121

U.S. Commission on Civil Rights. 1975. *The Voting Rights Act: Ten Years After*. Washington, DC: U.S. Commission on Civil Rights.

U.S. Commission on Civil Rights. 1977. The unfinished business: twenty years later. A report submitted to the U.S. Commission on Civil Rights by its Fifty-One State Advisory Committee. Washington, DC.

U.S. Congress, House of Representatives. 1924. Report No. 222.

U.S. Congress, House. 2006. Fannie Lou Hamer, Rosa Parks and Coretta Scott King Voting Rights Act Reauthorization and Amendments of 2006. 109th Cong., 2nd Sess., H.R. 9.

U.S. Congress. House, Committee on the Judiciary. 1975. *Voting Rights Act Extension*. 94th Cong., 1st Sess., H. Rept. 94–196. Washington, DC.

U.S. Congress, House, Committee on the Judiciary. 1992. *Voting Rights Language Assistance Act of 1992*. 102nd Cong., 2nd Sess., H. Rept. 102–655. Washington, DC: U.S. Government Printing Office.

U.S. Congress. House, Committee on the Judiciary. 2005. Oversight hearings on the Voting Rights Act. 109th Cong., 1st Sess. Oct. 18, 20, 25; Nov. 1, 8, 9, 15 www.judiciary.house.gov/oversightlist.aspx

U.S. Congress, House, Committee on the Judiciary, Subcommittee on Civil and Constitutional Rights. 1975. *Hearings on Extension of the Voting Rights Act*, Part 2. 94th Cong., 1st Sess. Washington, DC: U.S. Government Printing Office.

U.S. Congress, Senate, Committee on the Judiciary, Subcommittee on Constitutional Rights. 1970. *Hearings on Amendments to the Voting Rights Act of 1965*. 91st Cong., 1st and 2nd Sess. Washington, DC: U.S. Government Printing Office.

U.S. Congress, Senate. 1982. Report of the Committee on the Judiciary on S. 1992 with Additional, Minority, and Supplemental Views. Report No. 97–417. Washington, DC: U.S. Government Printing Office.

U.S. Congress, Senate, Committee on the Judiciary. 1975. *Voting Rights Act Extension*. 94th Cong., 1st Sess. S. Rept. 94–295. Washington, DC: U.S. Government Printing Office.

U.S. Congress, Senate, Committee on the Judiciary. 1992. *Voting Rights Language Assistance Act of 1992*. 102nd Cong., 2nd Sess., S. Rept. 102–315. Washington, DC: U.S. Government Printing Office.

U.S. Congress, Senate, Committee on the Judiciary, Subcommittee on the Constitution. 1992. *Hearing on Voting Rights Act Language Assistance Amendments of 1992*. 102nd Cong., 2nd Sess. Washington, DC: U.S. Government Printing Office.

U.S. Department of Education, Office of the Assistant Secretary for Elementary and Secondary Education. 1985. Complaint of Fort Belknap Community Council, In re: Financial Assistance Program for Harlem School District No. 12, Harlem, Montana. Washington, DC: U.S. Department of Education.

U.S. Department of the Interior. 1928. Quoted in the amicus curie brief filed by the National Congress of American Indians and the American Civil Liberties Union in *Harrison v. Laveen* 67 Ariz. 337, at p. 38.

U.S. Department of the Interior. 2004. Strengthening the circle: Interior Indian affairs highlights, 2001–2004. www.doi.gov

U.S. Department of Justice. 2000. "Benson County, North Dakota, to Change Its Method of Election, Under Agreement with the Justice Department." Press release. www.usdoj.gov/opa/pr/2000/March/107cr.htm

U.S. Department of Justice. 2006. Section 5 Objection Determinations. www.usdoj.gov/crt/voting/sec˙5/obj_activ.htm

Utley, Robert. 1993. *The Lance and the Shield*. New York: Henry Holt.

Valelly, Richard M. 2004. *The Two Reconstructions: The Struggle for Black Enfranchisement*. Chicago: University of Chicago Press.

Voting Rights Renewal Update. 2006a. Congressional Opponents of Voting Rights Act Become Aggressive. Atlanta, GA: Report prepared by the ACLU Voting Rights Project, June 13.

Voting Rights Renewal Update. 2006b. Bush Questioned on Voting Rights Act. Atlanta, GA: Report prepared by the ACLU Voting Rights Project, June 27.

Wagoner, Paula. 2002. *They Treat Us Just Like Indians*. Lincoln: University of Nebraska Press.

Walker, Samuel. 1999. *In Defense of American Liberties: A History of the ACLU*, 2nd ed. Carbondale: Southern Illinois University Press.

Washington Post. 2002. ACLU, Sioux settle election lawsuit. Nov. 9, A09.

Weber, Kenneth. 1989. Demographic shifts in eastern Montana reservation counties, an emerging Native American political power base? *Journal of Ethnic Studies* 16 (Winter): 101–16.

Weber, Ronald. 2000. A report on vote dilution issues for the case of *U.S. v. Blaine County*. Civ. No. 99-122-GF.

Weber, Ronald. 2001. A rebuttal report on liability issues for hearing in *U.S. v. Blaine County*. Civ. No. 99-122-GF.

Weisman, Jonathan, and Derek Willis. 2005. Democrat on panel probing Abramoff to return tribal donations. *Washington Post*, Dec. 14, A4.

Welch, Susan, and Albert K. Karnig. 1978. Representation of Blacks on big city school boards. *Social Science Quarterly* 59(1): 162–72.

Wilkins, David. 1997. *American Indian Sovereignty and the U.S. Supreme Court*. Austin: University of Texas Press.

Wilkins, David. 2002. *American Indian Politics and the American Political System*. New York: Rowman and Littlefield.

Wilkins, David, and K. Tsianina Lomawaima. 2001. *Uneven Ground: American Indian Sovereignty and Federal Law*. Norman: University of Oklahoma Press.

Wilkinson, Charles. 2005. *Blood Struggle: The Rise of Modern Indian Nations*. New York: W. W. Norton.

Will, George. 2005. VRA, all of it, forever? *Newsweek*, Oct. 10, 70.

Wolf, Darren. 2005. Commissioner, Thurston County, Nebraska. Phone interview, Jan. 20.

Wolfinger, Raymond and Steven Rosenstone. 1980. *Who Votes?* New Haven, CT: Yale University Press.

Wolfley, Jeanette. 1991. Jim Crow, Indian style: The disenfranchisement of Native Americans. *American Indian Law Review* 16(1): 167–202.

Woster, Kevin. 2004a. GOP plans hunt on rez. *Rapid City Journal*, Apr. 10, 1.

Woster, Kevin. 2004b. Rumors of vote buying continue. *Rapid City Journal*, Nov. 2.

Woster, Kevin and Denise Ross. 2002. Claims of voter fraud beget fraud claims. *Rapid City Journal*, Dec. 26. www.rapidcityjournal.com/articles/2002/12/14/news/local/news03.txt

Young, Robert W. 1968. *The Role of the Navajo in the Southwest Drama*. Gallup, NM: The Gallup Independent and Robert W. Young.

York. Bryan. 2002. Bad lands, bad votes. *The National Review*, Dec. 23, 32–6.

Zax, Jeffrey. 2003. Voting patterns in South Dakota state senate districts 26 and 27 in the 1996, 1998, 2000, and 2002 general elections. Prepared for the Office of the Attorney General, State of South Dakota. Jan. 22.

Zelden, Charles L. 2002. *Voting Rights on Trial: A Handbook with Cases, Laws, and Documents*. Santa Barbara, CA: ABC-CLIO.

Cases

Many of the case materials, including judicial opinions, used in this book have not been published in readily available sources. To adapt these materials to social science citation format, we have adopted the following conventions. For judicial opinions that are readily accesible through standard printed or electronic sources, the date in parentheses in the text is the year of the published judicial opinion most relevant to the immediate point. In the Case reference list that follows, published opinions in a given case are listed in sequence from earliest to latest.

For cases with no published judicial opinion, the date in parentheses in both the text and the reference list is the year of the case's initial filing. An asterisk following the date indicates that this is the year of filing, not of the decision. Sometimes several years may pass between filing and a court's published or unpublished decisions. In addition to the year of filing, the unpublished cases are identified by their civil action or docket number. Docket numbers are unique identifiers assigned by the court to each case in sequence upon its filing, which are used to track all documents associated with a given case. Where letters follow the numbers, they refer to the city within the judicial district where the case was filed and/or the initials of the judge assigned to that case. If a case is appealed to a higher court, that court assigns the case a new docket number.

Specific documents referenced in the cases are listed in chronological order below the main entry for each case. One exception to this practice is reports by expert witnesses, which have named authors and thus are listed in the general References.

Unpublished case materials may be obtained by writing to the court where the case was heard, although many courts centrally archive materials after some number of years. Many federal courts now have cases on a shared electronic system called PACER for Public Access to Court Electronic Records (pacer.psc.uscourts.gov). Other courts maintain their own Internet-based records access, which vary in terms of how many years back the records go and whether they require registration and charge fees.

ACLU of Minnesota v. Kiffmeyer. 2004. 2004 U.S. Dist. Lexis 22996 (D. Minn.).
Consent Decree. September 12, 2005.

Alden v. Board of Commissioners of Rosebud County. 1999*. Civ. No. 99-148-BLG-DWM (D. Mont.).
Order. December 29, 1999.
Order. May 9, 2000.

Allen v. Merrell. 1956. 305 P.2d 490 (Utah); 6 Utah 2d 32; 1956. cert granted, 352 U.S. 889; 1957. vacated as moot, 353 U.S. 932.

Allen v. State Board of Elections. 1969. 393 U.S. 544.

American Horse v. Kundert. 1984*. Civ. No. 84-5159 (D. S.D.).

Apache County v. U.S. 1966. 256 F. Supp. 903 (D. D.C.).

Apache County High School District v. U.S. 1977*. Civ. No. 77-1815 (D. D.C.).
Memorandum Opinion. June 12, 1980.

Arizona v. Reno. 1995. 887 F. Supp. 318 (D. D.C.); 1996. cert. granted but dismissed pursuant to Rule 46, 516 U.S. 1155.

Beer v. U.S. 1976. 425 U.S. 130.
Black Bull v. Dupree School District. 1986*. Civ. No. 86-3012 (D. S.D.).
Blackfeet and Gros Ventre Tribes v. U.S. 1967. 18 Indian Claims Commission. 241.
Blackmoon v. Charles Mix County. 2005a. 386 F. Supp. 2d 1108; 2005b. reconsideration denied and partial summary judgment granted, 2005 U.S. Dist. LEXIS 27551 (D. S.D.).
Bone Shirt v. Hazeltine. 2002. Section 5 opinion, 200 F. Supp. 2d 1150 (D. S.D.); 2004a. order denying defendant' motion to strike McCool, 2004 U.S. Dist. LEXIS 28775; 2004b. order denying summary judgment, 2004 U.S. Dist. LEXIS 28778; 2004c. Section 2 opinion, 336 F. Supp. 2d 976; 2005. remedial order, 387 F. Supp. 2d 1035; 2006. aff'd 2006 U.S. App. LEXIS 21409 (8th Cir.).
Complaint. Civ. No. 01-3032 (D. S.D.). Decemeber 26, 2001.
Defendants' Brief in Support of Motion for Summary Judgment. July 18, 2003.
Plaintiffs' Brief in Opposition to the Defendants' Motion for Summary Judgment. August 11, 2003.
Plaintiffs' Proposed Findings of Fact and Conclusions of Law. March 22, 2004.
Defendants' Proposed Findings of Fact and Conclusions of Law. March 29, 2004.
Bowannie v. Bernalillo School District. 1988*. Civ. No. 88-0212-JP (D. N.M.).
Buckanaga v. Sisseton School District. 1986. 804 F. 2d 469 (8th Cir.).
Consent decree. 1988. 15 Indian Law Reporter 3119 (D. S.D.).
Bush v. Vera. 1996. 517 U.S. 952.
Canady v. Lumberton City Board of Education. 1981. 454 U.S. 957.
Casuse v. City of Gallup. 1987. 746 P.2d 1103 (N.M.); 106 N.M. 571.
Cherokee Nation v. Georgia. 1831. 30 U.S. (5 Pet) 1.
Choctaw and McCurtain Counties v. U.S. 1976*. Civ. No. 76-1250 (D. D. C.).
City of Boerne v. Flores. 1997. 521 U.S. 507.
City of Mobile v. Bolden. 1980. 446 U.S. 55.
Clark v. Holbrook Unified School District. 1989. 703 F. Supp. 56 (D. Ariz.).
Clark v. Roemer. 1993. 500 U.S. 646.
Cottier v. City of Martin. 2002. 445 F.3d 1113 (8th Cir.).
Cousin v. Sundquist. 1998. 145 F.3d 818 (6th Cir.).
Crank v. Utah Judicial Council. 2001. 20 P.3d 307. (Utah); 2001 UT 8.
Cuthair v. Montezuma-Cortez, Colorado School District. 1998. 7 F. Supp. 2d 1152 (D. Colo.).
Daschle v. Thune. 2004*. Civ. No. 04-4177. (D. S.D.)
Temporary Restraining Order. November 2, 2004
Easley v. Cromartie. 2001. 532 U.S. 234.
Elk v. Wilkins, 1894. 112 U.S. 94.
Emery v. Hunt (In re Certification of a Question of Law). 2000. 615 N.W.2d 590 (S.D.); 2000 SD 97. Certified from 2000*. Civ No. 00-3008. (D. S.D.).
Emison v. Growe. 1992. 782 F. Supp. 427 (D. Minn); 1993. rev'd 507 U.S. 25.
Estevan v. Grants-Cibola County School District. 1984*. Civ. No. 84-1752-HB (D. N.M.).

Farrakhan v. Washington. 2003. 338 F.3d 1009 (9th Cir.); 2004. rehearing and rehearing en banc denied, 359 F.3d 1116 (9th Cir.); 2004. cert. denied sub nom *Locke v. Farrakhan*, 543 U.S. 984.
Felipe and Ascencio v. Cibola County Commission. 1985*. Civ. No. 85-0301 (D. N.M.).
Fiddler v. Sieker. 1986*. Civ. No. 86-3050 (D. S.D.).
Fortson v. Dorsey. 1965. 379 U.S. 433.
Frank v. Forest County. 2002. 194 F. Supp 2d 867 (E.D. Wisc.); 2003. aff'd 336 F.3d 570 (7th Cir.).
Georgia v. Ashcroft. 2003. 539 U.S. 461.
Goddard v. Babbitt. 1982. 536 F. Supp. 538 (D. Ariz.).
Goodluck v. Apache County. 1975. 417 F. Supp. 13 (D. Ariz.); 1976. aff'd 429 U.S. 876.
Grinnell v. Sinner. 1992*. Civ. No. A1-92-066 (D. N.D).
Harrison v. Laveen. 1948. 196 P.2d 456(Ariz.); 67 Ariz. 337.
Opening Brief of Appellants.
Appellee's Reply.
Brief, Amicus Curiae, of the NCAI and ACLU.
Brief, Amicus Curiae, of the United States.
In re By-a-lil-le, 1909. 100 P. 450 (Ariz.); 12 Ariz. 150.
In re Primus. 1978. 436 U.S. 412.
Independent School District of Tulsa v. Bell. 1976*. Civ. No. 76-C-573-B (N.D. Okla.).
Intertribal Council of Arizona v. Brewer. 2006*. Civ No. 3:06-01362-JAT (D. Ariz.).
Jepsen v. Vigil-Giron. 2001*. Civ. No. D0101 CV 2001-02177 (N.M. Ist Jud. Dist.).
Johnson v. McIntosh. 1832. 21 U.S. 543.
Johnson-Lee v. Minneapolis. 2004. 2004 Lexis 19708 (D. Minn.).
Kirk v. San Juan College Board. 1986*. Civ. No. 86-1503 (D. N.M.).
Kirkie v. Buffalo County. 2003*. Civ. No. 03-CV-3011-CBK (D. S.D.).
Consent Decree. February 10, 2004.
Klahr v. Williams (originally *Klahr v. Goddard*). 1972. 339 F. Supp. 922 (D. Ariz.); 1974. 388 F. Supp. 1007 (D. Ariz.).
Kramer v. Union Free School District. 1969. 395 U.S. 621.
Large v. Fremont County. 2005*. Civ. No. 05-CV-270-ABJ. (D. Wyo.).
Largo v. McKinley Consolidated School District. 1984*. Civ. No. 84-1751 (D. N.M.).
Little Thunder v. South Dakota. 1975. 518 F. 2d 1253 (8th Cir.).
Maine v. U.S. 1975*. Civ. No. 75-2125 (D. D.C.).
Stipulation of Dismissal without Prejudice. July 5, 1977.
Matt v. Ronan School District. 1999*. Civ. No. 99-94-M-DWM (D. Mont.). Order. January 13, 2000.
McConnell v. Blaine County. 2002. 37 Fed. Appx. 276; 2002 U.S. App. LEXIS 10883 (9th Cir.).
Meyers v. Board of Education of the San Juan School District. 1995. 905 F. Supp. 1544.

Miller v. Johnson. 1995. 515 U.S. 900.
Montoya v. Bolack. 1962. 372 P2d. 387 (N.M.); 70 N. M. 196.
Navajo Nation v. Arizona Independent Redistricting Commission. 2002. 230 F. Supp. 2d 998 (D. Ariz.).
New Mexico v. U.S. 1976*. Civ. No. 76-0067 (D. D.C.).
Old Person v. Cooney. 2000. 230 F.3d 1113 (9th Circ.); 2002. Remand sub nom *Old Person v. Brown*, 182 F. Supp. 2d 1002 (D. Mont.).
Opsahl v. Johnson. 1917. 163 N.W. 988 (Minn.); 138 Minn. 42.
Porter v. Hall. 1928. 271 P. 411 (Ariz.); 34 Ariz. 308.
Prince v. Board of Education. 1975. 543 P.2d. 1176(N.M.); 88 N.M. 548.
Quick Bear Quiver v. Nelson (originally *Quick Bear Quiver v. Hazeltine).* 2005. 387 F. Supp. 2d 1027 (D. S.D.); 2005. stay denied, 2005 U.S. Dist. LEXIS 27550 (D. S.D.); 2006. appeal dismissed as moot, 163 L. Ed. 2d 849; 2006 U.S. LEXIS 9.
Reno v. Bossier Parish School Board. 2000. 528 U.S. 320.
Reynolds v. Sims. 1964. 377 U.S. 533.
Sanchez v. King. 1982. 550 F. Supp. 13 (D. N.M.); 1983. aff'd 459 U.S. 801.
Findings of Fact and Conclusions of Law (on remand). Civ No. 82-0067. August 8, 1984.
Shakopee Mdewakanton Sioux Community and the U.S. v. City of Prior Lake. 1985. 771 F.2d 1153 (8th Cir.); 1986. cert. denied, 475 U.S. 1011.
Shaw v. Reno. 1993. 509 U.S. 630.
Shirley v. Superior Court. 1973. 513 P. 2d 939 (Ariz); 109 Ariz. 510.
Simenson v. Bell.[originally *Simenson v. Levi*]. 1976*. Civ. No. 76-59-HG (D. Mont.).
Memorandum and Order. January 24, 1978.
Sinajini v. Board of Education of the San Juan School District. 1975. 1975 U.S. Dist. LEXIS 15526; 1997. 964 F. Supp. 319.
South Carolina v. Katzenbach. 1966. 383 U.S. 301.
South Dakota v. U.S. 1980*. Civ. No. 80-1976 (D. D.C.).
Consent Decree. December 2, 1981.
Stabler v. Thurston County. 1997. 129 F. 3d. 1015 (8th Circ.); 1998. cert. denied, 523 U.S. 1118.
Swift v. Leach. 1920. 178 N.W. 437 (N.D.); 45 N.D. 437.
Thornburgh v. Gingles. 1986. 478 U.S. 30.
Trujillo v. Garley. 1948*. Civ. No. 1353 (D. N.M.).
Stipulation of Fact.
Conclusions of Law. August 11, 1948.
Defendant's Objections to Conclusions of Law.
Tso v. Cuba Independent School District. 1985. Civ. No. 85-1023-JB (D. N.M.).
U.S. v. Alamosa County. 2004. 306 F. Supp. 2d 1016 (D. Colo.).
U.S. v. Arizona. 1975. 417 F. Supp. 13 (D. Ariz.); 1976. aff'd 429 U.S. 876.
U.S. v. Arizona. 1988*. Civ. No. 88-1989-PHX-EHC (D. Ariz.).
Joint Motion and Order to Dismiss. December 13–14, 1995
U.S. v. Arizona. 1994. 1994 U.S. Dist. LEXIS 17606 (D. Ariz.).
U.S. v. Benson County. 2000*. Civ. No. A2-00-30 (D. N.D.).
U.S. v. Bernalillo County. 1998*. Civ. No. 98-156BB (D. N.M.).

U.S. v. Blaine County. 2001. denial of defendants' motion for summary judgment, 157 F.
Supp. 2d 1145 (D. S.D.); 2004. aff'd on merits 363 F.3d 897 (9th Cir.); 2005. cert denied 544 U.S. 992.
Complaint. Civ. No. 99-122-GF (D. Mont.). November 16, 1999.
Defendants' Answer to Complaint. January 3, 2000.
Defendants' Motion for Summary Judgment. January 31, 2001.
Memorandum in Support of Defendants' Motion for Summary Judgment. January 31, 2001.
Brief in Opposition to Defendants' Motion for Summary Judgment. February 27, 2001.
United States' Response to the Memorandum in Support of Defendants' Motion for Summary Judgment. February 28, 2001.
Reply to the United States' Response to Blaine County's Motion for Summary Judgment. March 14, 2001.
Defendants' Findings of Fact and Conclusions of Law. January 10, 2002.
United States' Proposed Findings of Fact and Conclusions of Law. January 10, 2002.
Findings of Fact and Conclusions of Law and Order. March 21, 2002.
U.S. v. Cibola County. 1993*. Civ. No. 93-1134-LH/LFG (D. N.M.).
U.S. v. Day County. 1999*. Civ. No. 99-1024 (D. S.D.).
Plaintiff United States' Required Statement of Material Facts. February 2, 2000.
U.S. v. Humboldt County. 1978*. Civ. No. R-78-0144 (D. Nev.).
U.S. v. McKinley County. 1986a*. Civ. No. 86-0028M (D. N.M).
U.S. v. McKinley County. 1986b*. Civ. No. 86-0029C (D. N.M).
Consent Decree. January 13, 1986.
U.S. v. New Mexico. 1988*. Civ. No. 88–1457-SC (D. N.M.).
U.S. v. Roosevelt County. 2000*. Civ. No. 00-50-BLG-JDS (D. Mont.).
U.S. v. San Juan County [New Mexico]. 1979a*. Civ. No. 79-507-JB (D. N.M.).
U.S. v. San Juan County [New Mexico]. 1979b*. Civ. No. 79-508-JB (D. N.M.).
U.S. v. San Juan County [Utah]. 1983a*. Civ. No. 83-1286W (D. Utah).
Complaint. November 22, 1983.
Agreed Settlement and Order. April 4, 1984.
U.S. v. San Juan County [Utah]. 1983b*. Civ. No. 83-1287 (D. Utah).
Complaint. November 22, 1983.
Agreed Settlement and Order. January 11, 1984.
First Amended Settlement and Order. October 11, 1990.
Joint Motion for Termination of Consent Decree and Entry of Order. July 19, 1995.
Order. December 21, 1998.
U.S. v. Scanlon. 2005. Crim. No. 05-411 (ESH) (D. D.C.). Violation: Count One: 18. U.S.C. Sec. 371.
Plea Agreement. November 17, 2005.
U.S. v. Sioux Nation of Indians. 1980. 448 U.S. 356.
U.S. v. Socorro County. 1993*. Civ. No. 93-1244-JP (D. N.M.).
U.S. v. South Dakota. 1979*. Civ. No. 79-3039 (D. S.D.).
U.S. v. South Dakota. 1980. 636 F. 2d. 241 (8th Cir.).

U.S. v. South Dakota. 2001. 132 F. Supp. 2d 803 (D. S.D.).
U.S. v. Thurston County. 1978*. Civ. No. 78-0-380 (D. Neb.).
U.S. v. Town of Bartelme. 1978*. Civ. No. 78-C-101 (E.D. Wisc.).
U.S. v. Tripp County. 1978*. Civ. No. 78-3045' (D. S.D.).
Order. February 6, 1979.
Vigil v. Lujan. 2001. 191 F. Supp. 2d 1273 (D. N.M.).
Defendants Speaker Lujan and President Pro Tempore Romero's Motion to Dismiss Consolidated Cases . . . , Civ. No. 01-1077-BB/RLP-ACE.
February 8, 2002.
Response of the Jicarilla Apache Nation and Carson Vicenti in Opposition to the Various "Expedited Motions" for Appellate Review . . . , February 8, 2002.
Response of the Navajo Nation to the Expedited Motions . . . , February 8, 2002.
Order. March 15, 2002.
Wedell v. Wagner Community School District. 2002*. Civ. No. 02-4056-KES (D. S.D.).
Whitcomb v. Chavis. 1971. 403 U.S. 125.
White v. Regester. 1973. 412 U.S. 755.
Windy Boy v. Big Horn County. 1986. 647 F. Supp 1002 (D.Mont.).
Winters v. U.S. 1908. 207 U.S. 564.
Worcester v. Georgia. 1832. 31 U.S. (6 Pet.) 515.
Yanito v. Barber. 1972. 348 F. Supp. 587.
Zephier v. Cihak. 2004*. Civ. No. 04-91 (S.D. 1st. Jud. Cir., Charles Mix County).
Zimmer v. McKeithen. 1973. 485 F.2d 1297.

Statutes

Act Providing for Elections. 1897. Laws of the State of Utah. 1897. 2nd Session: 163.
Act of November 6, 1919. U.S. Statutes at Large 41: 350.
Act of March 3, 1921. U.S. Statutes at Large 41: 1249.
Act of Feb. 27, 1951, Ch. 471, 1951 S. D. Laws, 432 (repealing Sec. 65.0801 of 1939 S. D. Code).
Act of April 4, 1985, ch. 202, 1985 N.M. Laws 1238 (school boards); ch. 203, 1985 N.M. Laws 1239 (municipalities), and ch. 204, 1985 N.M. Laws 1242 (counties). Now codified as NMSA §22-45-1.1, §4-38-3, and §3-12-1.1.
Civil Rights Act of 1866. 1866. Statutes at Large of the USA 14: 27
Civil Rights Act of 1957. 1957. U.S. Statutes at Large 71: 634.
Civil Rights Act of 1960. 1960. U.S. Statutes at Large 74: 86.
Civil Rights Act of 1964. 1964. U.S. Statutes at Large 78: 241.
Dawes Act. 1887. U.S. Statutes at Large 24: 388.
Fannie Lou Hamer, Rosa Parks, and Coretta Scott King Voting Rights Act Reauthorization and Amendments Act of 2006. 2006. U.S. Statutes at Large 120:577.
First Montana Assembly. 1866. Acts, Resolutions and Memorials of the Territory of Montana Passed by the First Legislative Assembly. Virginia City: D. W. Tilton.

General Laws and Memorials and Resolutions of the Territory of Montana Passed at the Fourth Session of the Legislative Assembly. 1868. Virginia City: D. W. Tilton.

General Laws, Memorials and Resolutions of the Territory of Montana Passed at the Seventh Session of the Legislative Assembly. 1871. Virginia City: D. W. Tilton.

Indian Citizenship Act. 1924. U.S. Statutes at Large 13: 253.

Indian Reorganization Act. 1934. U.S. Statutes at Large 48: 984.

Laws, Memorials and Resolutions of the Territory of Montana Passed at the Ninth Regular Session of the Legislative Assembly. 1876. Helena: *Helena Daily and Weekly Herald*.

Laws, Regulations and Memorials of the State of Montana Passed at the Seventh Regular Session of the Legislative Assembly. Helena: State Publishing Co. 1901.

Laws, Regulations and Memorials of the State of Montana Passed at the Tenth Regular Session of the Legislative Assembly. 1907. Helena: State Publishing Co.

Laws, Regulations and Memorials of the State of Montana Passed at the Twenty-second Regular Session of the Legislative Assembly. 1919. Helena: State Publishing Co.

Laws, Regulations and Memorials of the State of Montana Passed at the Twenty-sixth Regular Session of the Legislative Assembly. 1932. Helena: State Publishing Co.

Montana Enabling Act. 1889. U.S. Statutes at Large 25: 676.

Oklahoma Enabling Act. 1906. U.S. Statutes at Large 34: 267.

S. D. Laws. 1895. Ch. 84, Sec. 7.

S. D. Laws. 1901. H.J.R. 6, ch. 147, 1901: 248.

S. D. Laws. 1939. Ch. 65.08, Sec. 65.0801 (1).

South Dakota revised Civil Code. 1903, Sec. 26.

Territorial Laws of Dakota Territory. 1862. ch. 32, Sec. 51, approved May 15.

Territorial Laws of Dakota Territory. 1866. "A Memorial and Joint Resolution Regarding the Appointment of an Indian Agent," ch. 38, 1866: 551.

Territorial Laws of Dakota Territory. 1867a. "A Memorial to General Grant, Relative to Indian Matters in the Northwest," ch. 17, 1867: 120.

Territorial Laws of Dakota Territory. 1867b. "A Memorial to the President of the United States, Relative to the Removal of the Santee Band of Sioux Indians," ch. 18: 122.

Territorial Laws of Dakota Territory. 1867c. ch. 18, 1, approved Dec. 30.

Territorial Laws of Dakota Territory. 1869. "Memorial and Joint Resolution to the Secretary of the Interior," ch. 352.

Territorial Revised Civil Code, Dakota Territory. 1866. An Act to Establish a Civil Code, Sec. 26: 1.

Voting Rights Act of 1965. 1965. U.S. Statutes at Large 79: 437. Now codified as 42 U.S.C. § 1973.

Voting Rights Act Amendments of 1970. 1970. U.S. Statutes at Large 84: 314.

Voting Rights Act of 1965, amendments of 1975. 1975. U.S. Statutes at Large 89: 400.

Voting Rights Act Amendments of 1982. 1982. U.S. Statutes at Large 96: 131.
Voting Rights Language Assistance Act of 1992. 1992. U.S. Statutes at Large 106: 921.

Attorneys General Opinions

Biennial Report of the Attorney General, State of Montana. 1897.
Biennial Report of the Attorney General, State of Montana. 1912.
Official Opinions of the Attorneys General of the United States. 1856: 746.
Opinion of the Attorney General, State of Utah. 1940. Oct. 25.
Opinion of the Attorney General, State of Utah. 1956. Mar. 23.
Report of the Attorney General, State of South Dakota. 1908. Vol. 1907–8, letter of Aug. 29: 123.
Report of the Attorney General, State of South Dakota. 1912. Vol. 1911–12, letter of May 9, 1912: 400.
Report of the Attorney General, State of South Dakota. 1917. Vol. 1917–18, letter of Dec. 28.
Report of the Attorney General, State of South Dakota. 1918. Vol. 1917–18, letter of Sept. 17: 1918: 277.
Report of the Attorney General, State of South Dakota. 1919. Vol. 1919–20, letter of July 26: 169.
Report of the Attorney General, State of South Dakota. 1924. Vol. 1923–4, letter of Dec. 18: 204.
Report of the Attorney General, State of South Dakota. 1932. Vol. 1931–2, letter of June 2: 360.
Report of the Attorney General, State of South Dakota. 1963. Vol. 1963–4, letter of July 5: 115.
Report of the Attorney General, State of South Dakota. 1977. Vol. 1977–8, Opinion no. 77–73 of Aug. 25: 175.

Index